Easy Does It

Cheap and Simple Ways to Solve Common Household Problems

Publisher's Note

The editors of FC&A have taken careful measures to ensure the accuracy and usefulness of the information in this book. While every attempt has been made to assure accuracy, errors may occur. We advise readers to carefully review and understand the ideas and tips presented and to seek the advice of a qualified professional before attempting to use them. The publisher and editors disclaim all liability (including any injuries, damages or losses) resulting from the use of the information in this book.

The health information in this book is for information only and is not intended to be a medical guide for self-treatment. It does not constitute medical advice and should not be construed as such or used in place of your doctor's medical advice.

"Now I exhort you, brethren, by the name of our Lord Jesus Christ, that you all agree and that there be no divisions among you, but that you be made complete in the same mind and in the same judgement."

1 Corinthians 1:10

Table of Contents

Do-it-yourself appliance care

Banish dirty blender blues. Blender cleanup can be easy if you do it as soon as you finish mixing that milkshake or chocolate pudding. Just squirt a little dish detergent inside, add a cup of warm water, replace the cover, and give it a spin.

Top-notch treatment for your dryer. Be sure to clean the lint catcher on your dryer every time you use it. For loads of clothes that have a lot of lint, stop and clean the filter in the middle of the drying cycle. You'll save money, improve the efficiency of the machine, and eliminate a fire hazard.

Disasters in the dryer. Sometimes items like crayons and ink pens go through the wash without causing a problem. But watch out if they reach the dryer. Tumbling a load of clothes with a melted crayon or a leaky ink pen or marker can really stain them. And these substances can coat the dryer's drum and get passed on to the clothes in the next load. So if this happens, it's important to clean the insides of the dryer thoroughly before drying anything more. Remove as much melted crayon as you can with a non-flammable all-purpose cleaner, like Top Job, Mr. Clean, or Soft Scrub. (Read the label to be sure it's non-flammable.) Apply it with a clean sponge or cloth. Do not pour or spray it directly on the inside of the dryer. Wipe it off with rags or paper towels. Put some old rags in the dryer and tumble them until no more residue comes off.

Lengthen the life of your appliances

Today's appliances have an average life span of 30 years. Yet, they can't live to that ripe old age without a little help from you. To keep them blending, toasting, and whipping, you'll need to carry out routine maintenance, cleaning, and minor repairs. Check your owner's manuals.

Dry your clothes efficiently. Don't overload your dryer, always empty the lint filter, and make sure your dryer has proper ventilation. These strategies will help you save money.

Be wary of lint buildup. Clean the exhaust vent system at least once a year. Be sure it is never clogged. Never vent a dryer inside the house. It should always be vented to the out-of-doors.

Boot out dryer stains. To remove ball-point or felt tip marker ink from the dryer drum, you may need to use a household cleaner containing a flammable solvent such as Fantastic, Formula 409, or Pas. Be sure the drum is cool before cleaning. Put some undiluted cleaner on a cloth or pad of paper towel and rub it on. Do not spray or pour the cleaner into the dryer drum. Wipe the drum with a damp cloth or paper towels. Be sure to remove all solution. Leave the dryer door open for several hours to be sure all the vapors from the solvent have evaporated.

Wipe away dryer residue. The dryer can also get spotted from starch or tinted items. Moisten a cloth with a diluted bleach solution and wipe the interior. Remove the bleach with a sudsy sponge or cloth, then rinse and dry.

Scour with baking soda. Baking soda is a great replacement for scouring powder. It's also especially good for removing stains and odors from refrigerators and coffee pots.

Serve great-tasting coffee. Save your coffee maker — and your taste buds — from foul-tasting mineral buildup. Mix a quart of water with one-quarter cup of baking soda. Run it through your coffee maker and follow with a pot of plain, cold water.

Exercise caution with warranty. Wait to send in your appliance's warranty card until you're sure it works properly. Most stores will let you return a "lemon" within 30 days if it doesn't work. If you already mailed in the warranty card, you might have to send your appliance to the manufacturer to be repaired. That could be a bigger hassle than it's worth.

Urn your keep. If you have a large coffee urn for serving big groups, always store it with the spigots open to prevent the handles from sticking. Wash it thoroughly before storing it.

Clean out your coffee maker. For best care and the best coffee, clean out your drip coffee maker about once a month. Fill it with equal parts water and distilled vinegar, then run it through the brew cycle. Rinse it out with another cycle using just plain water.

Flatten it and forget it. You've just bought a computer, and you think you might be moving in a year or two so it makes sense to save the box it came in. But there is nowhere to store that bulky box. Simply slit the tape holding the box together and flatten it out. Now you can store it under a bed or flattened against the back wall of a closet. If you don't have any place to keep the Styrofoam packing, try to recycle it or discard it if you need to. When the time comes for moving, wadded newspaper or household linens can substitute for the packing, and your computer can move safely to its next home.

Clear the air. If your humidifier begins to smell musty, add a tablespoon of bleach to the water and let it run for a while. This should kill any germs the humidifier is harboring, and once the bleach smell is gone, the water vapor will be fresher.

Stave off streaks and spots. Hard water hard to wash with? Add some baking soda to your next dishwasher load. Your dishes will come out free of those annoying mineral streaks and spots.

Deal with a musty dishwasher. Your dishwasher could start to smell like your basement if you keep it closed most of the time. Flush out that musty odor with two tablespoons of baking soda and a run through the rinse cycle.

Wash half your dishes at half the cost. Save money on your water and energy bills and use the forgotten cycle on your dishwasher — the rinse-and-hold cycle. If your dishwasher isn't full, this is perfect. The rinse-and-hold cycle will wash food off your dishes before it gets caked on, but it won't waste the hot water and the electricity of a full cycle.

Enhance your dishwasher's performance. A safety pin can help you get maximum performance from your dishwasher. That's because it's great for de-clogging the spray holes in your dishwasher's arms. Usually the bottom arm has the most clogs since it sits in the water, but make sure to clean the top arm's holes, too. For a complete cleaning, give the arms a bath under a sink faucet. Take the arms out of the dishwasher by removing the racks and then undoing the hubcap that holds them in place.

Tie up loose items. Small, loose items, like plastic lids, can bounce around in your dishwasher. Secure them by putting them in a small, mesh bag closed off with a rubber band. Then use the rubber band to attach the bag to one of the hooks on the top rack.

Get out grease and grime. If you want your dishwasher sparkling clean and smelling as fresh as a grove of citrus trees, put powdered lemon or orange drink mix in the detergent dispenser and run it through a whole cycle. You'll find that rust stains will vanish, too.

Give your appliance a facelift. Remodeling your kitchen doesn't mean you have to buy a new dishwasher. Your old dishwasher might come with its own remodeling kit. Just inspect inside its door. Sometimes the door panel has another color on the other side, or other panels are stored behind the door. If these colors still don't match your new kitchen, take the door panel to an auto body shop and have it repainted to match your new decor.

A bath for the dishwasher. Sometimes even your dishwasher needs to be cleaned. The first sign of buildup is a film left on the glasses and plates. An easy way to clean your machine is to fill a bowl with one cup liquid bleach and put it on the bottom rack of the dishwasher. Run the dishwasher on a setting that excludes the "dry" cycle. Open the machine and fill the bowl with one cup of white vinegar. Run the dishwasher through a full cycle. Repeat if necessary.

Super clean your dish drainer. Every week or so, run your dish drainer through the dishwasher. This will get the grunge off those hard-to-reach places.

Dishes are just the beginning. You can clean a lot of things in your dishwasher. It's ideal for figurines, knickknacks, and baby toys. Some shelves and bins from the fridge are dishwasher safe. And do you know the easiest way to clean your stove's burner liners? That's right. Pop them in the dishwasher once a week, and you can put off replacing them a lot longer.

Unbend a bent beater blade. If a beater blade on your electric mixer is bent, lay it on a cutting board and press down on it with the round side of a teaspoon.

Foil a noisy food processor. If your food processor makes a racket every time you turn it on, put it on a large, plastic pad. The best pads are those used in offices to keep printing and copying machines quiet. Look for them at office supply stores.

Avoid costly, unnecessary purchases

The best money-saving tip you can follow is to consider these things before making a major purchase.

- Make sure it's something you need. Is it the best buy for the money?

- Think about the emotional reasons you might be buying it, like overcoming sadness or showing off. Will it improve your life? You might find that you can get along without it.

- Look at the price to figure if it's a good value. Some luxury items lose their value quickly. Is this one of them? What would happen if you don't buy it?

- Gauge how costly the upkeep will be. You might have to give up a lot to own it. Whether it's worth it, of course, is up to you.

Communicate with your freezer. To avoid food poisoning, don't eat food that has been thawed and refrozen. But how can you know if your freezer ran continuously while you were on vacation? Easy. Place a plastic bag containing a few ice cubes in the freezer before you leave. If the power goes off for any length of time, the ice cubes will melt and refreeze into a block. If you come back to ice cubes, all is well. But if you return to a frozen block of water, throw out your frozen food.

Fill er up! Your freezer can be a wonderful time and money saver, but to really work efficiently, it needs to be at least two-thirds full. If you don't have enough food to keep it this full, fill plastic milk jugs or plastic food storage containers with water and place them in the freezer. Once the water turns to ice, you can count on a peak performance from your freezer.

Organize your deep-freeze. Do you have a large freezer that's become a mixed-up jumble of frozen foods? Organize it with plastic milk crates. They're easy to stack and lift. And you can even sort your foods by color — perhaps green for vegetables, red for meats, and a yellow crate for your frozen fruits.

Defrost by using your oven. Need to defrost but have a freezer full of food? If you have a self-cleaning oven, you're in luck. Stash everything inside, close the door, and get to work on the freezer. The oven is so well insulated that nothing should thaw for at least a couple of hours.

Dispose of garbage disposal goofs. If you've ever scared yourself silly by turning on the garbage disposal when you meant to flip on the sink light, here's a tip that could save your ears and your nerves. Dab colored nail polish onto the disposal's switch, and you'll never get the two confused again.

Bid adieu to disposal pewh. Remove food debris and leave a fresh scent in the garbage disposal. Put in about a half-dozen ice cubes, run the system, and flush it well with cold water. Then put in half of a lemon and grind it up. Or for a warmer deodorizing, pour in one-half cup of salt, then add hot water and run the disposal.

Get the funk out of your trash compactor. Line the bottom of your trash compactor with several layers of newspaper to fight nasty odors. The newspaper will suck up much of the smell of decomposing food and protect the bottom of the compactor from sharp, damaging objects.

Clean your hair dryer with a toothbrush. If your hair dryer smells like burning hair, it usually means hair and lint is trapped in the air intake. Rubbing an old toothbrush over the holes of the intake will get rid of the problem.

Organize your electrical cords. Keep your electrical cords from getting tangled with ponytail hair bands. You can buy them at any discount drug store for a few cents apiece. They'll help keep your cords in neat little bundles.

Blow away wrinkles. Your plastic shower curtain or tablecloth has been packed away and now it's wrinkled. You can't iron plastic, so what do you do? Just blow away those wrinkles with your hair dryer. As the plastic gets warm, the wrinkles fall out.

Unclog your steam iron. Return your clogged iron back to its old, steamy self with a half-and-half mixture of vinegar and water. Pour the combo into the water chamber, sit the iron upright, and select the "steam" setting. After five minutes, unplug your iron and let it cool. Empty out the water chamber, and your iron should be clog free.

Foil a dirty iron. Don't you just hate it when the face of your iron gets coated with burnt starch or residue from polyester fabric? Fortunately, you can remove it easily. Rub it with aluminum foil, or apply a baking soda paste with a soft cloth. Even an iron with a nonstick coating can get a buildup of starch. To get rid of it, scrape it away gently with a scrubber made for cleaning nonstick cookware when your iron is cool.

Cord care. To get the longest life from your appliances, take care of the cords. If a cord gets knots or crimps in it, it can break and cause a short. And heat can do a lot of damage so don't let the cord touch any hot surface — like a hot iron or toaster oven. Also, don't wrap the cord tightly around an appliance, especially if it's hot. It's better to store it with the cord coiled loosely beside it.

Water works. Keep water handy for your steam iron by storing it in a recycled sports water bottle or mineral water bottle with pop-up top. The small spout is the right size for pouring water into the iron's water tank.

Make your iron glide. To keep your iron gliding smoothly along, occasionally run it over a fabric softener sheet.

Protect yourself from microwave mishaps

Liquids heated in microwaves can "superheat" and erupt. That's because your microwave can heat inner layers of liquid to a boiling point while the surface remains calm. When you move the container, the inner layer can explode and cause serious burns.

To make sure this doesn't happen to you, use a conventional stove for heating liquids whenever possible. When microwaving, always use a container at least one-third larger than the liquid being heated.

Before heating a liquid in the microwave, stir it well, and place something in the container to spread out the heat energy. You can use a tea bag or stirring stick. Break up heating time and stir liquid at least twice while microwaving, and again when it's done. Never exceed the recommended heating time.

Zap microwave smells with a lemon. If your microwave still smells like the fish you cooked last week, get out a lemon and cut it in quarters. Place the lemon and a cup of water in a microwave-safe dish. Cook on "high" for three minutes.

Throw in the towel for a dirty microwave. A wet paper towel is all you need to clean your microwave. Place the towel inside and "cook" it for four minutes. Let it sit for another minute or two, and then use it to wipe down the inside of your microwave.

A steamy affair. The microwave oven is one of the most popular kitchen appliances these days. Lots of use means lots of baked on food spills inside. Take the work out of cleaning up your microwave by boiling a cup of water in it for a few minutes. The steam from the water softens the debris and makes wiping it clean a breeze. Never use abrasive powders or soap pads to clean the microwave oven.

Say no to a hot dish. Want to know if a glass container can be used in the microwave oven? Do a quick test by putting the empty dish in the microwave on high for one minute. If it's still cool, you can safely use it for cooking. If it's lukewarm, it's OK for short periods of reheating. If it's warm, don't use it in the microwave oven.

Clean out the microwave. Your fridge isn't the only appliance a little baking soda can help. Think of the good it can do for the splattered-on walls of your microwave. Use a quart of warm water mixed with four tablespoons of baking soda to scrub and deodorize the inside.

Effortless microwave cleaning. Remove cooked-on food from your microwave the easy way. Put one-fourth cup of white vinegar and one cup of water into a glass bowl, and microwave on high for about five minutes. The moisture from the vinegar water will soften food splatters while it deodorizes the interior of your microwave. Let the water/vinegar mixture cool, and use it to wipe off the softened mess.

Don't cook with recycled paper towels. Paper towels made of recycled materials should not be used in the microwave. They may contain pieces of metal.

Release grease from oven fans. That disgusting, greasy buildup on the fan filter above your oven isn't hard to clean. All you need to do is take the filter out, put it on the top rack of your dishwasher, and run it through a full wash cycle.

Shake off oven spills. Make cleaning up nasty oven spills a cinch by sprinkling them with salt before they have a chance to bake on. When you're through cooking, the stain will be a pile of ash that you can easily wipe away. Here's another salt tip. The next time you drop an egg on the floor, sprinkle it with salt and let it sit for about 10 minutes. The egg will absorb the salt, and you'll be able to wipe it up easily.

Fight kitchen grease. White vinegar is a safe, economical cleaner for cutting the grease buildup on your stove top. It also prevents grease from building up on the inside of your oven. Just wipe down your oven walls with a cloth dipped in water and vinegar.

Encourage finicky oven racks. Grease and grit can build up on your oven racks, and this causes trouble sliding the racks in and out. Clean the racks by rubbing their edges and guides with a soap-filled steel wool pad. For extra slide, grease the edges with vegetable oil after they've dried.

Give oven cleaning a head start. Cleaning your oven doesn't have to be a time-consuming chore. Just set your oven at 250 degrees. After five minutes, turn it off and put a small, glass bowl of ammonia on the top shelf. On the bottom shelf, put a large pan and fill it with boiling water. Close the oven door and let it stay overnight. By morning, cleaning your oven should be a cinch. But remember — don't use this tip if you have a continuous-clean oven.

Protect your oven light. When cleaning your oven, cover the light bulb with a paper cup. You'll still have some illumination while protecting the bulb from oven cleaner.

Better burning stove. If the holes in your gas burner get clogged or caked with spilled food, use a pipe cleaner to get rid of those troublesome clogs. It's just the right size.

Save money when you cook. On an electric stove, you can usually turn the heat off about five minutes before the cooking time is over and the residual heat will finish cooking your food. This is also true for foods you cook in your oven.

Repel refrigerator smudges easily. For a refrigerator that's as clean and shiny as a new car, give it a rubdown with car wax, inside and out. The wax will help keep it clean, making spills, stains, and fingerprints easier to wipe off down the road.

Guard your fridge from odor. If you're going on a long trip, place several opened boxes of baking soda in your refrigerator before you leave. When you return, your refrigerator will smell sweet and fresh.

Check your refrigerator gasket. Every so often, check the condition of your refrigerator gasket. It's the rubber lining around the door that seals in the cold. One way to check it is to close the door on a newspaper page. Try to pull the paper out. If it rips, the seal is good. Or leave a dollar bill in the door. If it's difficult to pull out, the seal is tight. Here's another quick test. Leave a flashlight turned on in your refrigerator. Point it so the light shines to where the door closes. Your seal is good if you can't see the light when the door is shut. If the gasket fails any of these tests, have it replaced.

Ward off yellow stains. Unsightly yellow stains on any appliance don't stand a chance with this homemade cleaning solution — one-half cup of bleach and one-quarter cup of baking soda mixed with four cups of warm water. After you wash the appliance with this solution, wait 10 minutes and rinse with clean water.

Detail the dings on your appliances. The touch-up paint for your car could also cover up scratches and dings on your appliances. If you don't have a matching color at home, pay a visit to your local automotive parts store. They're sure to have a rainbow of shades to pick from.

Arrange your appliances to save money. Help your refrigerator and stove last years longer with this simple tip — make sure the two appliances aren't next to one another. Putting a "cold" appliance next to a "hot" one makes them both work harder to maintain their temperatures. Moving them apart will save you big bucks over the years.

Snap a lid on refrigerated liquids. Cover that open can of soda before you stick it in the refrigerator. Otherwise, you'll overwork your refrigerator. Refrigerators remove humidity to help keep food cold. An open container of liquid keeps your refrigerator busy constantly.

Good 'scents' for your refrigerator. If odors don't come out with a regular sudsy washing, spread one of these in a container and place it in your smelly refrigerator or freezer. Let the appliance run empty for a few days: activated charcoal; cat box litter; imitation vanilla extract (not pure extract); ground coffee.

Keep stored appliances smelling fresh. Tie some charcoal in a pantyhose foot, and put it inside a refrigerator or freezer before a move. Even if the appliances are closed up for some time, they'll come out smelling sweet and fresh.

No more musty smell. If you have major appliances that are bound for storage, whether it's for a couple of days or a couple of years, make sure they don't come home with a musty odor inside. Fill an old pantyhose leg or knee-high stocking with fresh-ground coffee (unused), knot it closed, and toss inside.

Seal with approval. Use rubbing alcohol to clean the gasket that keeps your refrigerator door sealed tight. Then rub it with a little mineral oil to prevent cracking.

Hang up on pricey cell phone cases. You carry a small cellular phone in case of emergencies. But it shouldn't take an emergency spending plan to pay for your cell phone case. To protect your phone — and your pocketbook — use a simple cloth eyeglass case instead.

Clean recharging contacts with eraser. Use a pencil eraser to wipe off the metal recharging contacts on the handset and base of your cordless phone. Your phone will get a better recharge. Try this also for the battery contacts on your TV and stereo remote controls.

Make contact with your portable phone. If your portable phone is sounding kind of fuzzy, perhaps it isn't charging properly. Check the metal contact points on the phone and the base. If they are dirty, they can't do their job properly. Clean them regularly with an eraser to keep your calls coming in loud and clear.

Regain control over broken remote. You push and push the buttons on your remote control, but it still doesn't work. Instead of mashing the buttons senseless, get a sheet of aluminum foil and tear it into small squares. You'll need one small square for each broken button. Then remove the face of your remote and its circuit board. With a little bit of contact cement, attach the foil to the broken buttons. Reattach the board and the remote face, and you're ready to channel surf.

End TV and VCR interference. If a snowstorm seems to hit your television any time you turn on your VCR, try this tip before you call in a repairman. Lay a sheet of aluminum foil between the TV and the VCR. The static could be caused by interference between the two appliances. If this is the problem, the foil will help control it.

Hit 'PLAY' to vanquish VCR troubles

You might not be able to figure out how to program your VCR. But chances are you can fix it if it starts acting up. About one-quarter of all VCR problems stem from dirty heads. Too many particles on the heads can cause your TV screen to turn blue suddenly while you're trying to watch a video. One easy and effective way to clean the VCR heads is just to play an ordinary tape for about an hour. Eventually, the tape will remove the gunk from the heads, and your picture will return to normal.

Keep your remote under your control. Leave your TV remote control where you need it — right where you're sitting. Stick a strip of fabric fastener, like Velcro, on the back of your remote, and the other half on the arm of your couch or chair. It's best to stick the hooked half of the fastener on your remote and the soft half on your furniture.

Book 'em. Always store videotapes on their ends, like books. Give them their own shelf away from the magnetic fields produced by televisions and other appliances.

A remote in the hand is worth two under the cushions. Attach a bit of Velcro sticky back tape to the side of your television. And put another piece on the back of the remote control device. When you turn the TV off, just stick the remote control to the side. You'll never have to hunt for it again.

See your reflection in your appliances. It's easy to get that showroom shine back on your kitchen appliances. Polish the chrome trim with a cloth dipped in rubbing alcohol.

Short-circuit safety. Do not leave toasters, blenders, can openers or any small countertop appliance plugged in after you use them. If an electrical component malfunctions, the appliance could catch on fire.

Go small for big savings. Your toaster oven preheats in less than half the time it takes to heat the range oven. And it uses a lot less energy. It's great for browning foods, crisping casserole toppings, toasting nuts, warming a slice of pizza, even baking a potato. If you have an electric skillet, use it. Stovetop cooking burns up about three-and-a-half times as much energy as an electric frying pan. And don't forget about your reliable old pressure cooker. It may not be glamorous, but it cooks faster than conventional methods while using 50 to 75 percent less energy.

Scrub away melted plastic. If plastic wrap has melted on your toaster or toaster oven, you can get rid of the mess with a damp cloth and some baking soda.

No waffling with your waffle iron. Use a clean, soft toothbrush to oil and clean your waffle iron.

Unstick your waffle iron. Has your waffle iron lost its nonstick ability? You can restore it by inserting two sheets of wax paper into the waffle iron and letting it heat. When the paper gets dark brown, remove it. Now your waffles should come out easily again.

Recycle a vacuum bag. If your vacuum cleaner bag fills up and you don't have a replacement, don't empty it through the little hole in the front. Instead, take the whole bag out and cut a slit in the back, down the middle. After you've emptied it, hold the edges of the slit together, fold them closed, and seal the opening with strong masking or duct tape. This recycled bag won't hold as much dirt as before, but you'll be able to continue vacuuming.

Stand up right. When you go to the store to buy a vacuum, you'll find a dizzying array of machines to choose from. If you can, go for an upright vacuum cleaner over the canister type. They generally do a better job.

It's in the bag. You'll get the best results from your vacuum cleaner if you make sure the bag isn't too full of dirt and dust. Once the bag is filled to a height of about 8 inches, you need to replace it. What if you haven't finished vacuuming and you don't have any more bags? You can remove the bag, put on a rubber glove, and take some of the dirt out by hand. Then reattach the bag and continue.

Flea free. If you have a pet, you may sometimes find it necessary to vacuum up fleas from your carpet. Put two or three mothballs in your vacuum bag before you begin, and the fleas should be dead before you turn off the machine. Immediately remove the used vacuum bag. Put it in a plastic trash bag, close it up tight, and take it outside to the garbage can.

Silence a clunky washer. If your washing machine often acts like a Mexican jumping bean, a remnant of flame-retardant carpet could settle it down. Just lay the carpet underneath the washer, and it should stop its vibrating racket.

Brighten wash by cleaning washer. If your clothes come out dull and faded, don't reach for extra-strength detergent. Your washing machine might need cleaning. Once a year, run a half gallon of vinegar through a wash cycle. It's an easy, all-natural way to clean out dirt and soap residue.

Make old appliances look like new. Buff your washer, dryer, and other metal appliances with car wax at least twice a year. The wax will preserve the finish and make them shine like new.

Top-of-the-line care for your washer. Taking care of your washing machine will make it last longer and run more efficiently. Protect the top of your washer by wiping up spills of laundry products at once. Some surfaces and plastic parts can be damaged by ammonia, chlorine bleach, abrasives, and solvents.

Use soil and stain-removers in the sink. Carefully follow the label instructions for clean up.

Fill in nicks in your washer. Sometimes your washing machine develops small nicks in the tub that can rust and stain your clothes or snag them. To prevent this, cover up those nicks with clear nail polish.

Clean hoses with vinegar. Vinegar can help keep washer hoses clean. It also removes soap residue and reduces the build up of mineral deposits in the machine. Add one to one-and-a-half cups of vinegar to a normal wash cycle (without any clothes) every couple of months. But be sure to continue through the rinse cycle. You don't want to leave vinegar on the surface of porcelain enamel tubs. It contains acid that can etch the surface if it remains in contact too long. This can cause rust and rough spots that could damage your clothes.

Remove dishwasher film with vinegar. Adding a cup of white vinegar to an empty dishwasher and running it through a full cycle will remove soap film.

Clever cleaning solutions

Rev up your vacuum. To get the most dirt-sucking power out of your vacuum, wipe its brushes with a wet paper towel before hitting the carpet.

Don't exhaust your options. To clean those stubborn exhaust fan filters that get coated with kitchen grease, soak them in a strong solution of grease-cutting dishwashing detergent and water. After soaking for an hour or so, clean with a scrub brush or old toothbrush.

Add shine to your bathroom fixtures. To remove hardwater stains on your bathroom fixtures, apply a paste of baking soda and vinegar. When you're finished, carefully drape a towel over the fixtures. After about an hour, wipe clean, rinse, dry, and marvel at the shine.

Put the squeeze on mineral deposits. Lemon juice is a powerful, all-natural corrosive that can remove built-up mineral deposits on your faucets. Try slicing a lemon in half and squeezing the juice on the metal. After waiting a few minutes, rub the faucet with the lemon slice and rinse. Repeat the process using the other half of the lemon if needed.

A sprinkle a day. Recycle a small spice jar with a sprinkler top to keep by your bathroom sink. Fill it with baking soda and use it with a sponge daily to keep your basin and faucets sparkling clean. If you have stains on your porcelain, a gentle scrubbing with cream of tartar sprinkled on a damp cloth should remove them.

Quick clean-up. Keep a supply of fabric softener sheets in your bathroom for quick in-between cleanups. Your tub, faucets, and fixtures will shine like new.

Spray away shower scum. Commercial shower cleaners can clean out your wallet if you use them every day, so make your own daily cleaner instead. Pour 8 ounces of rubbing alcohol in a 32-ounce spray bottle and top it off with water. Spray this concoction on your shower walls and curtain after every shower. You won't even have to rinse it off.

Stop mildew before it starts. Scrubbing mildew off your shower tiles can be as much fun as going to the dentist. Instead, prevent mildew from growing in the first place by running a squeegee over your tiles after every shower. Keep the squeegee in your shower stall so you won't forget to use it.

Double your shower power. It does a good job cleaning you, so it makes sense that a hot, steamy bath or shower can also loosen the dirt off your bathroom fixtures, tiles, and tub. Wait to clean your bathroom until right after you've taken a hot shower or bath. Or if you want, lather up your shower tiles while you're lathering up yourself.

Call in a ringer for bathtub cleaning. If a ring forms around your tub no matter what you do, don't reach for the power sander. Put on your rubber gloves and get down and dirty with undiluted ammonia. Rubbing the ring with a wet sponge saturated with baking soda can work, too. In a worst-case scenario, attack the ring with automatic dishwasher detergent or a vinegar-soaked cloth. Whatever tactic you use, finish the job by rinsing the tub clean and wiping it dry.

Whiten your bathroom caulking. Return your caulking to its original pearly whiteness with a solution of one-quarter cup bleach to one gallon of water. Rubbing alcohol can clean caulk, too. It's also good for getting chrome and glass to glitter again.

Banish mildew easily. Here's a tip for getting rid of mildew from your bathtub that requires practically no effort. When it's time to clean your bathroom, start by dipping cotton balls in bleach and pressing them into the tub's corners, where mildew is most likely to sprout. Leave them there while you finish cleaning. When you're done, remove the cotton balls and rinse the corners with water.

Safeguard your shower with car wax. Follow this two-step tip to chase away shower grime and mildew. First, do a thorough job of removing soap and water residue from the tiles. Then rub on a layer of paste wax, like car wax, and buff with a clean, dry cloth. You'll only need to reapply the wax about once a year.

Teach your shower curtain to glide. If your shower curtain seems about as flexible as the Iron Curtain, try rubbing some baby oil on the shower rod. A bar of soap also works well. Either way, your curtain will slide more smoothly.

Overwhelm shower curtain mildew. Mildew can't stand salt water. So either take your new shower curtain to the beach or dip it in salt water at home before you hang it. That unsightly mildew will look for another place to call home.

Clean fiberglass for pennies. Gently clean your fiberglass tubs and sinks with nonabrasive cleaners, like dishwashing soaps and liquid laundry detergent. You can make your own cleaning solution by diluting one tablespoon of trisodium phosphate (Spic & Span) in one gallon of water. A baking soda and water paste is an effective cleaner, too. Just make sure to wet the surface of the fiberglass before applying the paste. Or go all-natural by rubbing a freshly cut lemon on light stains. Whatever you use, let it soak in for an hour before rubbing it off with a sponge or a brush made from a nonabrasive material, like nylon, polyester, or polyethylene. When you've finished cleaning, give your fiberglass a good rinse.

Muscle out bathroom mildew. Cleaning your bathtub and shower regularly can stop mildew in its tracks. That's because a clean bathroom doesn't contain the things mildew thrives on, like soap scum, shampoo residue, and body oils. To deprive mildew of the moisture it needs, leave shower doors or curtains open right after you've bathed or showered. Keep the bathroom door open to dry the room out, too.

Get your shower back on track. Bathe the track of your sliding shower door with full-strength vinegar to make it like new. Let the vinegar sit in the track for a few minutes and then rinse it out.

Baby your shower doors. Baby oil can help your shower doors repel dirt, soap scum, and hard water deposits. Rub a light layer of baby oil on your shower doors to keep them crystal clear for months.

Erase dirty grout this 'elementary' way. Erase dirt between your bathroom tiles with a circular typewriter eraser. Simply roll it along the grout to rub it clean. Many of these erasers come with brushes to sweep away the eraser dust left behind.

A lemon-fresh view. Keeping your glass shower doors clean may seem like a full-time job. After cleaning the glass, wipe it with a little lemon oil to help keep it from getting cloudy.

Give your tub a good shampoo. Is your tub greasy from bath oil or other dirt? There's a product in your bathroom that will clean it in a flash. Pour some shampoo on a rag and wipe off the greasy ring with ease.

This will do for mildew. No need for expensive mildew and mold cleaning solutions for your bathroom tile or shower. Add liquid bleach to a spray bottle, label the bottle "bleach," and spray away the fungus. Be careful though; bleach fumes can be irritating, and you don't want to inadvertently spray bleach in your eyes or on fabrics.

A mildew-free zone. Keeping mold and mildew out of the bathroom is a tough problem for many people. As a professional house cleaner, Donna Harp knows how much work it takes to maintain this particular room. She suggests you give your tile and grout a good scrubbing, then get in the habit of maintaining it. "Spray the problem areas with a mildew-removing spray or an all-purpose cleaner a couple of times a week before you step into the shower," she advises. "Then take a minute to scrub down the walls and rinse them. Just be sure you have plenty of ventilation when you're using strong chemicals."

Help shower doors stay cleaner. Spraying your glass shower doors with furniture polish or lemon oil will help keep them clean longer.

Remove sticky decals. Ever try getting bathtub decals off? It can be a back-breaking, fingernail-bending process. Instead, set your hair dryer on the hottest setting, and let it blow on the decals. The heat should loosen the adhesive enough so they peel right off.

Say good bye to soap scum. Attack soap scum on ceramic tile with a solution of four parts water to one part vinegar.

It's curtains for mildew. Don't let unsightly mildew build up on your shower curtain. Wash it now and then with a load of towels. They'll give it a good scrubbing. Then add a cup of vinegar to the rinse cycle for a sparkling clean spin.

Polish off your bath. Tired of constantly scrubbing mold and mildew off your bath tile and grout? Then seal it with car wax. Cleanup will be quick and easy. And you'll only need to reapply the wax about once a year.

Remove resistant rust. To get rid of rust stains on tubs and sinks, sponge them with white vinegar, and rinse. If stains remain, rub on some kerosene with a cloth, wash with soapy water, and rinse.

Master the art of cleaning mini-blinds. For the cleanest mini-blinds in town, slip an old sock on each of your hands. Dip one sock into warm, soapy water and rub the mini-blind between your fingers. Dry the blind with the sock on your other hand.

Secret dust remover. Use a fabric softener sheet to wipe off your blinds. They'll come out clean and repel dust, too.

'Glov'erly way to clean slats. Turn a fleece-lined glove inside out, put it on, and spray the fingers with your favorite cleaner. Then run your fingers between the slats of the blinds. Or you can slip on cloth gloves over rubber gloves. Dip your fingers in a solution of one teaspoon ammonia and one quart water. Rub each slat between your fingers and thumb.

Sock it to louvered doors and blinds. Cleaning louvered doors and mini-blinds is always a challenge. Make your own specialized cleaning instrument with an old sock and a ruler or yardstick. Slip the sock over the ruler and secure it with a rubber band. Spray with a commercial dust-attracting spray or with rubbing alcohol, and wipe across each slat.

Must books stay musty smelling? No, not when there's baking powder in the house. Put the offending book in a brown paper bag with a bit of baking powder. Leave it for a week, and say hello to a sweet-smelling tome.

Kiss tarnish goodbye. Use a tangy salad ingredient and salt to shine tarnished brass and copper — not harsh chemicals. Salt and vinegar, mixed into a paste, make an excellent metal cleaner.

How to make metals shine. To clean copper, bronze, brass, or pewter, dissolve a teaspoon of salt in a cup of white vinegar. Mix in enough flour to make a paste. Coat the item with the paste, and let it sit for 15 minutes to an hour. Rinse with warm water and polish dry with a clean cloth.

Buff up the brass

Try these easy brass polishers for a no-fuss shine:

- Clean tarnished brass by coating it with a paste of lemon juice and cream of tartar or baking soda. Let it stay on for five minutes. Wash in warm water, rinse, and polish dry.

- Sprinkle baking soda directly on a slice of lemon and rub the brass with it.

- Pour vinegar over tarnished brass items and sprinkle with salt. Rub, rinse, and polish.

- After cleaning, rub brass with a little olive oil. It will brighten the brass and retard tarnishing so you won't have to polish it as often.

Like a new penny. Try this home formula to make copper pots or pots with copper bottoms look beautiful. It's cheaper and faster than commercial copper cleaners. Mix three tablespoons of salt with four cups of vinegar. Spray it on the copper. Let stand for a few minutes and then rub clean. If you don't have any vinegar on hand, you can use liquids that have salt and vinegar in them — like Worcestershire sauce, ketchup, or sauerkraut juice. You can use these cleaners on tarnished brass as well.

Choose copper cleaners carefully. Avoid using cleaners containing ammonia on your copper and brass pieces; they can corrode these surfaces. As with any other metal valuables, consult an expert before removing the tarnish on very old pieces since it could decrease their value.

Polish brass in an instant. Make a paste of equal parts vinegar, salt, and flour and rub in well. It is especially good for brass pulls on wooden antique furniture, since commercial cleaners can leave white marks on the wood that may require professional restoration. They can also make the brass look unnaturally bright for antique pieces. Be sure to rinse the paste off carefully after you buff it to prevent corrosion.

Polish metals. To clean brass, copper, bronze, or pewter, dissolve a teaspoon of salt in a cup of white vinegar. Mix in enough flour to make a paste, coat the item, and let it stand for 15 minutes. Rinse with warm water, and dry with a soft, clean cloth.

Peel off lacquer easily. If the lacquer finish on your brass item is flaky or spotty and needs to come off, try soaking the piece in soapy water for about 15 minutes, then rinse with hot water. Rub with a soft cloth until what's left of the lacquer begins to peel off. You can also use denatured alcohol, applied with a soft cloth. Remember that once you completely remove the lacquer, the exposed surface is going to tarnish more quickly, so it will require more frequent care.

Hot or cold, cleanup's a snap. There are two easy ways to remove the dripped candle wax from your glass candlesticks. Put them in your freezer for a couple of hours, and the frozen wax will pop off easily. Or turn them upside down on a few layers of paper towel in the microwave oven. Heat them on low for three minutes. The paper towel will absorb the wax that drips off. Don't use the microwave method on lead crystal candle holders.

Put the bite on pet stains. Don't worry about that dog-gone stain Sparky left on your carpet. Mix a teaspoon of a mild detergent — one without alkalis or bleaches — with a cup of warm water. Pour a bit on the stain and blot with a clean towel. Next, apply a mixture of one tablespoon ammonia in a half cup of water and blot. Now hit the trouble spot with the first mixture again and blot. Then mix one-third cup of white vinegar with two-thirds cup of water. Treat the stain with this and blot. Finally, sponge the spot with clean water, blot one more time, and the carpet should be stain free.

Choose your carpet stain cleaner. These three carpet-cleaning recipes will work against any spill under the sun. For oily messes, as well as tea, mustard, and colas, mix together one tablespoon of mild detergent, one-third cup of white vinegar, and two-thirds cup of water. For starchy or sugary spills, like blood, eggs, milk, and chocolate, mix one cup of water, two tablespoons of ammonia, and one tablespoon of mild detergent. If you don't know what the stain is, then try this old standby — one-quarter teaspoon of dishwashing soap in one cup of warm water. Whatever the stain is, always scrape off and blot the excess before applying the carpet cleaner. Then gently blot the stain with a clean towel dipped in the solution. Finish by laying several paper towels on top of the wet spot, weighing them down with something heavy, and leaving them there until the carpet dries.

Lengthen your carpet's life. Your carpet looks beautiful and fluffy. If you want to keep it that way, vacuum it at least twice a week. Always wipe up spills immediately, and get it deep cleaned every 12 to 18 months.

Wipe up wine stains. Don't whine when someone spills red wine on your carpet. Just pour a little white wine on it. This will stop the red wine from staining the fabric. If you don't have any white wine handy, shake salt onto the stain and dab with club soda. You could also blot the stain with one teaspoon of mild detergent mixed with one cup of warm water, followed by one-third cup of white vinegar and two-thirds cup of water. Finish by sponging the spot with clean water.

Send coffee stains packing. Coffee stains on your carpet can give you the jitters — unless you know how to remove them. Mix a half teaspoon of mild detergent in two cups of water. With a clean, white towel, blot the stain. If the stain is still there, continue blotting with this super solution — a half-and-half mixture of white vinegar and water. Here's another common household product that can remove coffee stains — an egg. Just rub a beaten egg yolk into the stain with a clean, white cloth and rinse with warm water.

Clean your carpet with peanut butter. Gum stuck in your carpet? Turn to the tried-and-true solution mothers have been using for years — peanut butter. Scrape up the excess gum. Then rub the peanut butter into the carpet fibers. After you wipe up the peanut butter, dab the spot with a mixture of one teaspoon dishwashing detergent and one cup of lukewarm water. Blot the area with paper towels to help it dry faster.

Foam away greasy rug stains. For a cleaner carpet, spread aerosol shaving cream on your greasy carpet stains. Gently work the foam into the carpet fibers. After it dries, vacuum away the shaving cream and the stain.

Discourage dog 'accidents.' Never clean dog urine from a carpet with an ammonia-based cleaner. Urine has ammonia in it, and your dog might think the spot has been permanently marked for his use. Try a mixture of three parts club soda to one part white vinegar instead.

Blast gum out of carpets. To remove gum in your carpet, start by heating it with a hair dryer set on warm, so the carpet fibers don't melt. When it's good and mushy, press a small plastic bag onto the gum and pull as much of it up as possible. Then rub methyl salicyclate, an ingredient in Extra Strength Ben Gay, into the remaining gum and repeat the hair dryer process again. Finally, after all the gum is up, wash the spot with a gentle detergent and rinse with water.

Perform a carpet miracle in 5 minutes. Company is coming in a half hour, and your carpet is filthy. You don't need an expensive carpet shampoo — just five minutes and a half cup of ammonia and two cups of water. Using a mop, lightly rub the mixture on your carpet. You won't need to use much. Before you begin, test the solution on a hidden area of your carpet to make sure it doesn't cause any damage. And never use ammonia on wool carpet.

Color away stains with crayons. If your carpet gets a tough grease stain or bleach spot, borrow a child's box of crayons. Pick one that best matches your carpet, and color the spot with the crayon. To set the color, lay a piece of wax paper over the area, and melt the crayon into the fibers with a warm, not hot, iron. You can do this as often as needed.

No bare feet allowed. Taking off your shoes and walking on plush carpet may make you feel like a kid again running barefoot in the grass. But it may not be as good for the carpet as it seems. Professional carpet cleaner Robert Clay recommends that you adopt the Japanese custom of removing your shoes at the front door. But don't go completely barefoot. "It may be pleasant to walk around your house this way, but the oil from your feet rubs off and attracts more soil to your carpet," Robert notes. "Slip on a pair of clean white socks instead." Tennis-style socks, which only come to your ankle, might be a comfortable compromise between sock feet and bare feet.

Don't let stain remain. When you get a spot or stain on your carpet, deal with it immediately. The longer you wait, the less likely you are to get it out. Begin by removing as much of the stain-causing substance as possible. For thick, "gloppy" stuff, use a paper cup, a spatula, or a credit card to lift the substance up and away. For liquids, blot it with paper towels or a clean, white cloth. If it's a dry mess, vacuum it up.

Don't play chicken with your carpet. You trip on the way to the dining table spilling greasy fried chicken on the floor. Never fear. Your kitchen cupboard has the carpet cleaning remedy you need. Remove the chicken and scoop up all the grease you can. Pour baking soda over the remaining stained area and rub it in. Wait for about an hour so the oil can be absorbed. Then run your vacuum cleaner over the soda. You'll squawk with delight at the results!

If you delay, your nose will pay. Nothing smells worse than an old pet stain in carpet, so you need to act quickly if your pet has an accident. Blot up all of the urine and rinse the area with warm water. Then apply a solution of one teaspoon of white vinegar, one teaspoon of liquid detergent, and two cups of warm water. Work this into the carpet and let it stand for 15 minutes. Rinse and dry the area. (Caution: vinegar may affect dark colors so be sure to test this formula in an area that is hidden.)

Restore a shine to wood floors. Bring back that old shine to your finished wood floor with vegetable oil and white vinegar. Just mix equal parts in a pump-spray bottle. Squirt it over the floor and rub it in with a cotton rag or a wax applicator. Make sure to wipe up any leftover solution with a clean cloth. Then buff your floor until it won't shine any more.

Carpet freshener. You can make your own custom carpet freshener. Just combine three-fourths cup of baking soda with one-fourth cup of talcum powder, two tablespoons of cornstarch, and your favorite scent. Sprinkle mixture over your carpet, let stand for at least 15 minutes, vacuum, and enjoy the aroma.

Get blood out of a carpet. It is almost as hard as getting blood out of a turnip, but if the stain hasn't set, you've got a chance. Make a paste of cornstarch and cold water. Rub it in gently and then let it set. It will get hard so you may have to soften it by hitting it with a hammer or mallet. Vacuum the powder. Repeat if necessary.

Shocking solution to static electricity. If winter time means you're constantly generating static electricity in your carpet, try this easy solution. Mix one part fabric softener with five parts of water into a spray bottle. Spritz your carpet and no more shocks. Your carpet should stay cleaner as well.

Make shampooing your carpet a snap. Don't worry about moving your furniture into the garage when you shampoo your carpet. Simply pull a plastic grocery bag up over each furniture leg, using a rubber band or tape to secure it firmly in place. Move each piece only as much as necessary, then move it back into place.

Remove spots from carpet. Do you automatically reach for soap to clean spots in your carpet? Next time, reach for club soda first. The carbonation loosens dirt so you can blot it up, and it doesn't leave a sticky residue like soap does.

Lift carpet stains. To pick up a recent stain in your carpet, mix half a cup each of white vinegar and warm water. Add one tablespoon of dishwashing liquid and stir. Dab this solution onto the stain, then blot it with a clean towel. Repeat this process until all the stain color is transferred to the towel. When you finish, cover the area with a clean white towel to dry.

Fight fruit stains on carpet. Wet the stain with water, and gently rub in salt. Let it set for a few minutes, then brush it out and vacuum. Repeat if necessary.

Make mattress stains disappear. Mix together cornstarch and water until they form a thick paste. Pat this on the stain, and let dry for at least four hours. Vacuum off, and your stain should be gone.

Spend less and clean more

Never be without these five household super heroes — ammonia, white vinegar, baking soda, bleach, and liquid dish detergent. These super solutions can clean your house from top to bottom.

Double your steel wool supply. To double the number of uses you get out of your next box of steel wool soap pads, cut the pads in half. As an added bonus, your scissors will get sharpened, too.

Get disposable gloves for free. Need to get down and dirty? Save those plastic produce bags you tear off in the grocery store and turn them into disposable gloves. Slip the bags over your hands and hold them in place with rubber bands. When you're done, just toss them out.

Clever cleaning with simple stuff. You can make a good general cleaner by mixing one-half cup of borax in one gallon of hot water. This solution disinfects your bathroom, too.

Take a shine to it. If you need to shine your bathroom quickly, get out the bottle of rubbing alcohol and a soft cloth.

Isopropyl (rubbing) alcohol shines chrome faucets and fixtures and cleans hairs pray film from mirrors.

Bleach alert. When doing laundry or other household chores, never mix vinegar, ammonia, or anything else with chlorine bleach! This could produce toxic fumes and make you very sick.

Dust and wax your floors easily. If you want your wood floors to shine but you don't have the time, rely on this simple, but effective, technique. Place a small piece of wax paper under your dust mop. The mop will sweep up the dirt, while the wax paper shines the wood.

Do-it-yourself formulas save money

What are you really paying for when you buy those expensive cleaners advertised on TV? Mostly water! Save money and clean without harsh chemicals by mixing your own. Here are two tried-and-true formulas that outshine the commercial brands.

All-purpose cleaner: 1/4 cup baking soda, 1 cup ammonia, 1/2 cup white vinegar, 2 pints warm water. Fill a spray bottle or use with a mop or rag.

Drain opener: 1 cup baking soda, 1 cup salt, 1/2 cup white vinegar. Mix and pour down the drain. Wait for 15 to 20 minutes and then pour a big pot of boiling water down the drain. This drain opener doesn't damage the pipes. Do not use this method, however, if commercial drain cleaner has been used and is still present in the standing water.

Emergency cleanup solution. For a quick and easy solution to messy floors, make a substitute dustpan out of half a paper plate.

Clean your teeth, then everything else. When your toothbrush loses its oomph, don't toss it just yet. You can use it to clean a whole host of things — the tiny spaces around faucets, tile grout, your fingernails after gardening, mud from the grooves on the bottom of your sneakers or hiking boots, small plastic or wooden toys (especially those from garage sales), can openers — and whatever else you can think of.

Get the most from vinegar. Although vinegar is quite handy and versatile around your house, it isn't a good cleaner for most household grime — at least not by itself. That's because most of the soils in your home contain fats or oils, which need an alkaline solution (like baking soda) to break them up so they can be wiped away. Vinegar is acidic, which makes it good for cleaning water stains and lime deposits, and it's a great rinsing agent because it dissolves soap scum. Vinegar may work wonders on some jobs, but make sure you're using it to its best advantage.

Versatile vinegar

Vinegar is the mainstay of your non-toxic cleaning arsenal. Try these concoctions to clean everyday problems:

Copper pots — scrub with a pinch of salt and vinegar.

Bathtub film — remove with vinegar alone if it's not a porcelain enamel surface.

Windows — spray with equal parts of water and distilled vinegar, dry with soft cloth.

Grout stains and mildew — apply a straight solution of vinegar and wipe clean.

Get the dirt on antique glass. Found an antique glass medicine bottle in the old privy? Here's how to clean it. Soak it for a full day in a solution of water, detergent, and water softener. After soaking, pour out half the water in the bottle and add a couple of tablespoons of uncooked rice grains or fine sand. Shake and swish it around for a few minutes to help scour the inside surface.

Give ivory a new luster. If you have genuine ivory pieces, you need to clean them carefully. Mix one tablespoon of lemon juice into one-fourth cup of plain yogurt. Rub this onto your ivory, and let it sit for a couple of minutes. Rinse off, and enjoy the new luster to your old treasures.

TLC for your trophies. If you're a hunting or fishing enthusiast, you may be concerned about keeping your wall trophies in top condition. Professional taxidermist Larry Reese of Centreville, Md., says the best way to clean furred animal mounts is with a vacuum cleaner. "They can be vacuumed with a brush-type attachment, or you can use a cotton rag and a spray furniture polish, like Endust. Wipe from the head toward the tail." For fish and birds, Larry recommends using a feather duster. Any glass or wooden parts can be cleaned with regular window or furniture cleaner.

Banish permanent marker stains quickly. You can remove permanent marker stains from appliances and counter tops by using rubbing alcohol on a paper towel.

Choose baking soda for countertop stains. It's easy to banish coffee and tea stains from your countertops. All it takes is a good rubbing with baking soda and water made into a paste.

Clean stains from countertops. Bleach is a great stain remover, and white countertops and porcelain sinks are perfect candidates for its power. For particularly stubborn stains, soak paper towels in bleach, and put them over the stain. Be sure to wear rubber gloves to protect your hands. Cover with another paper towel soaked in water. Leave overnight and the stain should be gone in the morning.

Rub countertops clean. Those purple pricing ink stains will come right off food containers and onto your countertops. But you can wipe them away with a little rubbing alcohol. It not only removes stains but disinfects as well. And rubbing alcohol will remove grease stains, too.

Choose the right cleaner. A regular soap or detergent is all you'll need for most household cleaning. If you need something a little stronger — for cleaning utensils and countertops after contact with raw meat for example — use a fast-evaporating chemical like chlorine bleach, alcohol, hydrogen peroxide, or ammonia. They remove potentially dangerous bacteria but do not stick around doing damage after they have done their job.

Make purple ink stains disappear. What if you have an ugly purple stain from a grocery pricing label that stuck to your wet countertop? Spray on a generous amount of your regular household or kitchen cleaner and allow it to liquefy the stain. Blot with a paper towel and rinse with clean water. Repeat this process until the stain is gone.

Enjoy dust-free curtains and spreads. Freshen heavy curtains and bedspreads at home by placing them, one at a time, in your dryer on the delicate setting with a damp towel.

Fluff up your down with 'sole.' To perk up a saggy comforter, run it through a low heat cycle in your dryer. Before you start the dryer, toss in a pair of old, but clean, sneakers.

Put the squeeze on stains with lemons. To clean, deodorize, and bleach away stains on your wooden cutting board and utensils, turn to Nature's unmatched bleach and odor remover — lemon juice.

Germ warfare. You can sanitize wood or plastic cutting boards by first spraying a mist of vinegar over the surface. Follow that with a mist of hydrogen peroxide. This combination can even kill bacteria on meat or produce without harming the food. Bacteria require moisture to survive more than a few hours. So keep cutting boards and other food surfaces dry when not in use.

Rub out stubborn stains. To get rid of unsightly stains on a wooden board, first sprinkle it with ordinary table salt. Then take a lemon wedge and rub the salt in. If the stain is particularly stubborn, this might not complete the job. In that case, pour liquid laundry bleach over the stains. Leave it for about 10 minutes, then rinse it off. Sometimes you must do this a second time to remove the worst stains.

Say good-bye to stinky boards. Clean odors from your cutting board by sprinkling it with salt and rubbing with a damp cloth. Then wash in warm, soapy water.

Clean odors from your cutting board. That cutting board can get pretty rank after a few rounds of onions or garlic. To help lift the stink such foods leave behind, rub the surface with a fresh slice of lemon. Afterward, just rinse and wipe dry, and voila, no lingering odor.

Remove adhesive from glass. Dab a small amount of oil on the object with a paper towel or napkin, and rub firmly. If the adhesive is stubborn, use some toothpaste (as an abrasive) along with the oil. When all the adhesive is removed, wash the object with warm soapy water. Avoid using the abrasive on plastic as it can leave tiny scratches.

Chase away porcelain stains. Cream of tartar, a white powder that comes from old wine casks, can also clean your delicate porcelain. Just sprinkle some on a damp cloth and rub it in. It works especially well on light stains.

Rescue Corelle from ugly spots. It's easy to clean
Corelle dish ware. Just get out your baking soda, sprinkle some
on a damp cloth, and rub on the stains, especially metal or
hard-water spots. For temporary discolorations, turn to another
old favorite, vinegar. Mix three tablespoons vinegar with one
cup of hot water, and let the solution bathe the stain for several
minutes. Then wash and rinse as usual.

Don't splurge on detergents. Don't fall for those expensive, name-brand, concentrated dish detergents. Use the cheapest
brand you can find but add a few tablespoons of vinegar to the
wash water. The amazing power of vinegar cuts the grease and
leaves the dishes squeaky clean.

'Wooden' a light wax be 'lov-er-ly'? Dry your wooden
salad bowl thoroughly as soon as you wash it. Then rub it inside
and out with wax paper. This light coat of wax will reseal the
surface of the bowl.

No stained history here. If your prized family heirloom
china has dark stains from years of use, return it to like-new
condition. Mix equal parts of white distilled vinegar and salt,
apply, and let the solution dissolve the discoloration.

Cut grease with soft hands. Add a tablespoon of baking
soda to your dishwater. It will cut grease and soften your hands
at the same time.

Put the shine back into dull china. Your good dishes
can glow like new again. Rub them with Vaseline, let them sit
for an hour, then polish with a soft cloth.

Stretch the soap. You can make your dishwashing liquid
go further by adding a few tablespoons of vinegar to the dishwater. This works with even the cheapest brand.

Treat fine china with care. A dishwasher is a great time
saver, but when it comes to your fine china, you're better off

taking the time to wash and dry by hand. The heat from the drying cycle can damage it. Save the dishwasher for your every-day dishes.

Make your china cups sparkle. For tea or coffee stains in the bottom of your china cups, add one-and-a-half teaspoons of chlorine bleach to a cup of water and pour into the cup. Let stand for about two minutes, then pour it out and rinse the cup immediately. To gently scrub stains from fine china, use dry baking soda. And if china gets dull, bring back the shine with petroleum jelly (Vaseline). Just rub it on, let it sit for about an hour, and polish.

Here's the wrap-up. To clean louvered doors, use a sock or a piece of cotton fabric wrapped tightly around a plastic ruler, spatula, or stiff paint brush. Secure the sock or fabric in place with a rubber band if you like. Spray with a dust-attracting spray or saturate it with rubbing alcohol and wipe across each slat for thorough cleaning. This method works well for plastic mini-blinds, too.

Banish dust to boost brightness. Chances are you don't need new light bulbs to make your home brighter. Dusting the bulbs you have could give you 50 percent more light. Just make sure you turn off the lights and give the bulbs a chance to cool before wiping them with a cloth.

Paint your collectibles clean. A soft, dry paintbrush makes an excellent duster for your precious collectible pottery and figurines. To get dust and loose dirt out of hard to reach cracks, give the collectible the once-over with a hair dryer.

Sock it to dust. A simple, more effective alternative to a dust cloth — an old athletic sock! Wear it over your hand and wipe around behind and over every nook and cranny.

Put a damper on flying dust. Vacuuming just seems to make the dust fly around on hardwood floors. So use a dust mop instead. You can spray it with a little commercial dusting spray if you'd like to help attract the dust.

Get dust off your dustpan. If you want to get dust and dirt into your dustpan without them permanently sticking there, try this. First, wash and dry your dustpan thoroughly, and then spray it with furniture polish and buff lightly. Next time you use it, the dirt should slide right out and into the trash.

Clean silk flowers. Your feather duster doesn't seem to make a dent in the dust accumulating on your favorite floral arrangement. Try using your hair dryer on the lowest setting to blow the dust off silk or dried flowers.

Recyclable dust rags. Those shoulder pads you rip out of all your sweaters make great palm-sized dust rags. They're soft, washable, and reusable.

Close the door on soot. To wipe soot from your fireplace doors, spray or wipe on a mixture of one-eighth cup of white vinegar, one tablespoon of ammonia, and one quart of warm water. Scrub off the soot and finish by rinsing the door and drying it with a clean cloth.

Make soot scoot. Toss a handful of salt into your fireplace occasionally. It helps prevent soot accumulation and makes more colorful flames.

Keep down the dust from ashes. You can minimize the mess from cleaning out a fireplace. When you are ready to take the ashes out, sprinkle moist coffee grounds over them. They'll stay put while you remove them.

Put a gleam on your fireplace. After washing and drying your slate hearth, coat it with lemon oil for a killer shine.

Freshen your garbage disposal. The baking soda in your refrigerator has worked for months getting rid of food odors. And it's not done yet. When it's time for a new box, pour the old baking soda down the drain. It will clean and deodorize your garbage disposal.

Freshen drains and disposals. A spray mildew remover will clean drains or garbage disposals if it contains chlorine bleach. Or you can pour a little undiluted bleach down the drains, and let it sit for a while before running the water. Turn on the disposal as you run water through it. This will clean, disinfect, and remove most odors.

Add sparkle to crystal. A handful of salt and some vinegar can make your crystal glassware shine like never before. Just add the two common, but amazing, ingredients to your dishwater.

Overpower hard-water stains. If hard-water stains on your glassware are hard to deal with, dip some steel wool in vinegar and scrub them away with ease.

Make drinking glasses sparkle. Cloudy drinking glasses will be sparkling clean again if you soak them in warm white vinegar for about an hour. Then rub gently with a dishcloth to remove the film.

Shake mineral deposits with salt. Scrub away those ugly hard water stains in your clear vase with salt and a wet cloth. Finish the job by washing with soap and warm water.

Shake, rattle, and rinse. Trying to clean a vase or bottle with a tiny opening can be frustrating. But here's a trick to save time and energy. Grind up some eggshells and mix with water and vinegar. Pour the solution into the container, cover, and shake until it's clean. Rinse and you're done.

Insurance for butterfingers. When washing your prized glass possessions, line the bottom of your sink with a thick towel. This will soften the blow if you happen to drop a piece. It will also contain all the glass if something should get broken.

Rub out glass stains and scratches. Non-gel toothpaste provides just enough mild abrasive to rub out tiny scratches on glassware or acid-rain stains on windows.

Be careful with crystal. If your crystal glassware has deep etchings, lather it up with an old-fashioned shaving brush. The bristles are stiff enough to get into those hard-to-clean crevices but gentle enough not to cause any damage.

Small-mouthed glasses sparkle. Glasses, jars, and vases with openings too small to get your hand into can be a nightmare to clean. Just put in a handful of rice, add some water and dish detergent, shake it around, and rinse it out. The rice will help scrub it clean.

Foil grimy grills without elbow grease. You don't need a metal brush and lots of elbow grease to clean your grill. Instead, tear off a sheet of aluminum foil big enough to fit your grill. Lay it shiny-side down and turn the grill on for 10 to 15 minutes. When you take the foil off, the greasy mess will be gone.

Clean your grill with newspaper. Steam clean your dirty barbecue grill while you relax. Here's how. When you're finished grilling, soak yesterday's newspaper in water and leave it on top of your warm grill rack with the lid closed. After about 45 minutes, open the lid and wipe off the greasy grime. Just remember — don't let the newspaper sit on the grill rack too long, or it will dry out and become a bigger mess.

See it in the right light. Planning a party and don't have time for a thorough house cleaning? Replace your regular light bulbs with low wattage bulbs and use candles for "atmosphere."

Mop up marble stains. You don't need fancy chemicals to clean marble. Just make a paste using baking soda, water, and lemon juice. Scrub the stain, rinse, and dry. Amazingly, the same mixture works for slate, too.

Double your cleaning power. Kill two birds with one spray can. Use air freshener to clean all of your mirrors. It will keep them crystal clear and also wipe out any bad odors in your house.

Give glass a glistening glimmer. Use a blackboard eraser to make all kinds of glass surfaces shine. You can clear a fogged-up mirror or wipe a car windshield clean as a whistle.

Back away from mirror damage. Spray glass cleaner onto a cloth, and then wipe your mirror. Don't spray it directly on the glass. It could get to the back and damage the reflective coating.

See yourself clearly. To prevent your bathroom mirror from fogging up, rub in foamy shaving cream with a paper towel until the cream disappears.

Bring a bright polish to chrome. Gently shine chrome surfaces with a soft cloth dampened with apple cider vinegar. For the insides of chrome teapots, dip a vinegar-moistened cloth into some salt and scrub.

Shield your cooler from musty odors. You better hold your nose when you open that ice chest or cooler you haven't used since last summer. It could be a Pandora's box of smells — unless you put newspaper inside it before you stashed it away. Newspaper will absorb any leftover moisture and banish musty odors from your cooler.

Banish bathroom moisture with charcoal. To soak up moisture in your bathroom, hide some charcoal around the room. It also helps cut down on musty and unpleasant odors.

Bounce odors with fabric softener. Freshen the scent of your bedroom or bathroom without throwing away money on fancy-smelling air fresheners. Just put a fabric softener sheet in your wastebasket.

Try a bright idea for a fragrant room. Make a room smell better with the flick of a switch. Just squirt a bit of perfume or cologne near a light bulb. When you turn on the light, the bulb will heat up and spread the fragrance throughout the room.

Freshen the air with wintergreen. You can deodorize your house for pennies. Just put a few drops of wintergreen oil on cotton balls. Set them in several open glass containers, and your house will smell clean and fresh for months.

Vacuum smells away. Spread a fresh smell throughout your house every time you vacuum. Leave a scented fabric softener sheet in the bag of your upright vacuum. Just remember to replace the sheet every few weeks. For a change, you could also try whole cloves, carpet freshener, baking soda, or potpourri.

Spice up the air. Did you know that commercial air fresheners don't really freshen the air? What they do is cover up the odor with a stronger, more pleasant scent. Or they deaden the nerve endings in your nose so you just don't smell the bad smells. You can make a safe and fragrant alternative to a commercial air freshener from two popular kitchen spices — cinnamon and cloves. Tie them in a piece of cheesecloth for an easy cleanup. Then boil them together and fill the air with a pleasant scent.

Are those fajitas I smell? Plastic storage containers really come in handy for storing leftovers. But chili, pesto sauce, and other strong-smelling foods can leave them with a permanent aroma. Crumple black and white newsprint and place it inside the offending container. Cover and leave for a day. The smell should be gone when you remove the paper.

Get rid of odors. The next time you have a bad odor in a small, enclosed space like a closet, freezer, or pantry, try setting out a bowl of fresh coffee grounds. Pretty soon things will smell country fresh.

Clear the air. You gave a party without enforcing your usual no-smoking-in-the-house policy. Now your living room smells awful, and it's too cold outside to open the windows to air it out. Place a few fabric softener sheets around the room and close the door. Chances are, in a day or two, the smell will be gone. This tip works well for your car, too.

No smoking, please. If you've got the lingering odor of cigarette or fire smoke hanging about, banish it with vinegar. Fill a dish and let it sit in the room, or put some in a humidifier. You'll be surprised at the results.

Freshen your kitchen for just a few 'scents.' No need to buy expensive air fresheners. You can get rid of bad odors in the kitchen easily. With the oven door open, "cook" an entire, unpeeled lemon in the oven at 300 degrees for 15 minutes.

Scare off baked-on food. No need to break down crying at the sight of a casserole dish with baked-on food. Add two tablespoons of baking soda and enough boiling water to cover the mess. After an hour or so, the food will loosen up and wash off easily.

Shine your aluminum with apples. Restore the shine to your dull pots and pans by using them to cook apples, rhubarb, lemons, or tomatoes. You can get the same benefit by boiling one to two teaspoons cream of tartar in a quart of water. Or try two tablespoons of vinegar in a quart of water. Boil these mixtures in your aluminum pots and pans for 10 minutes.

A cool end to rust frustration. A wet, soapy, steel wool pad makes quick work of cleaning baked-on food from a metal pan. But have you ever reached for one only to have it disintegrate in your hand, leaving you with a palm full of powdered rust? What a mess! But keep your cool. Your used soap pad doesn't have to get rusty. Just drop it in a zip-lock plastic bag and stash it in the freezer until you need it again.

Ah, but here's the scrub. Burnt-on food in the bottom of a saucepan can take you all night to clean. Here's the easy way. Pour baking soda in the pan covering the burned area well. Add enough water to make the consistency like paste. Let the pan sit for several hours then scrub, rinse, and see how fast the cleanup is!

But does it soften the dishes? To clean a difficult casserole dish, save your used laundry softener sheets. Just put one or two used sheets in the pan, fill it with hot water, and let it sit for 20 minutes. It should wipe clean.

Help for dirty dinnerware. Pretreat baked-on foods on cookware you wash in the dishwasher (stainless steel, glass, ceramic, or porcelain). Put liquid automatic dishwashing detergent directly on the cooked-on food before putting it in the dishwasher.

Mama mia — now that's a solution! Plastic bowls with tops that seal good and tight are ideal for storing leftovers. But when dinner was your favorite Italian or Mexican dish, you may be left with unsightly grease and tomato sauce stains. Remove them by rubbing on a little dry baking soda with a damp paper towel or sponge, then washing in warm, sudsy water. You may have to do this several times to remove the stain.

Black is beautiful. Protect your iron skillets and pots from rusting by rubbing wax paper inside and outside the pan. Why does this work? The wax paper leaves a thin coat of wax on the pan and prevents air from interacting with the metal and any moisture. If you store smaller pieces of iron cookware stacked inside larger ones, leave pieces of wax paper between them. If light rust spots do appear on cast-iron cookware, remove them by rubbing with half a lemon dipped in salt.

Glassware is gonna clear up, put on a happy face. If your glass bakeware gets a cloudy appearance from mineral deposits, make it clear again by soaking it in a solution of hot water and vinegar.

Clean iron cookware. Iron cookware isn't as easy to clean as the nonstick type but even cooked-on food will loosen up with this solution. Put two teaspoons of baking soda and a quart of water into the pot and bring it to a boil.

Presoak ovenproof glass cookware. To remove baked-on sugars and starches from glass cookware, soak it in warm water and dishwashing detergent with a little baking soda added.

Make a scouring pad. A raw potato cut in half makes a good tool for removing rust from cookie sheets or other bake ware. Just dip the potato in baking soda or scouring powder and scrub away. The moisture from the potato holds the powder on, and the starch from the potato helps remove the rust.

Dissolve saucepan gunk. It's easy to remove burnt or stuck-on food from your pots and pans. Simply pour in a little fabric softener, and let it sit overnight. Next morning, wash and rinse, and you're ready to get cooking again.

Post-polish precautions. Always rinse your silver pieces well with water after using silver polish, then buff them dry with a soft cloth. This helps remove any residue from the silver polish that might cause damage if it isn't washed off.

The pewter polluters. Pewter, silver's first cousin in the metal family, is vulnerable to the same substances as silver. In addition, it can be damaged by oil or cheese. Be sure to use glass or plastic liners for your pewter pieces. Keep pewter items away from heating elements or flames, since pewter has a low melting point.

Renew pewter's smoky shine. Cigarette ashes make a good cleaner for dull pewter. Apply the ashes with a moistened piece of cheesecloth. As you rub, it will turn darker. But a good rinsing will reveal the new shine.

Flatter flatware with tender treatment. For the best results when washing your silver flatware, wash it by hand with mild soap and dry it with a soft towel. If your flatware is silver plated, do not put it in the dishwasher. The finish will be damaged and may wear off completely after a number of washings. However, you can safely wash your sterling silver flatware in the dishwasher if you follow these tips: (1) Put your silver in a separate section of the silverware basket away from your stainless steel flatware or utensils making sure they don't touch each other. The silver could be damaged by exposure to other metal especially under high heat conditions. (2) Don't wash hollow-handle knives frequently in the dishwasher. The heat and detergent can loosen the handles. (3) When you fill the dishwasher with powder detergent, don't spill any on your silverware. It can cause dark spots to form on the surface of the silver.

Find a lost shine. Here's a no-elbow-grease way to put the shine back on your silver. Line a baking pan with aluminum foil, shiny side up. Make sure it covers the pan completely. Add your silver pieces and cover with warm water and several tablespoons of baking soda. Wait 10 minutes and the tarnish will be gone without any work or expense.

A fruity way to make silver shine. Don't toss out those banana peels. Blend them in your food processor until smooth and use as a paste to shine your silver.

Toothpaste does the trick. If you don't have any silver polish handy and need to shine silverware or jewelry, toothpaste will work well. Use a very soft brush or cloth, and rinse thoroughly. This will work on other metals like copper and gold as well.

Give candlesticks a veggie scrub. A leaf of raw cabbage or leek will clean tarnish from pewter ware. Just give it a good rubbing, then rinse and dry it.

Say ta-ta to tarnish. Clean silver as soon as possible after it comes into contact with eggs, olives, vinegar, salad dressing, or salty foods. These substances can cause it to tarnish more quickly. They can even damage the surface if left on too long. And rubber can corrode silver as well. So don't store silver flatware on a rubber surface or wear rubber gloves when polishing a silver teapot.

Starch your silverware. If you are out of silver polish, you'll find a good substitute in the pot where you cooked potatoes. Soak your silverware in the starchy water for an hour, and watch tarnish disappear. Next, wash it in warm, sudsy water. Rinse and dry, and you're ready to set your table.

Remove rust from utensils. Place a knife or other rusty utensil inside an onion, and leave for a little while. Then move it around inside the onion for a bit. You'll remove a rust-free utensil.

Easy way to outsmart tarnish. For extra help in preventing tarnish on your silver utensils and serving pieces, you can line your silver drawer with Pacific cloth. It is specially made to absorb tarnish-promoting chemicals in the air. Buy it by the yard at a fabric shop and cut it to fit your storage areas. Get enough fabric to have a piece to put on top of your silver, too.

Be kind to silver. Don't wear rubber gloves when you polish your silverware or use rubber bands to hold pieces of it together because rubber will darken silver.

Brighten your stainless steel sink. If you have a stainless steel sink, you can brighten it in only a few minutes, as well. Polish it with a cloth dipped in a little vinegar or ammonia. Or use a bit of baking powder on a damp sponge. To remove streaks, rub with olive oil or club soda. But never scrub stainless steel with abrasive powders or scouring pads.

Sweeten up sour sponges. When your kitchen sponge gets that yucky, stale smell, you know it's full of germs and bacteria. Soak it in a mixture of two tablespoons of baking soda and one pint of water.

Keep your kitchen germ-free. Bacteria thrive in wet places and nothing gets wetter or germier than your kitchen sponges. Every time you wipe up a spill, you may be spreading bacteria from one surface to another. Eliminate this problem by running your sponges through the dishwasher. To prevent the sponge from dropping to the bottom, use a clothespin to clip the sponge to the top rack. If they're small enough, you can put sponges in the silverware basket.

Sanitize your sponge. Every few days pop your kitchen or bathroom sponge in the microwave oven. Wet it first, then zap it for about a minute and a half. You'll keep it fresh and free of bacteria. Just be sure you let it cool before you take it out.

Add sparkle to your sink. Make your stainless steel sink shine like the chrome on an old Cadillac. At the end of a hard day, pour some club soda or white vinegar on a cloth and give your sink a good rubdown. Then dry it with a clean cloth to prevent streaks.

Conquer stainless steel stains. Heavy-duty stains on your stainless steel sink might need a heavy-duty fix. Try rubbing an ammonia and water solution on the stain. If this doesn't work, make your own cleanser by combining borax and lemon juice. But remember — always be careful with borax. It's toxic.

Rehabilitate a scratched sink. If harsh cleaners and chemicals have damaged your stainless steel sink, head to your local auto parts store and buy chrome polish. With a little bit of elbow grease and a dab of polish, you can return your sink to its original luster.

Keep your coffeepot clean. To clean and remove lime deposits from your aluminum coffeepot, boil equal parts of white vinegar and water.

Clean your little teapot. Remove lime deposits from your tea kettle with this recipe: 1 cup apple cider vinegar, 2 tablespoons salt, 1 cup water. Boil this mixture in your tea kettle for 15 minutes. Let stand overnight then rinse it out with cold water.

Bring a shine to stainless steel cookware. It's supposed to be stainless. Put that's not always 100 percent certain. If stains do appear on your stainless steel cookware, scrub them with a stainless steel pad dipped in undiluted white vinegar.

Stay one step ahead of your guests. Keep your guest bathroom stocked with a clean rag, paper towels, and an all-purpose cleaner. That way, when your in-laws show up unexpectedly, you can excuse yourself for a moment and tidy up the place.

Say goodnight to cobwebs. Get rid of cobwebs in those hard-to-reach corners with this handy, homemade tool. Take a long-handled broom and slip a flannel pillowcase over the bristles. Secure it around the handle with string or a rubber band. The cobwebs will cling to the flannel. You can turn it inside out when it gets dirty, clean up some more, then throw it in the wash.

Two cleans in one. Alcohol can be used to clean your phone, too. For the small areas, use a cotton swab. For the larger areas, use a paper towel or cloth. The alcohol will tidy up the phone and kill germs at the same time.

Clean up spilled eggs. Crying over spilt milk is nothing compared to the crying you'll do over spilled eggs. They're so slimy and hard to clean up. Try pouring salt on top of the spill to cover the eggs, and then just wipe up with a paper towel, and you won't have to wipe away any tears.

From shoulder to knee. Next time you need to scrub the floor, protect your knees with shoulder pads. That's right, just sew a couple of elastic strips to those useless shoulder pads and presto — you have useful knee pads.

Extend your reach. Cover a straightened coat hanger with a sock or other fabric. Attach it with some sturdy tape. Use the hanger to clean hard-to-reach areas, such as the space between the refrigerator and cabinet.

Do away with ring around the toilet. Flush toilet rings down the drain with borax and lemon juice. First, be sure the sides of your toilet bowl are wet. Then, make a paste out of the two ingredients and rub it into the ring. Let it stand for two hours and scrub it off.

Dream about a simple solution. White vinegar can wash away the ring in your toilet bowl while you sleep. Just pour in one-half gallon of vinegar every month and let it sit overnight. The vinegar will do all the work. All you have to do is flush.

Easy cleaning while you're away. Next time you run an errand, pour one-quarter cup of bleach in your toilet bowl before you head out the door. When you get back, just flush, and you'll have a glistening bowl. But remember, don't put bleach in your toilet if you already have a tank-held cleaner, the kind that works each time you flush. It might contain ammonia. Mixed together, ammonia and bleach release toxic fumes.

Prevent trouble with baking soda. To put the lid on toilet bowl backups and odors, pour in one cup of baking soda once a week.

Give your bowl a smile. You have guests coming tomorrow and you'd like to clean and freshen the powder room toilet, but you just don't have the time. Do it effortlessly overnight. Drop a couple of denture cleansing tablets into the bowl before you go to bed, and in the morning, give it a swish with the bowl brush.

Commode cleaning. Forget expensive toilet cleaners! Flush your toilet to wet it down and sprinkle a little scouring powder over stained areas. After this has worked for a while, come back to it and swish it with a toilet brush. Use a liquid or spray all-purpose cleaner on the toilet seat. Scouring powder will leave it gritty and will eventually wear away a painted finish.

Tidy your toilet bowl. For space-age cleaning that adds a citrus freshness to your bathroom, sprinkle about half cup of Tang drink mix into your toilet. Leave it in for a couple of hours, then flush.

Clean the bowl with bleach. For a shine that puts to shame most commercial toilet cleaners, treat your bowl to a few minutes worth of soaking in undiluted chlorine bleach.

The cola solution. Did you buy a lot of cola the last time your grandkids visited, and now it's all gone flat? You can still put it to good use. Instead of pouring it down the drain, pour it into your toilet bowl. Let it soak for about an hour, and you'll end up with sparkling porcelain.

Ditch garbage can odor. Just because your garbage can holds garbage doesn't mean it has to smell awful. Keep your garbage can smelling fresh by emptying the trash often and cleaning the can as needed. Every month, sprinkle some borax in the bottom of your garbage can to kill odor-causing bacteria and molds. You'll find a pleasing fragrance in the most unlikely of places.

Try a little litter. Even though cat litter is associated with odor, unused litter is actually a great deodorant. Sprinkle some in the bottom of the garbage can to keep it smelling fresh. Change the litter after a week or so or when it becomes damp. Litter also works to prevent musty odors in a house that will be closed up for a while. Simply place a shallow box filled with cat litter in each room.

Mop up two messes at once. Next time you mop the floor, use your kitchen trash can as your suds bucket. You'll be cleaning two birds with one stone.

Stains take a powder. For a grease stain on your uphol-stered furniture, apply talcum powder generously and rub into the stain. Leave for a while until the grease is absorbed, then brush off with a stiff, dry brush, such as an old, clean toothbrush.

Get rid of cat hair. Use a fresh fabric softener sheet to get cat hair off furniture and drapes, wherever Fluffy likes to catch a catnap.

Baby wipes aren't just for babies. Try using a baby wipe on that stubborn spot. Some folks swear by them for stains on everything from carpet to upholstered furniture.

Brush your grater's teeth. Use a toothbrush to pick the leftover bits of cheese or whatever you grated out of the grinding surface of your grater to make things easier on your dishwasher.

Give new life to dull, greasy floors. A half cup of vine-gar added to a half gallon of plain old water makes a great everyday cleaner for vinyl and linoleum floors. Best of all, it removes dull, greasy film easily and quickly.

Soft on shine. Your floor needs mopping, but you hate to lose that high wax shine. Can you clean it and keep the sparkle? You bet you can. Just use a mixture of one cup of fabric softener in half a pail of water.

Scrub with the club. Remove wax buildup from your vinyl floor tiles with club soda. Pour it on a small section at a time. Scrub it in let it soak a few minutes then wipe it clean.

Mix-it-yourself cleaner. Use this formula to clean painted walls: 1/2 cup white vinegar, 1/4 cup baking soda, 1 cup ammo-nia, 1 gallon warm water.

Doughy cleaner for wallpaper. Use a few slices of crust-less, fresh bread to clean nonwashable wallpaper and other delicate surfaces. The softer and doughier the bread, the less abrasive it will be on your delicate surfaces.

Spray on resistance. Hallways and stairway walls attract plenty of fingerprints and grime especially if you have young children around. Try spraying these areas with a light coating of spray starch. The sprayed areas will resist marks longer and will be easier to wash off when the dirt begins to build up.

Brush on grease relief. You can't scrub grease spots on non-washable wallpaper. So what can you do? Try dusting on talcum powder with a powder puff or soft brush. Leave it on for about an hour, then brush it off. It may require a second treatment to make the grease disappear completely.

Erase spots from delicate wall coverings. An art gum eraser is the perfect soft solution for dealing with spots on non-washable wallpaper. Just remember to rub gently with the grain, if there is one.

Cheap and easy wall cleaning. Here's a natural solution for cleaning painted walls and other surfaces — mix a half cup of white vinegar, one cup of ammonia, one-fourth cup of baking soda, and a gallon of warm water.

Try these recipes for cleaner windows. Make your own window washing liquid with common household products. Mix two tablespoons sudsy ammonia with one quart water. For a window cleaner that's least likely to freeze, mix together one-half cup sudsy ammonia, two cups rubbing alcohol, one teaspoon hand dishwashing liquid, and one gallon water.

Add sparkle to your windows. Believe it or not, an ordinary coffee filter can make your windows sparkle better than a cloth or paper towel. They will leave lint streaks on glass, while a coffee filter will leave nothing but shine.

End window washing worries. If your windows are really dirty with soil and grease, you'll usually do better to clean them with an alkali, like ammonia, baking soda, or washing soda. But to remove hard water deposits and some soils, a mild acid, like vinegar, is best. Avoid harsh acids that can etch the glass.

Bring back sparkle and shine. To make your windows sparkle after washing and drying them, rub them with a clean blackboard eraser. Or dry your windows with coffee filters, and you won't leave any lint behind — just shine.

Improve your view. A solution of three parts water to one part ammonia works wonders on windows and anything else a commercial spray cleaner is used for. Cheaper, too.

A better way to clean windows. What's cheaper than paper towels for cleaning windows? Newspaper — and it's not only cheaper, it's better. Just crumple up a few sheets of yesterday's news and go to work.

No-streak window wiping. Need clean, streak-free windows and need them fast? Wipe them down with rubbing alcohol.

Cotton swabs aren't just for your ears. Use them to clean dust out of the corners of windows and picture frames. And they're particularly handy for surfaces with lots of small pieces, like a keyboard or the face of a radio.

Give windows a 'sill' of approval. A lot of dirt and grime can accumulate on those windowsills. But you can clean them in a snap if you give them a quick coat of wax. Most dirt won't stick, and any that does will wipe away easily.

Do away with dirt and fog. For cleaning and de-fogging your windows, mix either two tablespoons of vinegar to one quart of water or two tablespoons of sudsy ammonia per quart of water.

Blow away candle wax. The heat blast from your hair dryer can soften candle wax that has spilled on your wooden floor. Wipe up the softened wax with a paper towel, and clean the spot with vinegar and water.

A clean sweep. If you cut your child's hair at home or you have pets that shed, this tip will be a time saver. Tie a soft cotton cloth around the bristles of your broom and sweep up the loose hair. The cloth attracts the fine hair and keeps it from scratching.

Look like a million for pennies

Shop 90210 for used treasure. To find the best brands and latest styles at consignment shops, head for the wealthier zip codes. People with high incomes upgrade their wardrobes more often and will trade in many gently-worn, designer labels for you to choose from.

Discount duds. Get the best deals on clothing by checking out garage sales, thrift shops, and consignment shops. You can often find "gently worn" items or even brand new clothing with the tags still on for a fraction of their original prices. The quality of such clothing can be surprisingly good. Or consider having a clothing swap meet with friends or neighbors who wear clothing in sizes similar to yours or your family's.

Make the most of your closet space. Besides building a new closet, the best way to gain closet space is through better organization. For instance, you could hang all of your shorter garments — like shirts and folded slacks — on one end of the closet. That gives you room for another bar or a small chest of drawers. Another space-saving strategy is to remove all the clothes you haven't worn in a year. If you're not ready to toss some of these, put them aside for six months. You'll know it's time to give them up if you haven't worn them by then. Lastly, drop a shower curtain ring over each of your hangers and place another hanger through the loop. This gives you twice the closet space.

Save a fortune on your wedding dress

Take a chunk out of the cost of your wedding by buying a "pre-owned" or antique wedding dress. After all, you're supposed to wear something old, new, borrowed, and blue. Look in upscale thrift shops and watch for ads in newspapers. When you find a beauty in your size, buy matching shoes and borrow some elegant jewelry. You're on your own for something blue.

Chase mildew from your closet. If you live in a humid climate, or have a closet connected to your bathroom, the constant moisture could cause your clothes to mildew. But that's an easy problem. Install a light fixture in your closet, screw in a 40- or 60-watt bulb, and turn it on for a short time each day. Don't leave it on all the time, or your clothes might start to fade.

Protect your clothes from cedar chips. If you scare moths away from your closet with cedar chips, be sure the chips don't come in contact with your clothes. Cedar chips can cause clothing to yellow.

Keep dresses from slip-sliding away. Stop your dresses from sliding off their hangers and landing in a heap in your closet. Wrap rubber bands around each arm of the hanger, and your dress straps will have something to hang onto.

Clear your closet of clutter

Don't let your closet and drawers fall prey to clutter. Once or twice a year, go through your wardrobe and separate your clothes into three piles. One pile should be clothes that are keepers. These should fit you well and be in good repair. Make another pile of good clothes that need mending. In the third pile, place clothes you no longer want or that no longer fit you. Mend the second pile, donate or sell the third, and enjoy the extra space.

'Can' moisture in closets. Don't let your closets become damp or moldy. Put charcoal in coffee cans, punch some holes in the plastic lids, and put one in each closet. The charcoal will absorb moisture, keeping your clothes and possessions dry.

Store seasonal clothes in a suitcase. When winter rolls around, pack your summer clothes in a suitcase. Not because you're going on vacation — although that would be nice — but because suitcases make great storage containers. Put your folded clothes inside pillowcases or sheets before putting them in the suitcase. That way, you can remove them easily if you need the suitcase for a trip.

Repel moths, not friends. Moths hate mothballs, but so do people. So why not protect your clothes with something that smells good to people, but bad to moths — cloves. Put this spicy sweet alternative in the pockets of wool coats while storing them. You can also make a moth repellent for your closet by putting some cloves in cheesecloth. Sew it up and hang it with your clothes. Your closet will have a pleasant scent, but moths won't bother to visit.

Make your own pants hangers. Here's yet another ingenious use for a cardboard paper towel tube. If you don't have fancy hangers for your slacks, cut lengthwise down the cardboard tube and slip it over a regular hanger. Your slacks will rest nicely on the tube instead of wrinkling or having a crease at the knees.

End hanger hunts. As you're dressing, always return an empty hanger to the end of the clothes rod. When you put your garment back in the closet, you'll know exactly where its hanger is.

Reduce dampness in closets. To keep your closets dry and protect your clothes from mildew, tie several pieces of chalk together and hang them from a hook.

Top tips for wiser wear

Here are three things you can do to get the most mileage from your clothing:

(1) Make sure your clothes are clean when you put them away. A stain left in a piece of clothing can become a permanent one. Clean spots and spills as soon as possible.

(2) Repair small rips, tears, and pulls when they happen. The more clothing is worn, the worse the rips get and repairing them can be much harder later on.

(3) Store your clothes the right way. Keep them out of direct sunlight and away from damp moldy areas. Keep moths away from woolens. Don't hang stretchy clothing on hangers that can pull it out of shape.

Storing off-season clothes? Create your own dust covers for free. Instead of throwing out old pillowcases, make a small slit in the center of the seam opposite the opening and slip it over a hanger. No more dust on your winter suits. If you close up the opening by adding a fabric fastener, like Velcro, or a zipper, you can use it to store out-of-season blankets.

Create sachets. Put potpourri or spices in old shoulder pads and tuck into your drawers for pleasantly scented clothing.

Make hangers glide. If your clothes hangers stick, it can be difficult to flip quickly through your wardrobe. To make it easier, rub a piece of wax paper along the clothes rod. Hangers should slip smoothly along.

So many shoes have so little room. Make more shelf space for your footwear. Use bricks or stacks of books to support a board or two. Place shoes both on the shelves and on the floor underneath.

Make a cedar closet for pennies. For a great-smelling closet, fill the toe of one leg of an old pair of pantyhose with cedar chips. Tie the top to your closet rod, and — just like that — you're done.

Seal your closets. Tape pieces of wax paper on the inside of closet doors that have louvres or slats. You'll keep moths out, and your clothes will be dust free.

Make padded clothes hangers. No need to buy expensive padded clothes hangers for those delicate dresses. Just attach extra shoulder pads at the corners of plastic hangers.

Warn dry cleaner about spills. If you spilled a clear beverage on your clothes — even if you can't see a spot — tell the dry cleaner where it is. If it's not removed, it may show up later, especially when heat is applied, and it will be harder to get out.

Keep the blue in blue jeans. Some clothes, especially jeans and other denim items, will fade less and last longer if you turn them inside out before washing.

Clean your caps and saucers. Good news! Your husband no longer has to walk through a car wash to clean his baseball caps. Just put them in your dishwasher and wash as you would a load of dishes. Unlike the washing machine, which is too rough on a cap, the dishwasher will clean but not change the shape of your husband's favorite head wear.

Read it and stuff it. Cram hats and leather handbags with newspaper so they'll keep their shape in storage.

Prevent stretching when ironing. You are less likely to stretch your garments if you iron them with lengthwise strokes. On the other hand, ironing from side to side or with a circular motion could change the shape of some fabrics.

Getting the most from your iron

Do you know the difference between ironing and pressing? To iron, you generally go over the entire garment with long, smooth strokes. Pressing involves short lifting and lowering motions just where there are wrinkles.

Press without puckers. It is possible, believe it or not, to iron collars, cuffs, and hems without puckers and creases. Just press them on the underside first. Begin ironing collars at the points and press toward the center.

Help acrylics keep their shape. Take your time when pressing acrylic knits to avoid stretching them out of shape. Press one part completely and let it cool before moving on to the next section.

Cut ironing time in half. You can cut your ironing time in half by ironing only one side of your clothes. But how do you get the wrinkles out of the underside? Place aluminum foil beneath the ironing board cover. It will absorb heat and reflect it back up, allowing the pressure of the iron to smooth both sides at once.

Too many irons in the fire. Slight scorch marks in clothing from a too hot iron can be fixed in a flash. Dampen a cloth in white vinegar and place it over the area to be repaired. Iron using a low temperature, and the marks should disappear.

Pressing matters

Along with your iron and ironing board, one of the most useful tools for pressing is a "press cloth." It enables you to get wrinkles out of even the most delicate fabric without scorching or melting it. You can buy one at a fabric store or simply make your own out of an old cotton handkerchief or a large scrap of muslin. Just be sure you use a white or ivory cotton fabric about 12 square inches or larger.

To use your press cloth, smooth out the item you want to press on the ironing board, then lay the cloth out flat on top of it. Use the heat setting that is appropriate for the delicate fabric. The heat will transfer through the press cloth to smooth out the fabric underneath. Simply move the press cloth to cover each area as you iron.

Quick dry that water spot. You're dressed and ready for work when you discover water spots on your clothes. Luckily, your hair dryer is still handy for a quick blow dry, and you're on your way.

Don't ruin your pants. The iron won't leave your pants shiny if you use a clean, cloth diaper as a pressing cloth.

Turn back time on an old watch. You can make an old, scratched watch look new again by getting rid of the scratches. Using a cotton swab, gently spread a little nail polish remover on the face of the watch. Keep rubbing, and the scratches will disappear in no time.

Simplify your search for earrings. If you're like most women, your earrings are in a jumbled mess in your jewelry box, and finding a matching pair is a daily challenge. Solve that problem by lining a small drawer with a piece of Styrofoam or corkboard. Match each earring with its mate, and poke each set into the material.

Clean your jewelry for pennies. Why spend a lot of money on jewelry cleaner when you can make your own for pennies? Mix half a cup of ammonia with a cup of warm water and let your jewelry soak in it for about 15 minutes. Rub the jewelry with a soft cloth, then rinse with warm water. Dry on a clean linen towel or pillowcase. Pearls are too delicate for this cleaner. You can clean them gently with mild soap and water. Rinse and let dry.

Polish silver jewelry with toothpaste. Don't bother with expensive cleaners for your silver jewelry. You have some-thing at home that will work just as well — white toothpaste. Just dab a little on your silver, rub, and rinse with warm water. If that doesn't make your jewelry sparkle, try some baking soda made into a paste with a bit of water. Rub the mixture on your jewelry with a soft cloth, rinse, and pat dry.

Make gold jewelry glow. Make your real gold jewelry shine like new by washing it in warm, sudsy water. Gently nudge dirt from ridges and grooves with a soft toothbrush. Rinse with cool water, then rub dry with a soft cloth.

Fasten a bracelet with ease. Do you feel like a dog chasing its tail when you try to fasten a bracelet? Save time and avoid frustration by anchoring one end of the bracelet to your wrist with a piece of tape. Then you can calmly and leisurely find and fasten the clasp.

Erase earring disasters. If you lose the back of an earring at work, for a temporary replacement, cut an eraser off the end of a pencil. Take off your earring and push the post into the eraser to make a hole. Then put your earring back on with the temporary back. It will last until you get home!

Put your jewelry where your mouth is. Here's a jewelry cleaner you may not know about — denture tablets. Put your rings in a glass with a tablet of denture cleanser. After soaking for an hour or two, scrub them gently with a toothbrush just like you would scrub your teeth. Then rinse well and dry them with a soft cloth.

Baby your opals with the oil treatment. To keep your opals from drying out and cracking, wipe them every week with a small amount of baby oil or olive oil.

Pampered pearl protection. To keep your pearls from losing their natural luster, never wear them when you are spraying hair spray or perfumes. Even tiny amounts of chemical products will dull their shine and will never come off. After wearing them, wipe the strand with a damp cloth to remove any skin oils or other residues. Let them dry thoroughly before putting them away. If you wear your pearls often, get them restrung yearly.

A knotty problem. To get a tight knot out of your gold chain necklace, try this method. Lay the necklace on a piece of wax paper and put a drop of oil (salad or household) on the knot. Then use two straight pins to pull and loosen the knot until it comes undone.

Clean your silver jewelry in a flash. Here's how to clean jewelry with a chemical reaction. Put some short strips of aluminum foil in a small jar, fill it with cold water, and add a tablespoon of salt. Let your silver items sit in this solution for a few minutes, then rinse them off and let them air dry. Keep the lid on the jar between uses. One word of caution: Be sure the jewelry isn't plated silver and that it doesn't have any dark, oxidized areas that are part of a decoration. This technique may strip off the silver plating or lighten all the dark areas.

Quick cleanup. Clean your jewelry while you're getting dressed. For gold jewelry, add a little toothpaste or shampoo to a soft toothbrush and scrub gently. For sterling silver, sprinkle a little baking soda on a washcloth and polish until it shines.

Add new luster to gold. To put the shine back in your gold jewelry, pour a small amount of pale beer onto a soft cloth and buff gently.

Restring beads. When a string of beads breaks, whether glass or pearls, finding them all can be a challenge. Make sure that doesn't happen again by restringing them on dental floss.

Keep jewelry from tarnishing. Costume jewelry can be inexpensive and attractive, but it may also discolor your skin. To prevent this, paint clear nail polish on the jewelry wherever it comes into contact with your skin.

Make your diamonds sparkle. Clean your best friends with a bit of toothpaste and a small brush. Rinse with cold water and watch them shine.

Restore worn velvet. Rich velvet looks fabulous until it starts to wear. Shiny patches on elbows and collars can make a beautiful outfit look like a hand-me-down. You can restore velvet by spraying the shiny spots with a mist of water, then brushing against the pile with a clean nail brush.

Make bird droppings take wing. Your last outing in the park with the pigeons turned out like a scene from "The Birds." Now you're left with horrifying stains on your leather coat. Don't scream. Just rub a bit of petroleum jelly on the spot and wipe it off with a soft cloth.

Clean suede with pantyhose. Be careful when brushing suede. If you brush it too vigorously, the suede can become shiny and look worn. Instead, use an old piece of pantyhose to rub the material. The nylon will clean off lint and loose dirt without wearing out the suede.

Now you see it; now you don't. Did you just notice a sea of lint on your nice black skirt? You don't need a fancy brush or roller to get it off. Just wrap some masking tape or scotch tape around your hand, sticky side out, and lift the lint away.

Style yourself tall and thin

Want to look taller and slimmer? You can create that illusion by using darker colors rather than bold ones and matching your stockings to your skirts and shoes. Focus attention on your face by choosing interesting jewelry, scarves, and V-neck tops. And when wearing a jacket, leave it unbuttoned for a loose-fitting look. Before you know it, your friends will be asking if you've lost weight.

Look taller with fashion sense. To appear taller, don't wear horizontal stripes, wide belts, or chokers. Choose V-neck tops, pendant necklaces, and vertical lines that draw the eye up and down.

Oust mothball odors. Put garments with a mothball smell in a garbage bag or suitcase with a few fabric softener sheets. In a few days most of the odor should be gone. Air them out for a day or two, and they'll be ready to wear. If you need to wear an item right away, use your clothes dryer to speed things up. Put the item in the dryer with a couple of fabric softener sheets. Toss it with cool air, no heat, for 15 to 20 minutes.

Make play clothes work harder. Do your kids wear out their play clothes before they outgrow them? To make them last longer, iron patches on the inside of their pants at knee level. If you put the patches on before the pants are even worn, they'll last a lot longer.

Strike out pantyhose runs. If you can't wear pantyhose without getting a run, try washing them with a few drops of fabric softener added to the final rinse. The softener strengthens the fibers and keeps them run free longer. Or try soaking them in a bucket or sink of salty water before washing. Add a half cup of salt for each quart of water you use, and let them soak for about 30 minutes.

Make your outfit 'scentsational.' Your perfume will make a lasting impression if you dab some on your ironing board before pressing your outfit. As you iron, the perfume will be steamed into your clothing for a mysteriously pleasant scent that lasts all day.

Snag a sweater snag. Yikes! Your beautiful new sweater has a loose yarn that is threatening to unravel. Don't sweat it. Use a crochet hook or a bent paper clip to pull the yarn inside the sweater. Once you have it there, secure it to another piece of yarn with a knot.

A dab in time. These days the buttons on ready-to-wear clothing are sewn on with the shortest possible length of thread, sometimes working loose the first time you wear a garment. To avoid losing buttons from your new outfit, apply a little bit of Fray-Check or clear nail polish to the thread on the front of each button. Just be careful not to get any on the fabric. This reinforces the thread to help keep the button in place.

Keep buttons on clothing. Some manufacturers give you extra buttons with a new garment. But you can save yourself the hassle of sewing on replacements if you don't lose them in the first place. Before you wear a new item of clothing, squeeze a dot of super glue in the center over the threads. Your button should stay in place, and you can use those extra buttons in a more creative project.

No more ring around the collar. If your shirt collars are constantly stained, wipe your neck with rubbing alcohol each morning before you get dressed.

Say goodbye to drab white shoes. Warm weather is coming, and you're itching to wear your white shoes again. To get them ready, rub your shoes with a raw potato or rubbing alcohol before you attack them with white shoe polish. Then crumple a piece of wax paper and buff them. Once the polish dries, spray them with a touch of hair spray. No one's shoes will look quite as dazzling as yours.

Slip on whiter sneakers. New, white, canvas shoes sure look spiffy — for the first day or two. To keep that new look, spray them with plenty of starch.

Baby your white tennis shoes. If your white canvas shoes look a little tired between washings, sprinkle some baby powder on them. They'll look whiter and smell good, too.

Don't scuffle with scuff marks. Don't let scuff marks ruin the look of your white leather shoes or ice skates. Dab a little nail polish remover on a clean, soft cloth, and rub off the scuff marks.

Tame untied shoelaces. If your shoelaces untie themselves no matter what you do, there's an easy solution. Spray a bit of water on them and tie them while they're still wet. The bow will dry in that position and stay put.

Make shoe odor yesterday's news. Extra! Extra! Read all about it! Newspapers can help get rid of unpleasant odors in shoes and boots. Just crumple up newspapers, shove them in the offending footwear, and let the newspaper absorb the odors. When you put shoes away for the winter, stuff the toes with newspaper so they'll smell fresher when spring comes around.

Rebuff scuffs with olive oil. Never mind that you're out of shoe polish. Don't run out the door with those scuffed, leather shoes. Just pour some olive oil on a soft cloth and buff. You'll be on your way in no time with great-looking shoes.

Sneak cat litter into your sneakers. When you take off your sneakers, do people rush to open windows? You can combat stinky tennis shoes with cat litter and knee-highs. Pour some cat litter into a knee-high stocking, add a bit of scented powder, and leave them in overnight. Place these in your sneakers whenever you're not wearing them, and the odor will soon disappear.

Take a shine to new shoes. Want your new shoes to keep looking new long after you take them out of the box? Wipe them off, then coat them with a clear, cream polish before you wear them. You'll add an extra barrier against scuff marks, while moisturizing the leather.

Prolong the life of old leather. You can make old, scratched-up leather belts, shoes, and purses look great again with a permanent marker. Find a matching color and simply mark over the worn spots.

Treat your feet to shoes that fit

Walking is a great way to get out of the house and get some exercise. Unfortunately, a short trek can seem like a marathon if your shoes aren't comfortable. Experts offer three keys to finding the perfect pair. The first is flexibility. You should be able to bend and twist them with your hands. The second is flatness. That means no high heels, ladies. Last, but not least, is size. Your walking shoes should be one-and-a-half sizes bigger than your dress shoes, since your feet will swell after you've walked for a while.

An a-peel-ing tip. Don't throw away that banana peel! You can use the inside of a banana peel to polish your leather shoes. Then buff them with a soft cloth.

Warm your toes this winter. If you live in a cold, snowy climate, you know that cold feet are the worst part of winter. Give Old Man Winter the boot by lining your boots with carpet remnants. Simply trace the outline of your shoe onto a piece of carpet, and cut it out slightly smaller. You'll have a nice layer of insulation between your toes and the cold ground.

Make shoes smell sweetly. No more stinky sneakers. Simply tuck a new fabric softener sheet into each shoe.

Dry those wet sneakers. You can hang up freshly washed sneakers and other washable shoes to dry by bending both sides of a hanger up. Hang the hanger on a rod and slip a shoe over each upturned edge.

Lace your shoes with ease. When the ends of your shoelaces get a little frayed and difficult to lace, try dipping the ends in clear nail polish and letting them dry.

Stuff 'n dry wet shoes. If you got caught in the rain, you've probably got wet shoes. Here's a simple tip to prevent damage to your shoes. Stuff them with crumpled newspaper to absorb the moisture, then put them somewhere that's not too hot so they can dry slowly. If your shoes are really sopping wet, you may need to change the paper a few times.

Keep your feet warm and dry. Even the best-made snow boots and galoshes can leak. Keep your feet dry by slipping a plastic grocery bag over your socks before putting on your foul-weather gear. You can tuck the ends into your pants or tighten the bag around your ankle with an old shoelace. Either way — no more wet feet. This will also make sliding your foot into tight boots a little easier.

Loosen tight shoes. If your new shoes are pinching your feet, try swabbing the tight spot with a cotton ball soaked in alcohol. Walk around in the shoes for a few minutes to see if they've loosened up enough to be comfortable. If not, put on a different pair of shoes.

Remove ink stains from suede. You dropped your ball-point pen, and it left a mark on your suede shoe. Try removing it by rubbing the stain carefully with fine sandpaper. This will work for scuff marks and other stains as well.

Clean and easy shoe storage. A good way to store shoes is to slip them inside zip-lock bags. They'll remain dust free in your closet or attic. And if you're packing for a trip, bring out those baggies to keep the dirt from your shoes off the other items in your suitcase.

Clean white leather. Clean dirty white leather shoes with a white, non-gel toothpaste. Rub it on, rinse it off, and wipe shoes dry.

Away with wet sneakers. Use the floor in front of the refrigerator grille as a dryer. The fan in the fridge will dry tennis shoes overnight.

Tighten loose shoes. If your shoes are falling off your feet, try shrinking them. Wet the insides, then dry them outside in the sunlight.

No need to hold your nose. You can take the smell out of your shoes by filling them with baking soda. Leave them overnight, then remove the powder. They'll be fresh and ready to wear.

Don't cry over scorched fabric. You may be able to remove a scorch stain by rubbing it with grated onion. If it's really stubborn, soak it for a few hours in onion juice. Vinegar is another possible scorch remover, and peroxide might work on a cotton garment.

Out, out darn spot. Never rub a stain. Doing so can break the fibers on the surface of the fabric and may cause the stain to spread. It can also cause blotching and fading. Use a clean cloth sponge or maybe a soft toothbrush. Make a blotting or feathering motion (short light strokes) to remove as much of the staining substance as you can. If it has soaked through the garment, blot it from both sides if possible with a soft clean cloth. Work from the underside to move the stain out. When sponging or dabbing on a stain-removing substance, place the fabric face down on absorbent cloth or paper towel. By working from underneath, you'll push the stain out not in. Work from the outside edge of the stain toward the center to prevent making it larger. Be patient. Allow plenty of time for the agent to work before rinsing or laundering.

Nail that stain. You are giving yourself a manicure when your cat decides to get friendly, knocking over the fingernail polish in the process. Now how do you get that crimson stain out of your skirt? Quickly wipe up the excess. Then, unless the

fabric is acetate or triacetate, grab the nail polish remover. Place
the spot face down onto paper towels. Then sponge it with a
liberal dose of polish remover. Soak it in cool water. Apply
detergent to the stain and launder.

There's a fungus among us

Mildew is one of the toughest stains to get out. It is a fungus
that can grow and, in the advanced stages, weaken and
destroy some fabrics. If it occurs, treat it as quickly as possible with one of these solutions.

- Soak it in white vinegar.

- Dab on lemon juice and salt and put it in the sunshine.

- Blot repeatedly with hydrogen peroxide.

- Soak overnight in buttermilk or sour milk.

Don't sweat perspiration stains. Perspiration stains will
usually come out if you dampen them with cool water and rub
with bar soap. If the fabric has become discolored, sponge fresh
stains with ammonia or old stains with white vinegar. Rinse.
Launder with the hottest water the fabric can stand.

Deep freeze it. Sometimes an item of clothing gets stained,
but you don't have time to wash it right away. Put it in a plastic
bag and toss it in the freezer. Then wash when convenient, and
the stain will come out as if it just happened.

Get the yellow out. Some articles of clothing never go out
of style, so you can keep wearing them for years. However,
sometimes they yellow with age. To remove those yellow age
spots from washable wool or silk items, try sponging them with

a mixture of one tablespoon of white vinegar in a pint of water. Rinse and wash according to label directions.

Corny way to remove grease. Treat oily or greasy stains on your clothing with a paste of water and cornstarch. Apply, let dry, and brush off.

Give static cling the slip. Is static cling making you feel like a giant roll of plastic wrap? Give it the slip by rubbing some hand lotion into your palms, then smoothing it over your pantyhose or under your trouser legs. If you don't like the feeling of lotion on your clothes, try carrying several fabric softener sheets with you. Rub the sheet under the creeping, clinging material, and watch it settle down.

Wired up. Annoying static cling is often a problem during cold, dry winter months. If your skirt is sticking to your slip, try this diverting tactic. Run a wire coat hanger over your skirt or between your skirt and slip. The static energy should transfer from you to the wire. This also works for static-filled hair!

Don't hang an innocent sweater. Avoid hanging your sweaters in the closet. The sweater's own weight will stretch it out of shape. Instead, lay white tissue paper between folds and keep them in a sweater box. If sweaters are stacked, put the heaviest ones on the bottom of the pile and lightweight ones on top.

And the rust is history. For rust stains on white clothes, sprinkle with hot lemon juice, pat it in, then rinse with warm water. Or use lemon juice and salt and put it in the sunshine. Don't use chlorine bleach on rust stains. It can make the discoloration worse.

Zippity do-dah. When your zipper refuses to glide smoothly, try rubbing its little teeth with a candle, a pencil lead, or a bar of soap. The teeth should slip on down their tracks.

Be a kitchen magician

Make your pies shine. Ever wonder how professional bakers get that glossy shine on their pies? It's really quite simple. Beat an egg white and brush it over the crust before baking, and your pie will shine like a star.

Grease pans with ease. Save stick margarine wrappers in a plastic bag in your refrigerator. The bit of margarine clinging to the paper is perfect for buttering a cake pan or casserole dish without getting your hands greasy.

Cut classy cookies. Want refrigerator cookies that look like you got them from a bakery? Use a cheese slicer to cut uniform pieces from the roll. And for angels and gingerbread men with all their limbs intact, dip plastic cookie cutters in warm oil before using.

Fashion a fabulously flaky pie. If you want your pies to be light and flaky, sneak a teaspoon of vinegar into the cold water used to make the dough.

Slice a beautiful cake perfectly. Is there anything more frustrating than a beautiful cake that sticks to your knife and falls apart when you try to cut it? Serve perfect pieces for your friends and family by dipping your knife in a glass of cold water between slices.

Bake beautiful fruit pies. Use a glass baking dish when making fruit pies. Metal pans can react with the acid from fruit and discolor the pie. Just remember to reduce your oven temperature by 25 degrees when switching to glass.

Cap your dough to keep it moist. Use a clean, plastic shower cap to cover a bowl of rising dough. A large cap will allow enough room for the dough to rise without becoming uncovered. The cap can be washed and used again and again.

Score one for bar cookies. You can have perfectly cut bar cookies instead of jagged pieces if you score the cookie dough as soon as it comes out of the oven. Let it cool completely, then cut the bars along the lines you made.

Use flour power for cookies. You dropped them by rounded spoonfuls, and they looked perfect when you put them in the oven. So why did your cookies turn out like pancakes? Try adding a thin sprinkling of flour to your cookie sheet after greasing it. The flour will keep the cookies from spreading out too much, and it will also keep chocolate chips from sticking and burning.

Get rolling with refrigerator cookies. Refrigerator cookies will turn out beautifully if you follow this advice. You'll need the inner cardboard from a roll of paper towels. Cut the roll lengthwise, so you can open the tube. Line the inside with wax paper, then pack your cookie dough inside. Close it up, securing it with rubber bands, and chill the dough according to your recipe. When it's time for slicing, you'll have a perfectly shaped roll.

Leave leaky blueberries on ice. Don't bother to thaw frozen blueberries for pies, cakes, muffins, or any other baked goods. Thawing them will cause blueberry juice to run all over your creation.

Flour cake pans with cake mix. When a cake mix recipe calls for flouring the baking pan, use a bit of the dry cake mix instead of flour, and you won't get a white mess on the outside of your cake.

Test your cake with spaghetti. Don't have a wire cake tester to test for doneness? Do what grandma did. Grab a piece of uncooked spaghetti and gently poke the center of the cake. If the batter sticks to the pasta, it needs to bake a little longer. But if it comes out clean, your cake is done.

Put the heat on a stuck cake. You baked it to perfection, but now your masterpiece of a cake is stuck to the bottom of the pan. Don't panic. You need to heat the bottom of the pan to soften the hardened sugar and oil that are making it stick. You can do this by filling a large bowl with hot water and dipping the bottom of the pan in it. Or, if you have an electric stove, heat a burner then turn it off. Wait until it's warm but not hot, and place the cake pan on it for a few minutes. Either way, your cake should willingly exit the pan.

Crush cookies for creative pie crusts. Tired of graham cracker crusts? Add variety to your pie crusts by using all sorts of delicious ingredients. Each of the following when crushed will make approximately one cup of crumbs — 20 chocolate wafers, 30 vanilla wafers, or 15 gingersnaps. Your family will think you're a genius.

Measure without the mess. Use coffee filters to separate ingredients you've measured for a recipe, or to weigh food on a kitchen scale. You'll save yourself the trouble of washing several bowls.

Bake a potato in a flash. Cut the baking time on baked potatoes by choosing medium-size potatoes and placing them on end in a muffin pan. Bake as usual, only check back in half the normal time. You'll be amazed by how fast and well they cook.

Keep your peppers in shape. Looking for something to keep your stuffed peppers in shape while baking? Try lightly greased muffin tins. Just choose small peppers that will fit into the muffin cups.

Help for your chocolate cake. To keep chocolate cake brown on the bottom, dust the cake pan with cocoa rather than flour.

Simple way to get a cake out of the pan. Cake won't stick to the bottom of the pan if you cover it with wax paper. Use scissors to cut it to the shape of the pan. Spray the paper with cooking spray, then pour in the batter. When it's done, you can easily remove the cake from the pan and peel off the wax paper.

No more waste on baking day. Do you end up wasting more flour than you use when you're preparing pans for baking? Instead of piling flour into a greased pan with a spoon, try filling a large saltshaker with flour. It makes "dusting" quick and easy.

Bake better potatoes. If you insert a tenpenny nail into one end of a potato, it will conduct heat to the inside and bake your potato more quickly. Of course, don't do this if you're baking your potato in a microwave.

Keep cookies from sticking together. Few gifts are as appreciated as a freshly baked batch of homemade cookies in an attractive box or tin. To keep cookies from sticking together, separate the layers with paper coffee filters.

Kiss boring barbecues goodbye. Add a touch of exotic flavoring to your grilled food by placing fresh herbs on your hot coals. Try using rosemary, dried basil seedpods, and savory. As the coals heat up, the aroma will cling to your food and send a pleasing fragrance through your yard.

Make an organic marinade brush. Need a marinade brush for your meat? Don't run to the store and spend money. Just grab a green onion from your refrigerator and use the stem. Throw it away when you're finished and start fresh the next time you grill.

Ban bacteria from grilled food. You carefully carry the seasoned hamburger patties outside to the grill and cook them to perfection. Now it's time to bring your masterpieces to the table. Hold everything! You aren't going to put them back on the same plate, are you? If you do, your wonderful burgers could become contaminated with bacteria from the raw meat. The same goes for your utensils. Use clean plates and utensils to remove cooked foods from the grill, and wash your hands often. You and your loved ones will be glad you did.

Watch out for messy charcoal. Oh no! Your guests just arrived for your cookout and you're covered with charcoal soot from your grill. Next time you buy charcoal, fill paper grocery bags with enough charcoal for one fire each. When it's time to fire up the grill, just toss in one of the bags and light it. It will quickly burn and ignite the charcoal without getting your hands or clothes dirty.

Grill a fresh and fruity treat. Make a wonderfully easy summer dessert next time you barbecue. Place whole, unpeeled bananas right on the grill, and cook them for about eight minutes, turning often. Slice open, top with sauce or ice cream, and enjoy!

Enjoy delicious orange juice anytime. If you live alone, a carton of orange juice probably goes bad before you can drink it all. Try buying a can of frozen orange juice and keeping it in your freezer. When you want a glass of juice, pop off the metal lid and mix enough concentrate and water for just one serving. Keep the covered can in your freezer, and you'll be all set for a refreshing glass of juice the next time you get a craving.

Cube bread quickly. You love making bread stuffing and croutons from scratch like your mom did, but you hate cutting up all those little bits of bread. Next time, try using a pizza cutter. It cuts bread quickly and neatly.

Say 'so long' to soggy bread. Bread is on sale, and you'd like to stock your freezer. But you're afraid you'll get soggy loaves when you thaw the bread out. Go ahead and buy several loaves. Simply tuck a paper towel into each bag before you pop them in the freezer. When you defrost a loaf, the towel will absorb the moisture, and your bread will be free of dampness.

Keep bread fresh longer. Is your bread stale before you can enjoy it all? Try storing it in a plastic bag with a piece of fresh celery. Your bread will stay fresh much longer.

Flip fluffier flapjacks. Your family and friends will wonder what magical recipe you've stumbled across when you serve them pancakes lighter than air. The secret? Simply substitute club soda for the recipe's liquid ingredients.

Bag the bread crumbs. Save the end pieces and cut-off crusts from your loaves of bread in a plastic bag in the freezer. Next time you need bread crumbs for a recipe, get out the bag and run the bread through a food processor or blender to make crumbs.

Keep rolls warm longer. Those delicious yeast rolls you made for your dinner party will stay warmer longer if you put a piece of aluminum foil under the napkin in your breadbasket.

Homemade bread gets a new twist. If you make your own bread, be bold. Experiment with different liquids in your recipes.

You can substitute milk, fruit juices, even meat or vegetable broth for water. It will give your bread a wonderfully distinctive flavor.

Easy homemade croutons. If bread gets stale, you can use it to make delicious croutons. Choose your favorite herbs and seasonings and mix with olive oil. Brush both sides of the bread with this mixture. Cut into cubes and arrange in a single layer on a cookie sheet. Bake at 300 degrees until they are dry and crisp.

Become a chocolate expert. Mmmm. Homemade chocolate candy is so good — if you know what you're doing. For starters, cut chocolate into small pieces for quick melting. Place the pieces in the top of a double boiler, and keep the water hot but not boiling. If the temperature is too high, the flavor and consistency will be off. Be sure the top pan is not touching the hot water in the lower pan, since that could burn the chocolate. Stir it constantly to keep the heat evenly distributed. For a quick melt, use your microwave. Dark chocolate can be heated on medium heat at 50 percent power. Heat milk and white chocolate on low heat at only 30 percent power. Stop the microwave every 15 seconds to stir, and stop heating just before it's completely melted. Continue stirring until the remaining heat finishes melting the chocolate. If you need to soften hardening chocolate, add a bit of vegetable oil until it's liquefied. Never add water to chocolate, which is oil-based. It won't mix, and your batch will be ruined. Beware of drops of moisture on utensils and bowls that could spoil your hard work.

Drizzle chocolate like a gourmet chef. Decorate cakes or brownies like a pastry chef. Place half a plain chocolate bar in a small, microwavable plastic bag. Heat in the microwave until the chocolate melts. Then snip a tiny bit off a corner of the bag and squeeze as you drizzle a design on your creation.

Perk up your coffee with salt. If your coffee has been warming on your automatic coffee maker for over an hour, chances are it will taste less than fresh. Don't throw it out. Toss in a pinch of salt to improve the flavor and neutralize the bitterness.

Increase shelf life with plastic lids. Don't throw out the plastic lid from that empty coffee can. Slip it on the bottom of your new coffee can to protect your cabinet shelf from scuff marks.

Clean a thermos bottle. A thermos full of hot coffee can come in handy on a cold day, but coffee can stain the inside. To remove stains, fill it with water, drop in three denture tablets, and let them fizz your thermos clean.

Make a coffee filter. You simply must have your coffee in the morning, but you're out of coffee filters. There's no need to panic — as long as you have some paper towels in the house. Use one to make an emergency coffee filter.

Smooth out bitter coffee. If your brewed coffee has become bitter from sitting a bit too long, add just a touch of club soda (about one-fourth cup for every one and a half cups of coffee). Stir and enjoy.

Coffee lovers chill out. When that caffeine urge strikes, make yourself a cup of real coffee in an "instant." Just make a pot of very strong coffee. Pour it into an ice cube tray and freeze. When you want some coffee, toss a couple of cubes in a cup and add boiling water.

Brew fresher coffee with fresher beans. Your coffee beans will stay fresh longer if you store them in the freezer. This is especially helpful if you don't make coffee very often.

Pour batter easily. For little hands that want to help with baking, mix the batter in an extra-large measuring pitcher. That way, little ones will have a handle and pouring spout when it comes time to fill the cake or muffin pan. And the next time you're in the mood for waffles or pancakes, transfer the batter into an empty milk jug before hitting the griddle. You'll pour just enough batter each time, and if you have leftovers, just put the jug in your refrigerator.

Don't let cream sour your holiday. Yikes! It's a holiday and you need sour cream for your recipe. But the grocery stores are closed, and the convenience stores have been picked clean. Here's an easy substitution. Mix one tablespoon of lemon juice into a cup of evaporated milk. Leave the mixture at room temperature for 40 minutes, and you've got sour cream. No evaporated milk in the pantry? No sweat. Just mix three-fourths cup of buttermilk or sour milk with five tablespoons of melted and cooled butter.

Learn this great way to grate cheese. If you place your cheese grater in the freezer for several minutes before grating, cheese won't stick to the metal. Running it under cold water will work, too, but be sure to dry it completely before grating.

Udderly fresh. To double the shelf life of milk, add a pinch of salt when you first open it. And you can freeze it, too! So when your grocery store has a big sale, go ahead and buy a few extra gallons and store them in your chest freezer. It doesn't affect the nutritional value, but it may make the milk separate. Just shake well before using.

Put bad milk to good use. If your recipe calls for buttermilk but you have only fresh milk on hand, here's how to sour your milk and save yourself a trip to the store. Add one tablespoon of vinegar or lemon juice to a cup of fresh milk. Stir it and wait five minutes. Then just add it to your recipe. You can also substitute equal amounts of plain yogurt for buttermilk or buttermilk for plain yogurt.

Make cheese. Yogurt cheese can be a natural, low-fat alternative to cream cheese. You make this tasty cheese by removing the liquid from yogurt. Put 8 ounces of plain low-fat or nonfat yogurt that doesn't contain gelatin into a strainer lined with cheesecloth or three coffee filters. Don't try to use yogurt with fruit because the fruit tends to clog the strainer. Place the strainer over a bowl to catch the draining liquid. Cover and refrigerate for 24 hours. The liquid will drain into the bowl and leave behind a versatile yogurt cheese. You can season it with herbs and spread it on a bagel, or use it as a dip for chips, crackers, or veggies. You can even use it in place of cream cheese in your favorite cheesecake recipe. Make it with lemon yogurt to give your cheesecake a tangy twist.

Topsy-turvy keeps dairy foods fresh. If you store yogurt, cottage cheese, and sour cream upside down in your refrigerator, they will stay fresh longer. Just make sure the lids are on tight. Transfer these dairy foods to smaller containers when your supply gets low, and they won't go bad as quickly.

A salty solution. Ever make a hard-boiled egg only to have half of it stick to the shell? Here's a simple solution. Add a pinch of salt to the boiling water, and the shell will come off easily.

Peel hard-boiled eggs the easy way. Yes, yes, you know when eating hard-boiled eggs with the queen you should daintily tap the egg with your spoon and carefully remove the shell. But what about when you're making egg salad for 20? First, be sure the queen is nowhere in sight. Next, roll the hard-boiled egg on your counter while pressing down a bit. Finally, insert a teaspoon between the egg and its shell and gently move the spoon around the egg. The shell should easily fall off.

Keep eggs under cover. Never mind those cute egg holders that are built into your refrigerator door. Eggs are better off kept in their padded cartons where they can't soak up odors from other foods.

Save your eggs from a crackup. Save energy and make perfect hard-boiled eggs. Using a pot with a tight lid, cover your eggs with water, add a pinch of salt, and bring to a rolling boil. As soon as the water is boiling rapidly, turn off the heat and allow the pot to stand, unopened, for 10 minutes before removing your eggs. This allows the eggs to finish cooking without cracking and breaking.

Root out the rotten ones. Sometimes eggs lay around in your refrigerator for eons before you realize they're past their prime. To test an egg for freshness, fill a cup with water and add two teaspoons of salt. Gently place the egg in the water. If it sinks, it's still fresh. If it floats, toss it.

Scramble scrumptious eggs. Grandma knew how to stretch her food budget and make food taste good, too. Try her secret for delicious, fluffy scrambled eggs. Simply beat bread crumbs into the eggs before scrambling. You'll get more great-tasting servings per egg.

Color code the hard ones. Add a drop of food coloring to the water when boiling eggs. That way, when you put them back in the refrigerator, you'll immediately know which ones are hard-boiled and which aren't.

Plump up your deviled eggs. Want your deviled eggs to have plenty of filling? Mash the boiled yolks with some cottage cheese, then season and stuff as usual. Your eggs will taste and look super.

Beat eggs to a fluffy finish. Whip up unbelievably fluffy omelets and scrambled eggs with this secret. For each egg, add one-quarter teaspoon of cornstarch and beat well.

Humpty Dumpty should have tried this. If your egg cracks during boiling, add a splash of vinegar to the water to seal the crack and save the egg.

Perfect peels and super slices. You can peel hard-boiled eggs perfectly. As soon as they are cooked, put them in ice water for one minute. The cold water will cause each egg to shrink away from its shell. Then put them back into boiling water for 10 seconds. The hot water will make the shell expand away from the egg. Remove the eggs and crack the shells all over, then start peeling them at the large end. The combination of heat and cold will make peeling a snap.

When only the hen knows for sure. You can figure out how fresh an egg is by placing it in the bottom of a bowl of cold water. If it lies on its side, it's fresh. If it stands at an angle, it's at least three days old. If it stands on end, it's at least 10 days old

Easy-does-it deviled eggs. A simple, no-mess way to make deviled eggs is to put all the ingredients for the filling into a zip-lock bag, seal, and mix by kneading the bag for a few minutes. Then just cut a small hole in one corner of the bag, and pipe the filling into the egg white halves — no bowl, spoon, or pastry tube to clean!

Improve boiled eggs. Don't you just hate it when an egg cracks while it's boiling? If you add a couple of tablespoons of vinegar to your water before you boil, you can prevent that, and the eggs will peel more easily when they're cooked, too.

Slicing is simple. Use an egg slicer for fast and easy sliced mushrooms.

Store 'egg'stras in the freezer. If you have more eggs on hand than you can use right now, freeze some for later. Just crack one egg into each mold of an ice cube tray and freeze. When the egg cubes are hard, transfer them to a plastic freezer bag. Be sure to wash the trays in hot, soapy water afterward. Raw eggs can harbor harmful bacteria that can make you sick.

Save a yolk. Leftover egg yolks will last for a couple of days in the refrigerator. Slip unbroken yolks into a container of cold water and seal airtight until you are ready to use them. Or put them in a small bowl with two tablespoons of salad oil.

Whip cream into shape. Why won't your whipped cream ever stand up for you? Maybe it's not cold enough. Try using a metal bowl and putting it and your beaters in the freezer for a while. If your cream and utensils are icy cold, you'll soon have whipped cream standing up to salute you.

Put bad bananas on ice. Don't worry about bananas that are too ripe. Just hide them in your freezer — peel and all. They'll turn a brownish color, but it won't affect the taste of your banana bread or muffins. Pull them out to thaw a few hours before you need them for a recipe. They'll mash nicely with a fork.

Squirrel away nuts in the freezer. Go ahead and buy a pile of nuts on sale. They'll keep for years in a freezer if you put them in a coffee can with a plastic lid. When you want nuts for baking or nibbling, just remove some from the freezer and leave them at room temperature for a few hours.

Freshen up frozen fish. Do your frozen fish fillets taste like they've been in your freezer since the ice age? They'll taste fresher when you serve them if you place them in a cup of milk to thaw.

Shape up your soup. Freeze soup and other liquids in a plastic bag inside a coffee can. This makes a shape that's easier to store. Once the food is frozen, you can remove the can and use it again.

Fixings in the freezer. Keep two containers in your freezer for soup fixings. Use one for meat scraps and bones. Put vegetable leftovers, like celery leaves and carrot tops, in the other. Use for meat broth and vegetable stock.

Freeze up perfect hamburgers. Save the plastic lids from coffee cans, and layer them between raw hamburger patties. When you've got a good stack, put them in a container and freeze.

Replace freezer tape. Masking tape works as well as the more expensive freezer tape. You can write on it, and it sticks tight. Cellophane tape, on the other hand, won't hold when frozen.

Freeze a spare. If you are making a casserole, make an extra one and freeze it for another meal. Just take it out of the oven about 10 minutes before the one you'll eat right away, and let it cool. If using a dish that can handle sudden temperature changes, set it in a pan of ice. If you think you'll need the baking dish before you're ready to eat the casserole, plan ahead. Before filling the dish, line it with aluminum foil. After the casserole is frozen, lift it out and wrap it so it's air tight. When you're ready to reheat it, slip it back into its original container. If there's a crumb topping, leave it off until you're ready to heat it.

Enjoy summer's harvest all year long. When spring or summer berries are in season — whether growing in your garden or plentiful at the supermarket — freeze some to enjoy in winter. Put them in the freezer on a cookie sheet. When they are frozen, transfer them to freezer containers. They won't stick together, so you can use just the amount you need without defrosting extras.

Cold wrap is less clingy. Tired of fighting with your roll of clear plastic wrap? Freeze it. If you store it in the freezer, it will unroll and tear more easily, and it won't stick to itself until it thaws out. Anytime you have trouble getting it to stick to your bowl, try moistening the outer edge of the dish before you wrap it.

Stretch summer's abundance. Don't let those extra tomatoes from your garden go to waste. Instead, wash them, cut out the cores, and freeze them whole for soups and stews. When you're ready to use them, hold them under running water, and the skins will slide right off.

Freeze liquids without splashes. When you want to freeze a liquid in a plastic bag, put the bag inside a plastic cup or food container. It will hold its shape while you pour and freeze it. Once it's frozen, if you want the container for other uses, remove the bag. When you are ready to defrost it, slip the frozen liquid out of the bag and return it to the same or a similar container to thaw.

Flatter means a faster thaw. If you buy hamburger in bulk and freeze it in smaller portions, try this tip. Separate it and put it into zip-lock bags. Flatten each one evenly with a rolling pin. Seal and freeze. It takes less space in your freezer, stacks neatly, and thaws out more quickly.

Squeeze more juice from a lemon. When life hands you lemons, you're supposed to make lemonade. But don't ruin the opportunity by wasting juice. Take lemons, or other citrus fruit, out of the refrigerator a few hours before squeezing to get them to room temperature. If you forget to take the fruit out early, simply run them under warm water for a minute. Then roll them back and forth on a hard surface under the pressure of your palm. Now when you squeeze your lemons, you'll get plenty of juice.

Store strawberries carefully. Keep strawberries fresh in an uncovered colander in your refrigerator. And don't wash them until you're ready to use them. Strawberries are like little sponges. To keep them from soaking up too much water after washing, toss them in a salad spinner and spin them around a few times. After most of the water is gone, go ahead and cut off the tops. Use your cleaned strawberries at once for best flavor.

Bring out your berry best. If you want your berries to be their best, pull them out of the refrigerator an hour or two before you serve them. Room temperature brings out a berry's best flavor.

Soften hard sugar with an apple. Has your bag of brown sugar turned into an unusable mound of rock candy?

Place a slice of apple in the bag and reseal it. In no time, your sugar will be soft.

Prevent apples from turning brown. Go ahead and make fruit salad hours before your company arrives. And don't worry about the apple slices looking rusty. Simply squeeze a little lemon juice on the apple pieces, and they'll stay snowy white.

Crack a coconut with confidence. Opening a coconut is a delicate operation. If you just smash it with a hammer, you'll be in for a surprise. Coconuts contain a whitish juice called milk, which will make a mess if you don't drain it first. Find one of the "eyes" of the coconut by looking for round, hairless areas that are slightly indented and softer than the rest of the shell. Poke a hole in one of the eyes and drain the milk into a bowl. Now you're ready to crack it open — almost. Coconuts crack better when they're cold or hot. You can put it in the freezer for an hour, or heat it in a 350-degree oven for 20 to 30 minutes. If you heat it, be sure to let it cool before cracking. Cover the coconut with a towel and use a hammer to gently whack it all over. It will eventually break open, allowing you to cut out the meat. Enjoy.

Make a honey of a fruit salad. Ever made a beautiful fruit salad only to have it turn brown before you could serve it? A bit of light-flavored honey mixed into the fruit will take care of that. The small amount of natural acid in honey keeps fruit looking fresh.

Keep grapefruit fresh and juicy. You can keep grapefruit in a fruit bowl on your counter for about a week. If you want them to last longer, put them in your refrigerator in a plastic bag or in the fruit and vegetable bin.

Ripe and ready. Most fresh fruit you buy at the grocery store is gathered before it is fully ripe. But it will taste better if you allow it to ripen fully before eating. Some fruits like peaches, pears, and tomatoes will ripen faster if you place them in a brown paper bag. Just punch a few holes in the bag and place pieces of fruit inside in a single layer, not stacked on top of each other. Fold over the top of the bag and leave it on the counter. Check every day to see if it's ready to eat. When it's ripe, eat what you wish and store the rest in the refrigerator.

Keep kiwi for months. Unripened kiwi, which are very firm, can keep in your refrigerator as long as six months if they haven't started to ripen. When you want them to ripen, leave them at room temperature until they soften.

Freshen food with salt water. Keep your apples, pears, and potatoes from turning brown as you slice them. Just drop them straight into lightly salted, cold water. They'll look freshly cut until you serve them.

Is your pineapple ripe? Do you have trouble figuring out whether a pineapple is ripe? Try plucking a leaf from the crown. If it comes out easily, it's ripe.

When you're craving banana bread. Your bunch of bananas has ripened, but you don't have time to eat them. Here's an easy alternative to the old idea of freezing them in their skins. Peel and slice the bananas, puree them in the blender, and add a little lemon juice to keep them from browning. Store them in a bag in the freezer for up to six months. Then when you're ready to make banana bread or a refreshing fruit smoothie, just thaw overnight in the refrigerator.

Pleasingly plump. If raisins dry out, soak them in hot water for a few minutes to soften them before putting them in your recipes.

Savor the tart taste. If your recipe calls for only the juice of the lemon, don't waste the peel. Cut it up and freeze it to use later when you need freshly grated lemon peel.

Put the lid on your grapefruit. If a half of grapefruit is part of your breakfast routine, keep the other half fresh in the fridge by placing it upside down on a clean coffee can lid.

Keep fruit from turning brown. You want your fruit salad to look perfect for the party, but it would save your schedule if you could chop up the fruit ahead of time. Go ahead. Just toss it all in some lemon juice, and it won't turn brown. The fruit will stay fresh-looking, and the flavor will remain fruity.

Store fruit at peak of freshness. Some fruits, like blueberries, cranberries, and strawberries, do not ripen anymore after they are picked and should be refrigerated immediately. Bananas, on the other hand, are always picked green, but they ripen quickly. When they have brown speckles called "honey spots," they are very sweet and ready to eat. You can store them in the refrigerator. The skins will turn black, but the banana inside will stay fresh for several days.

Banana math. And in case you need to know, three or four medium-size bananas will make a pound. A pound will yield about one and three-quarters of a cup of mashed bananas.

Freeze meat for stir-fry. A stir-fry dinner means quick cooking and cleanup. Streamline the process even more by freezing beef, pork, and boneless, skinless chicken breasts for 10 minutes before slicing. They'll cut neatly, making your job that much easier.

No more fish odor. Do you love fried fish but hate the lingering smell in your house? Next time you're ready to fry up a batch, drop a small amount of peanut butter into the pan with the fish.

Fry without splatters. Do you avoid frying bacon because you always get zinged with hot grease? Try adding a little salt to your frying pan, and say goodbye to dangerous popping grease.

Overpower garlic with lemon. Your hands will smell lemony fresh after chopping garlic if you rub a cut lemon on your fingers.

Spices A to Z. If you take a few minutes to alphabetize your spice rack, finding spices when you are in the middle of preparing a meal is easy. Also, when you are preparing your shopping list or using a new recipe, you can quickly check to see if you have the necessary ingredient without looking at all your spice bottles to make sure. This is a real time saver.

Cut the clinginess. Herbs like parsley, cilantro, sage, and rosemary can cling to a cutting board. Use kitchen scissors to cut them, letting them fall directly into a dish or glass measuring cup. It will be easier, and you'll have less waste.

Slip sliding away. A clove of garlic, on the other hand, tends to slip around on the cutting board when you are trying to mince it. To keep it still, sprinkle the board with salt, crush the garlic by pressing down on it with the flat side of the knife blade, then chop it.

Save your blood pressure. So you made a little mistake and put too much salt in the casserole? Don't throw it out. Add an apple sliced into thin strips to the dish for a while. Then take out the apple and the salt goes with it! Also, try this to remove the bad taste when foods and sauces burn. If it's salty soup you're having trouble with, add a peeled potato. It will absorb the extra salt. Just toss it out when the soup's done.

Shake salt freely. Few things are more frustrating than a shaker that won't give up its salt. If you add a few grains of rice to your shaker when you fill it, your salt will stay dry and free flowing.

Do a slow shake. Need to cut back on salt? Make it easier on yourself by shaking it from a pepper shaker. With fewer and smaller holes, you'll reduce the chance of overdoing it.

Make your ice cubes sparkle. You go out of your way to make fresh-squeezed lemonade for special guests. Don't ruin it with cloudy ice cubes that look like they were chipped out of the pond last winter. For crystal clear ice cubes, simply boil water, let it cool, then pour it into your ice cube trays. Boiled water freezes clearly because it contains less oxygen.

Remove fat from soup. You're on a diet, and you're trying hard to eat low-fat. Try sliding a few ice cubes into your soups and stews to remove excess fat. The fat will congeal around the cubes as they melt, and you can fish it all out with a spoon. Reheat, and you have an ultra-low-fat dish to enjoy.

Fresh-tasting rice the second time around. Reheat leftover rice in the microwave with an ice cube on top. The added moisture will really perk up the taste.

Get a grip on jars. If it seems like jars are getting harder and harder to open, try wrapping a rubber band around the lid or donning a pair of rubber gloves. Either way, it will help keep the lid from slipping out of your grasp.

Tenderize tough meat with vinegar. Does your inexpensive stew meat turn into shoe leather after cooking? Try this. Add a tablespoon of vinegar to the water while boiling. The vinegar will tenderize even the toughest meat so you can cut it with a fork.

Tenderize meat with a tropical fruit. Try something exotic to tenderize your meat tonight. Kiwi — that cute, little green fruit — contains the enzyme actinidin, which works great on tough meat and lends an interesting flavor.

Prevent roasts from sticking. Don't settle for roasts and poultry getting stuck to your roasting pan. Prop it up with a few stalks of fresh celery before cooking. The celery will lend a bit of flavor and make cleaning up a breeze.

Defrost meat safely with your microwave. A big problem with defrosting meat is not knowing if the center is thawed. If it's still frozen, your meat won't cook evenly, and even worse, the still-cold center could harbor bacteria. That's where your microwave comes in. Microwaves heat from the inside out, which is not good for cooking a roast, but it's great for defrosting one. Use the "defrost" setting, and microwave about 10 minutes for each pound of meat. Be sure to turn the meat regularly for even thawing. If you don't have a "defrost" setting, check your microwave's manual for recommendations.

Roast a juicy chicken. If your roasted chicken makes people gasp for water, try juicing it up with an apple. Just stuff a whole apple inside the chicken and roast as usual. Throw the apple away and serve your moist and tender chicken with pride. Or try a lemon. Start with a large roasting chicken, and season it with salt and pepper inside and out. Cut a lemon in half and squeeze the juice over the chicken, then pour a quarter cup of water on it. Toss the lemon halves inside the chicken for extra juiciness and place the bird in a greased baking dish. Bake in a 300-degree oven for about three hours, basting it with water as needed.

Keep frozen meat frost free. Freezer burn can ruin perfectly good meat. To keep it from chipping away at your food budget, store meat in plastic freezer bags, and carefully press all the air out of the bag before storing. Frost is less likely to form without air. In addition, label everything you put in the freezer, and be sure to note the date.

Make your roast cook your vegetables. Why waste time, extra pots, and energy cooking vegetables separately from your roast? Use a roasting pan with a good lid, and place the vegetables around the roast. Cut potatoes and onions into small pieces and throw in some baby carrots. Add half a cup of water and about 10 minutes to the roast's cooking time. Your entire meal will be done at once.

Tenderize tough meat with tea. A tough cut of meat will soften up nicely if you braise it in black tea. Place four table-spoons of black tea leaves in warm — not boiling — water and allow to steep for about five minutes. Strain the leaves from the water and stir in a half cup of brown sugar until dissolved. Season 2 to 3 pounds of meat with salt, pepper, onion, and garlic pow-der, and place it in a Dutch oven. Pour the mixture over the meat and cook in a preheated, 325-degree oven until tender. Because the meat cooks slowly, it will take about an hour and a half, but it will turn out so tender you'll be able to cut it with a fork.

Mess-free meat loaf. Make meat loaf and you make a mess, right? Not necessarily. Put all the ingredients in a large zip-top bag, push out most of the air, and seal the top. Then knead and blend the ingredients from the outside of the bag, form into a loaf shape, remove from the bag, and put into the pan to bake.

A brush with the sauce. For basting meats or brushing on sauces, use a natural bristle paint brush. It will be flexible and easy to clean. And when grilling, dip the brush in olive oil and spread it on the grate to keep the meat from sticking.

Be fast on the thaw. There's an easy way to store ground beef so that it will thaw faster when you're ready to cook it. Put about a pound of ground beef in a large zip-lock freezer bag and then flatten it like a pancake. It stores more easily and thaws in half the time.

Bits about bacon. Keep bacon from sticking together in the package by rolling the package into a tube and holding it for a minute. The slices will loosen up and come out of the package one at a time.

Truss up that bird. Dental floss is a handy helper when trussing up turkey or other poultry for roasting.

Marinate meat. Zip-lock bags are the ideal no-mess method for marinating meat. You don't have to use as much liquid, and instead of having to turn or baste the meat, you just flip the bag over.

Keep the flavor, lose the fat. Skinless chicken is lower in fat, but the skin seals in flavor, vitamins, and moisture. So cook it first, then remove the skin.

Steam vegetables with ease. Save time cooking and cleaning pans by steaming vegetables in your microwave. Using a plastic bag made for use in the microwave, add fresh, cut vegetables and a few teaspoons of water. Don't completely seal the bag so steam can escape. Microwave for two or three minutes or until the veggies are tender.

Make your microwave work smarter. Arrange food carefully in your microwave so everything will be finished at the same time. Place thicker and larger pieces of food on the outside edges of a plate, and smaller pieces toward the middle. For example, when you microwave stalks of broccoli, put the heads pointing toward the middle, and aim the thick stems toward the rim of the plate.

Crack nuts in your microwave. Don't use a sledgehammer to crack nuts open. There's an easier way. Put hard nuts, like walnuts, Brazil nuts, and pecans, in a bowl of water and cover. Heat on a high setting until the water boils. Let the bowl stand in your microwave until the water cools a bit, then drain. You should now be able to open the shells easily. Crack them over a bowl to catch excess water.

Peel chestnuts easily. Chestnuts roasting in the microwave. It's not the stuff songs are made of, but it helps their skins fall right off. Here's how. Make a small slit in the round end of each of several chestnuts. Place them in a bowl of water and heat on high for three to four minutes or until boiling. Allow the water to boil for another minute, then turn off the microwave. Let the bowl cool for five to 10 minutes. When the water is cool enough, remove one chestnut at a time and peel. The water will keep the others soft until you get to them.

Toast nuts quickly and easily. Toast nuts and seeds quickly in your microwave. Coat a microwavable plate with a thin layer of oil or butter. A spray works well. Scatter sunflower, sesame, or pumpkin seeds on the plate and microwave on high for three or four minutes. Stir every minute or so. When they begin to turn brown, they're toasted.

Cold corn for hot popping. Store microwave popcorn in the freezer to keep it from getting stale. This will also reduce the number of those irritating unpopped kernels when you pop it.

Cook healthier bacon. If you love bacon, but not the fat, cook it in your microwave. Lay a few strips side by side on a paper towel, then place the paper towel on a plate. Cover with another paper towel and cook. The paper towels will absorb the fat, leaving you with crispier, leaner bacon.

Skin garlic cloves. The simplest way to quickly remove the skin from garlic cloves? Zap them in the microwave for about 15 seconds.

End of the line for hands. Get rid of that fishy smell on your hands by washing them with toothpaste.

Stop throwing out salad. Make a crisp, tossed salad the day before your holiday gathering and spend time mingling with your guests. Here's the secret. Choose a large bowl and add lettuce, celery, cucumbers, cabbage, radishes, broccoli, cauliflower, green and red peppers, carrots, and green onions. Don't add any tomatoes. Cover the salad completely with water and refrigerate. When it's time to serve your guests, drain the salad well and add tomatoes. Your salad will be as fresh as if you just made it.

Cook pasta like a pro. Cooking pasta to perfection is a delicate operation, so don't be heavy-handed. Use a lightweight pot, and the water will boil faster and return to a boil quickly after you add the pasta. Best of all, your spaghetti won't clump together or stick to the bottom of the pot.

Protect pasta from hidden peril. You'd never know by looking at it, but the pasta you have in pretty glass jars on your counter is under attack. Once fortified pasta is exposed to light, its vitamins start to break down. You'll have to use it within a month or two to get the benefit of the vitamins. For long-term storage, hide pasta in airtight containers in a dark place. You can keep it up to 18 months when stored properly.

To rinse or not to rinse. Experts say you shouldn't rinse pasta destined for sauce since its slightly sticky starch helps hold the sauce on your spaghetti. But if you're making lasagna, go ahead and rinse the wide noodles for better handling. Also, rinse any pasta you'll use in a cold salad. Cold, starchy pasta doesn't taste so hot.

Smart boiling secrets. If you place a spoon in a pot of pasta before boiling, it won't boil over. Another trick is to treat the pot with nonstick spray before adding the water, or adding a dash of oil and salt to the water. Whatever you do, never add the pasta before the water boils. If you do, you'll slow down the boiling process, and your pasta will stick together.

Keep spaghetti out of sight. Once you use some spaghetti from the 1-pound box, you're left with dry pasta falling out in your pantry. Next time, put the rest of the uncooked pasta in one of those cartons that stacked chips come in. Just be sure to label it so you don't accidentally take dry spaghetti to a picnic.

Don't let kitchen fires pan out. Reach for a cookie sheet when you have a pan fire on your stove. Smothering the fire with the sheet will extinguish it faster than you can say "chocolate chip."

Save dinner from going up in smoke. If you frequently forget about food cooking in the oven, wear a timer around your neck. Set the alarm so even if you snooze you'll know it's time to take your dinner out of the oven.

Shake, rattle, and put out the fire. Always keep a super-size shaker of salt, baking soda, or baking powder on your stove to help put out small cooking fires.

Improve a child's grip. Children sometimes have a difficult time holding onto a water glass. A wide rubber band, slipped around the glass, can improve their grip and lessen the chance of spills.

Keep cutting boards in place. Does your cutting board slide around whenever you chop something vigorously? Wrap a couple of rubber bands diagonally across each corner, and it will stay put so you can hack away at those veggies with as much gusto as you like.

Save sauce from garlic overkill. Were you a little heavy-handed with the garlic in your sauce or soup? Don't throw it out. Put a few parsley flakes in a tea infuser and place it in the garlicky brew for a few minutes. The parsley will attract and absorb the garlic, and your sauce will be saved.

Doctor a bitter sauce. If your spaghetti sauce tastes bitter, try adding a pinch of sugar. Sugar brings out the flavor of cooked tomatoes.

Save gravy flavor, ditch the fat. If you've got delicious beef or poultry broth to use for soups or gravies, don't worry about the fat. Simply strain it through a paper coffee filter, and you're left with flavorful, fat-free broth.

Kiss grease goodbye. Another quick way to get rid of the grease floating on top of your soup — drop in a leaf of lettuce. It will attract the grease. When you're done, just toss the lettuce and serve the soup!

Downsize fruit for one. You can enjoy melons and pineapples even if you live alone and can't use a whole one. Just ask the produce clerk to cut one in half for you. Most grocery stores are happy to oblige.

Jog memory to save money. Coupons are great for saving money — if you remember to hand them over at the checkout counter. To jog your memory, bring a large paper clip with your coupons. As you find an item, clip the appropriate coupon to the front of your purse. When you go to check out, your coupons will be ready to save you money.

A cooler way to store perishables. For a perfect addition to your cooler — whether you're returning from the grocery store or going on an extended trip — fill a clean, plastic milk jug with water and freeze. Your perishables will stay cold, and you'll have cold drinking water, too.

Make grocery shopping less painful. Keep a couple of laundry baskets and a cooler in the trunk of your car. The baskets will make carrying a load of groceries into the house faster and easier. And the cooler is great for those spur-of-the-moment shopping trips or when you can't go straight home to unload.

Cut costs at the checkout. To save money at the grocery store, think ahead. Plan the week's menu before you go — and make a list. Otherwise, you may end up buying things you don't need and still not have all the ingredients to make dinner every night.

Pay attention to prices. Watch the price of items as they are scanned. If a price is different than the price marked, alert the cashier. Stores have various policies about scanner errors.

You may get the item free. At the very least, the store should correct the price.

Get the most fruit for your buck. All prepackaged bags of fruits and vegetables are not created equal. Even though they may be labeled 5 pounds, some will weigh more than others. Test a few on the scale and purchase the one that weighs the most.

Check out the salad bar. If your recipe calls for just a few broccoli or cauliflower florets, buy them in the supermarket salad bar. You won't have leftover parts that might go to waste, and you'll save preparation time as well.

Bake cookies that stay fresh. Do your homemade cookies turn into rocks before they can all be eaten? Substitute honey for the recipe's sugar and your cookies will stay moist longer. For every cup of honey you use, decrease other liquid in the recipe by one-fourth cup.

A kinder, gentler nutcracker. For an easy way to crack nuts that leaves the nut meat intact, soak walnuts or pecans in salty water overnight and then gently crack them the next day.

Decorate a cake with ease. Need a pastry bag with a decorating tip? Make one from a zip-lock plastic bag. Spoon frosting into the bag, press out the air, then snip off a bottom corner. Give a squeeze and decorate your cake with no fuss or muss.

Cutting the cake without the crumbs. Try cutting a hot cake with thread or even dental floss instead of a knife. Hold the thread taut on both ends and run through the hot cake quickly. It's much easier and won't cause a crumbly mess. Thread works well to cut angel food and chiffon cakes when they are cold, as well.

When it just won't cooperate. Has your opened box of brown sugar become so hard that you can't even scoop it out? Put a soft piece of bread in a plastic bag with the hardened brown sugar to soften it. Wait a few hours and you'll be able to measure it again.

Frosting that's easy as... cake. Out of frosting for your cupcakes? Don't worry. Plop a marshmallow on top of each one a minute or so before they're due to come out of the oven. Instant gooey frosting.

A great way to store crunchy veggies. It's easier to choose healthy snacks if they're readily available. Keep carrot and celery sticks fresh and crunchy in your fridge by using this handy tip. Take a clean, two-liter bottle and cut off the top to the desired height. Partially fill the bottom with cold water and a few ice cubes. Stand your veggies up in the water, and you'll always have healthy munchies on hand.

Lengthen the life of cooking oil. Store your cooking oil in colored, plastic bottles made for condiments. They're easy to pour, and the oil will last longer than in clear plastic or glass because light can't penetrate the container. Just be sure to label the bottles with a permanent marker so no one accidentally squirts oil on a hot dog.

Boycott smashed sandwiches. Do you hate to throw anything away? Now you'll know what to do with those boxes your sticks of butter come in. They're perfect for keeping a sandwich from getting smashed by the other food in your lunch bag. Wrap your sandwich in plastic, then slide it into the box. Come lunchtime, your sandwich will look freshly made.

Get the scoop on scoops. Why throw away the scoop that comes with your box of laundry detergent? You can wash it out and use it to scoop your flour, sugar, or coffee.

A no-odor way to store leftovers. Although you shouldn't store food in open cans for long, a leftover that will get used up in a few hours can still make your fridge smell awful — especially that half-can of tuna, dog or cat food, or sauerkraut. Just drop the whole thing inside an empty coffee can and snap on the lid, and you'll have no odors and no problem.

Foil pests in your pantry. Use clean, plastic ice cream buckets to store flour, sugar, and grains in your pantry. They'll keep everything fresh and bug free. Stick a label on the outside and finding the right ingredient will be a snap.

Learn to love leftovers. You can save money if you never throw away plastic margarine tubs. They're great for storing leftovers in the fridge or the freezer.

Pour some sugar. When you store sugar in a canister, you have to fill a sugar bowl or dip your spoon into the canister. Instead, store it in a clean, dry, plastic milk jug. The sugar will pour out easily into your spoon or measuring cup.

Keep cooking oil fresh. Store oil in a cool, dark location, and it won't turn rancid as quickly.

Arrivederci, tomato. You've made a double batch of spaghetti sauce but hate to store it in your plastic ware. In the past, tomato sauce has left stains that just wouldn't come out. But you can avoid that problem. Just coat the inside of your container with vegetable oil or nonstick cooking spray before pouring in the sauce.

Keep onions away from potatoes. Don't store onions and potatoes together because moisture from the potatoes will cause the onions to sprout.

Add years to a pot's life. Never store food in aluminum pots because chemicals in the food can erode the metal. While this doesn't cause food poisoning, it does damage your pots and make them unsanitary to cook with.

Keep rice fresh. If you store your rice in airtight jars, it will keep for a couple of years.

High or low grade oil? Olive oil comes in several grades with extra-virgin being the tastiest but most expensive. Save money by reserving that for salads and other cold uses. In cooking, you lose some of the flavor anyway so you might as well start with a cheaper variety. You can also save money by making your own nonstick cooking spray. Just put your olive oil into a spray bottle.

Put a stop to unsavory smells. To keep onion and cabbage odors from spreading through the house, simply boil a cup of vinegar in a saucepan at the same time they are cooking. Remove the onion smell from a pot with a tablespoon of vinegar in hot water.

Banish the smell of icky veggies. Simmering a small pot of vinegar on a spare burner will help get rid of ugly odors from cooking certain vegetables, such as cabbage or sauerkraut.

Protect iron skillets from rust. Iron skillets are so durable they often become heirlooms, handed down through generations. The one thing that might destroy their beauty and durability is rust. To prevent this, rub your skillets with wax paper inside and out. This puts a thin layer of wax on the skillet that keeps air from interacting with the metal and moisture. If you store your iron cookware stacked inside each other, separate them with pieces of wax paper.

A sticky solution. To cut sticky foods, like dates or figs, more easily, dip the knife in cold water frequently. Or use a pair of clean scissors. Just rub butter on the blades before cutting marshmallows or fruit, and the food won't stick.

Shine stainless steel. Make those pots and pans brighter, both inside and out. Just rub them with lemon juice on a cloth. Out of lemon juice? Vinegar works just as well.

Make measuring easier. Reading the measurements on a set of white plastic measuring cups can be difficult. To make it easier, paint over the numbers with red nail polish. When it dries, scrape the nail polish off the raised measurements. The background will be red and the numbers white. Now you'll be able to tell at a glance if you have two-thirds or three-quarters of a cup.

Make a disposable funnel. Cut off the pouring end of a clean two-liter bottle, and you have a great funnel for messy jobs in your kitchen or garage. When you're through, just toss it away.

Use utensils twice. When cooking, measure dry ingredients first, then liquid ingredients in the same measuring cup or spoon. This strategy will speed your cleanup.

Foil limp celery. Don't let your celery get limp in the refrigerator. Wrap it in aluminum foil as soon as you get it home, and it will keep for weeks.

Banish onion odor. You love the taste of onion in your food, but you could do without that lingering scent on your hands. Here's what to do. Rub your hands with salt before you wash them, and the onion smell should vanish into thin air.

Sweeten the pot for sweet corn. For deliciously sweet corn on the cob, add a bit of milk or a pinch of sugar to the boiling water. But never salt the water. The calcium in it will make your corn tough.

Treat tomatoes tenderly. Even if you love tomatoes, you can only eat so many from your garden. Leave what you can use in a few days on the counter for everyone to admire, but don't put any in the refrigerator. Tomatoes don't take kindly to cool temperatures and quickly lose their flavor. Yet, they freeze just fine. Spread them out on a cookie sheet and put it in the freezer overnight. Once frozen, store them in your freezer in freezer bags. When you need tomatoes for cooking, simply thaw a few.

Banish tears with a candle. Does slicing onions make you weep for happier meals? Try slicing the onion under running water into a colander in your sink. Or light a candle next to your work area before you begin slicing. The gasses that make your eyes water will burn off before they reach you. Besides, your spouse will think it's romantic.

Serve artichokes with 'gourmet' dips. Don't get stuck in a rut dipping artichoke leaves in butter. After steaming the vegetables until tender, try dipping the leaves in Hollandaise sauce, light mayonnaise blended with lemon juice, or plain yogurt mixed with Dijon mustard.

Wake up wilted asparagus. Fresh asparagus is so expensive you can't afford to let it wilt in your refrigerator. To keep it fresh, and to perk up wilted asparagus, cut off a half inch from the bottom of the stalk and stand the vegetable in an inch of warm water. Be careful not to get the tips wet. Your asparagus will look and taste great when you cook them for dinner.

Serve a classy salad. Want to impress your friends with a fancy asparagus salad? Steam the vegetable early in the morning and toss them with a bit of red wine or balsamic vinegar. Refrigerate the asparagus for several hours until they're completely chilled. Just before serving, add a dusting of chopped, toasted almonds. Serve, sit back, and enjoy the compliments.

Microwave tender asparagus. Why bother with pots and pans when you can microwave a pound of asparagus to perfection in less than 10 minutes? Using a large, microwavable container, lay the asparagus in a single layer with the tips facing the center. Cover and microwave on high for a total of six to 10 minutes or until tender. Rearrange the asparagus after half that time, exchanging pieces on the outer edges of the container with ones in the middle. Cover again and finish cooking. Watch out for steam when you remove the cover from your cooked asparagus.

Ripen an avocado with a banana. Avocados go all the way back to the 9th century — almost as long as you've been waiting for the one on your counter to ripen. To speed up the process, seal the avocado in a plastic bag along with a ripe banana. Keep the bag at room temperature until the avocado becomes soft and ripe.

Prevent cauliflower from turning brown. Don't serve cauliflower that has turned brown from boiling. Squeeze a teaspoon of fresh lemon juice into the water, and your cauliflower will stay white.

Be hip to hot peppers

Do you like a little heat with your peppers, but don't want a three-alarm fire in your mouth? Before you drench your enchiladas with a bottle of hot sauce, check out the ingredients. Here's how peppers rank from mildest to hottest.

El Paso (Very mild)
Anaheim
Jalapeno
Hidalgo
Serrano
Cayenne
Tabasco
Red Chile
Chiltecpin
Tabiche
Bahamian
Kumataka
Habanero (Very hot)

Keep your mushrooms in the dark. If you want your mushrooms to last as long as possible, don't wash them before storing. Put them in the refrigerator in a paper bag or colored, plastic container that keeps the light out. Wash them just before you use them. Mushrooms last longest when they're cool, dark, and dry.

Get spinach squeaky clean. Ever wash spinach carefully only to have your family complain that it's gritty? Next time, wash it with salt water, and say goodbye to grit.

Cut tears when chopping onions. Try these tricks for slicing onions without regret. Push a small piece of bread onto the point of your knife and carefully work it down toward the handle. Now when you cut your onion, the bread will absorb the fumes that bring tears to your eyes. Or try freezing the onions for about 15 minutes before you slice them. The cold will keep the eye-watering fumes at a minimum.

Keep refrigerated veggies crisp. Vegetables and fruits can get soggy in the refrigerator, and often have to be thrown out before you have a chance to use them. But if you place a dry sponge in your vegetable bin, it will absorb some of the moisture and leave your strawberries, onions, carrots, and other produce crisp and fresh days or weeks longer.

Put an apple in your potato bin. If your potatoes start sprouting buds before you have a chance to use them, toss an apple in your potato bin. The apple will slow down the sprouting process.

Get fresh with a cute tomato. Make your fresh tomatoes last longer by storing them with the stem-side down.

Simple way to peel a tomato. To peel a tomato quickly and smoothly, place it in boiling water for 20 to 60 seconds. The skin will come off easily.

Sack the celery. Celery may come in plastic bags from the grocery but that isn't the best way to preserve it in the refrigerator. Place celery in a paper bag and leave the outside stalks and leaves on it for best storage.

Keep the crunch to munch. Sagging veggies take the bite-appeal out of a green salad. Resuscitate limp lettuce by adding lemon juice to a container of cold water. Place the lettuce in the container and soak for an hour in the refrigerator.

Give limp celery a boost. Revitalize those rubbery celery stalks by cutting them into pieces or strips and store them in a plastic container with enough water to cover the bottom.

Watch for waste with pricey veggies. When you buy expensive fresh vegetables, be sure you use every part you can. Broccoli stems can be peeled and cut into small strips, then cooked with the broccoli florets. Eat as is or puree in a blender to add to soup stock.

Delay the toss. Leftover tossed salad won't last very long. One way to extend its crispiness is to place several sheets of folded paper towel in the bottom of the plastic bag or container you're using for storage. It soaks up excess moisture and keeps the vegetables from getting soggy.

Best way to prepare asparagus. Pricey asparagus yields more than you think, too. Prepare each spear by cutting off and discarding the dried, light-colored end, which is too tough to eat. Bend the stalk in several places down the stem until the tender part snaps off. Peel the tough green piece below the break with a sharp paring knife and cook with the rest of the asparagus for a tender treat.

Foil the sprouts. Onions will last longer and not sprout if you wrap them in aluminum foil. If you cut an onion and use only half, rub the remaining onion half with butter on the cut edge. The butter will keep it fresh longer.

For odor-free fingers. Have onions to chop? Rub your hands before you start and again afterward with white vinegar. Rubbing them with the end of a stalk of celery also works. To get the scent of fish off your hands or kitchen utensils, rub them with vinegar and lemon. And if all else fails, just get out your toothpaste and use it to wash your hands. The ingredients in toothpaste that clean and freshen your mouth will do the same for your skin.

Remove silk from corn. To make sure you get all the silk from an ear of corn after you husk it, rub it down with a damp paper towel.

Rub food stains away. After you've cut up brightly colored vegetables, like carrots or pumpkin, you may have stained fingers. A slice of raw potato, rubbed across your skin, will lift off those stains.

Chop without tears. Partially freeze your onion before you start to cook. It will be easier to slice or chop, and you won't shed a single tear.

Mash a better potato. Some say the best mashed potatoes are made from baked potatoes rather than boiled. And since potatoes cooked whole contain more nutrients than those that are cut up, they may be healthier, too.

Pop your cork with ease. Wrap a bit of wax paper around a cork, and next time it will come out of the bottle without the usual effort.

Freeze leftover wine for cooking. If you're not much of a drinker, you might be tempted to throw out wine left over from a dinner party. Resist the urge, and freeze it in an ice cube tray instead. You can use it later for casseroles and sauces that call for a splash of vino.

Let your wine recline

Ever wonder why wine racks are built so the bottles can be laid on their sides? There's a good reason. If you don't store corked beverages lying down, the cork will dry up and won't fit properly when you try to re-cork the bottle. Alcoholic beverages without a cork can be stored standing at attention.

Substitutes serve the purpose. Are you waiting to make a recipe because you don't have the right wine? Cranberry juice or red grape juice both work in place of red wine, while white grape or apple juice can substitute for white wine.

Pop your cork. You are ready to pour the wine, but that cork just won't budge. Take a hot, wet towel, and wrap it around the neck of the bottle. The heat will make the glass expand a little, and your corkscrew should finish the job nicely.

Creative crafts for every occasion

Update Christmas dough ornament recipe. Make traditional dough ornaments for Christmas, but try something new. Update your recipe by adding oatmeal, cornmeal, or coffee grounds. Mix one cup each of water and flour with two cups of oatmeal for a wonderfully textured dough. Add a small amount of cornmeal or coffee grounds to the dough for extra texture, as well as color.

Make your own holiday pillows. If you buy fancy holiday pillows, you'll clean out your wallet and then have to clean out a closet to stash your regular pillows. That just doesn't make sense. Buy holiday fabric in January when it goes on sale, and use it to make slipcovers for the pillows you already have.

Create a winter wonderland. Mix together equal parts of white craft paint and liquid dish soap. Paint your window with icicles, snowmen, stars, whatever suits your fancy. Cleanup is as simple as a quick wipe with a wet cloth.

Untangle yarn with a straw. You've finally worked out that complicated two-tone sweater pattern, but the two balls of yarn keep getting tangled. To knit or crochet in peace, string each ball of yarn through a straw. The straw sleeve will keep them from snarling, and let you pull the yarn freely as you work.

Turn knitting needles into rulers. To gauge your progress as you knit, mark your needles every inch with nail polish. As you finish a row, you can measure how far you have come, and calculate how far you have to go.

Keep hands smooth as a baby's bottom. Sprinkle your hands lightly with baby powder when you knit or crochet baby gifts. Not only will your hands stay dry and silky, your finished garment will smell as sweet as a newborn babe.

A nifty way to knit. Poke a hole in the lid of a clean, plastic ice cream bucket and store your knitting yarn inside. Feed the end through the hole, and you'll never have a tangled mess on the floor again.

Keep yarn from getting tangled. Make a holder from a two-liter plastic soda bottle, and you'll have a smooth flow of yarn when knitting or crocheting. Simply cut the bottom off, and insert the ball of yarn. Pull the strand out the mouth of the bottle. Then tape the bottom back on so the yarn won't fall out and roll across the room.

Immortalize your summer blooms. Why pay hothouse prices for a winter bouquet when you can enjoy one from your own garden? In the summer, trim the buds off your favorite daisies and violets and flatten them carefully between two paper towels. Choose a variety of small blooms and greenery, making sure they are fairly flat and not wet with dew. Dry them for six to 10 weeks between the pages of a large book. Come winter, you can spend many a cozy hour creating cards, bookmarks, and framed posies from your dried treasures. You can even use them to decorate candles and lampshades in true Victorian style.

Remember fall all year long. The colors of autumn are breathtaking. Here's how you can enjoy the beauty of the season all year. Gather the most colorful leaves you can find and spray them with hair spray. Arrange some in a pretty basket or decorate a table or sideboard. The leaves will maintain their color and shine for weeks, well into the cold and dreary winter.

Pick flowers to make unique place mats. If you're expecting a large crowd for dinner and don't have enough place mats, make your own with treasures from your garden. Pick small, flat flowers and leaves and arrange them artistically on a sheet of wax paper. Carefully lay another sheet of wax paper on top and iron gently in place. Your guests will be impressed with these unique place mats. You can even use this decorative paper to wrap gifts or make gift bags.

Wrap up summer in time for winter. Here's a great way to use the summer blossoms you discover sandwiched between the pages of a book. Arrange them attractively on a piece of wax paper. Dab some glue on the back of each bloom, letting it dry slightly before carefully securing it in place with tweezers. Peel a piece of clear contact paper and gently smooth it over the flowers, making sure you don't disturb the arrangement. Grace a frame, card, bookmark, or photo album with one of these little posies. They will never lose their sunny charm.

Craft some pretty candles. Tired of plain candles? You can dress them up with spring finery by adding pressed flowers to their surfaces. Purchase pressed flowers or make your own by gathering small fresh blooms and leaves and placing them between layers of wax paper. Lay several heavy books on top and in a week or so the flowers will be ready to use. Purchase wax as "paraffin" in the canning section of your local supermarket or recycle used white candles. In a tin can placed in a saucepan full of water, melt some wax until it is transparent. (If the wax begins to smoke, it's too hot.) Brush a small amount of wax on the candle then place a pressed flower over the wax and press it in place with a toothpick. Paint hot wax over the pressed flower and candle with an artist's brush while continuing to press the flower in place. One or two thin layers of wax should be enough.

Bookmark it. Create an original floral bookmark by placing small flowers on the sticky side of a piece of wide, clear tape. Cover it with a pretty piece of ribbon, a little bit narrower than the tape. Add another piece of tape, sticky side toward the ribbon, to form the back. Turn it over to see the flowers against the ribbon background.

A memento of fall. If you love the beautiful colors of leaves in the fall, save a few of them. Just lay the leaf between two pieces of wax paper, and put the wax paper between two pieces of brown paper. Then press with a warm iron.

Create an elegant doorstop. You can easily turn a brick into an elegant doorstop. Wrap the fabric from an old evening bag or tapestry pillowcase around a brick, tacking it down on the ends. You may be surprised how pleasurable it is to enjoy your discarded accessory in its new form.

Secure knots with nail polish. To keep thread knots from coming undone while you're working on your cross-stitch, dab them with a drop of nail polish. The knot will stay firm even when you wash and frame the finished piece.

Try floss for color harmony. Next time you don't have the right color thread to sew a button on your coat, ransack your cross-stitch project for embroidery floss. When you find the right color, separate one thread from the six and enjoy instant thread matching. Double the thread for extra-strength mending.

Serve your heirlooms coffee. Tea-dyeing is a well-known trick to make new linens look old. Unfortunately, the tannic acid in tea will destroy your heirloom in 30 to 40 years. As an attractive alternative, dip your linens in coffee. The rich brown color will give your cloth an antique look without damaging the fabric.

Banish grease on fabric with shampoo. If you notice a grease stain on your new fabric, treat the spot with shampoo made for oily hair before pre-washing.

Dining room downsizing. If your favorite tablecloth has acquired some large holes you can no longer cover up with your dinner plates, consider recycling it. Cut it up into large squares or rectangles and hem the edges by hand or machine to make napkins or place mats. You can also bind the edges with bias-cut fabric or bias binding in a matching color.

The law of averages. Survey your patterns and figure out the average amount of fabric you need to make a pair of slacks, a skirt, a blouse, a slim dress. a full dress, and any other clothing you make for your family. Write these average amounts on an index card and stick it in your wallet. Then when you see the right fabric, you can buy exactly the amount you need.

Pretend it's wrapping paper. The best way to store fabric waiting to be made into clothing or household items is to roll it up. An open bookshelf or a box turned on its side makes the perfect storage area for your rolled fabric. Fold and roll the yardage to fit the depth of your shelves or box, then secure each piece with a rubber band. You'll know at a glance whether you have the right green or that perfect shade of pink.

Mind the mothballs. To discourage insects like moths and beetles from making a meal of your antique textiles, you can use moth crystals or mothballs. Put them in an old sock and hang it in the top of the closet. But use this method only for short-term storage. Both forms of moth repellent contain para-dichlorobenzene, a strong chemical that should not directly touch valuable textiles. It must be kept out of the reach of children and pets, too. Cedar chests and cabinets provide a more natural solution, although they won't repel all kinds of insects.

Preserve valuable textiles. Another way to store antique textiles is to use a cardboard tube, like the ones that blueprints are stored in. First, wrap the tube in acid-free tissue paper or plain unbleached muslin. Then wrap the item around the covered tube with the design or decoration to the inside.

Keep your treasures in the dark. Light humidity and extreme temperatures are the enemies of all your textile treasures. Vintage clothing, quilts, embroidered items, linens, needlepoint, and lace should all be protected from any extremes of humidity and temperature, doing best at 50 percent humidity and a temperature of 60 to 65 degrees. Fluorescent and ultraviolet light will fade colors and damage fabrics, so take the time to store your valuable textiles out of the light.

Safe storage secrets. Where you choose to store your textile treasures will make a big difference in how long they last. Several things that should never directly contact your textiles are wood, cardboard, plastic, and colored gift-wrap tissue paper.

What 'scent' those moths running? Use cedar chips, lavender flowers, rosemary, mint, or white peppercorns to keep moths from attacking your stored fabrics.

Get the most from acid-free products. Acid-free storage boxes and acid-free tissue paper are available for storing delicate antique textiles. Replace acid-free items every three years or so to ensure ongoing protection.

Use muslin to protect valuable fabric. Unbleached muslin fabric that has been washed to remove excess chemicals makes an excellent stable wrap for protecting old textiles.

Stock a craft box for kids. Grand kids coming for a visit? Start filling up a craft box now. Save scrap material, ribbons, buttons, pipe cleaners, tissue boxes, cardboard, and any other interesting items you might have. Add some poster paints, scissors, and glue, and the kids will amaze you with their creations.

Personalize a pencil holder. Help your grandchild make this personalized pencil holder for a parent, sibling, or teacher. First cut out a magazine picture of something interesting. Find a clean, clear, glass jar and cut the picture to fit inside. Using white, paper glue, paste the picture to the inside of the jar so it shows through the glass. Be sure it's completely glued to the glass without any air bubbles. When the glue dries, paint the inside of the jar a complementary color with acrylic paints. Tie a ribbon around the rim, and your pencil holder is ready for giving.

Save that artwork for posterity. If you have children, you know that each drawing they bring home is precious. But pretty soon you can be up to your neck in finger paintings. For easy, safe storage, save all your empty paper towel and wrapping paper tubes and roll the artwork up inside. Stick a label on the outside with the child's name and date. These tubes are much easier to toss into storage, and you don't have to worry about ruining those little treasures.

Make a sun catcher. Grate small pieces of different colored crayons onto a sheet of wax paper. Place another piece of wax paper on top, and press with a hot iron until the crayon shavings are melted together. Let cool, thread a string through the top, and hang in the window.

Mix up some papier-mâché. Stir together a cup of flour with two-thirds cup of water. Cut newspaper into one- to two-inch strips. Dip each strip into the mixture and run your fingers along it to remove excess paste. Apply the strips to your form or empty container. Keep adding strips until your masterpiece is complete. Then let it dry, paint it, and coat it with varnish.

Entertain with finger puppets. Story time is more fun when finger puppets tell the tale. A permanent marker and a few fingers from an old cotton glove can quickly give you a whole cast of characters. To be even more creative, add features with buttons and yarn.

Roll on the glue. For crafts projects, make a handy glue dispenser from an empty roll-on deodorant bottle. Just pop off the ball top and wash the parts thoroughly. Fill the bottle with glue. Put the ball back in place, and you're ready to roll.

Bank on it. A potato chip can makes a neat coin bank. Just slit a hole in the top, and decorate it with play money.

Wrap your gift in flowers. Gifts for people with green thumbs are easy to find but hard to wrap. Whether it's a plant or a special tool, present your gift in true gardener's style. Save empty flower seed packets and seed catalogs. Cut out and glue your favorite blooms onto a plain paper bag. Use the front cover of a seed packet as a centerpiece and surround it with paper roses, daffodils and tulips. And don't forget to make a gift tag for your earth friendly bag.

Find new uses for tissue boxes. They are too pretty to throw away. Once those floral tissue boxes are empty, cut them up for gift tags or bookmarks.

Design your own dazzling jewelry. Accessorizing is effortless with these easy-to-make beads. Before you throw out small wallpaper scraps, rip them into long, triangular or rectangular strips — 1/2-inch wide and 12-inches long — and dip them in glue. Starting with the wide end, wrap the moistened strips around a wooden skewer and let them set. When your new beads begin to get stiff, take them off the skewer and let them dry. For a shiny finish, coat the beads with clear nail polish. String them on beading thread or dental floss. Experiment with different shapes and colors of paper for fun jewelry you and your friends will love.

Store beads in film canister. To keep the pieces of a broken necklace together until you can restring it, put the beads in an empty film canister and tape one of them to the outside. These handy containers are wonderful catchalls for many small items, like buttons, coins, confetti, and thumbtacks, that are easily lost.

Make better use of bits of time. Create a "waiting time bag" with a plastic grocery bag. Fill it with material for little projects — like postcards and pen so you can quickly write a note when stuck in traffic. Or put clothes that need mending and a film canister containing a threaded needle and buttons in your bag. Whip it out in the doctor's office while you wait for your checkup. Or carry a photo album and loose pictures. This could be a big project if done all at once. But done in bits and pieces, it's completed before you know it.

Stand your brushes at attention. Keep the tips of your paintbrushes dry and undamaged when they are not in use. Flip a plastic berry basket upside down and organize your brushes in the plastic grid, handles down.

Create a disposable paint palette. Instead of buying an expensive paint palette, mix watercolor or acrylic paint in an empty, foam egg carton. The egg cups can hold standard tube paints while you mix your custom colors on the attached lid. Cut out one of the egg cups to make a handy finger insert for your disposable palette.

Blow bubbles to jazz up paper. This easy alternative to marbled paper will blow you away. Mix poster paint with water and a little liquid soap. Pour it into a shallow bowl and use a straw to blow air into the mixture. The paint will soon froth, the colorful bubbles growing until they tower over the edge of the bowl. Lay a clean piece of paper over the bubbles to create a pattern of intersecting circles. Continue to blow bubbles and move the paper until it's covered with a pleasing pattern. When the paper is completely dry, use it for cards, gift tags, wrapping paper, or book covers.

Paint on a little snow. If you want white paint to look like snow for a craft or decorating project, mix very fine sand or sawdust with white acrylic paint, and you've got your snow.

Speed your pine cone's bloom. Do you want to make a pine cone wreath, like the ones pictured in decorating and craft magazines, but picked your cones too early for the full-blown effect? To open closed cones, warm them for an hour in a 250-degree oven. Open the oven door when the smell of fragrant pine fills your house, and you will discover fully opened cones. Be sure to shake out all remaining seed pods before using them for your craft project.

Make an easy decoration. Find a basket and fill it with pine cones. Adorn the basket with ribbon, and you have a pretty centerpiece. You can use it every day, or save it just for the holidays.

Crafty way with pine cones. Before working with pine cones, you should condition them in your oven to melt the sap and add a nice glaze. Use an old cookie sheet or cover a sheet with foil. Place the pine cones on the cookie sheet and bake them at about 200 degrees until the sap is melted and the pine cones are open. You might want to test one pine cone first to get the right temperature. As an added bonus, your house will smell wonderful!

Sweeten your home with spices. Don't let musty smells dampen your day. Mix up a batch of fragrant ingredients to sew into a handkerchief or make into a sachet for your closet. Combine half a cup of lemons zest with one tablespoon each of coriander, nutmeg, and whole cloves. Add lavender buds for bulk and one teaspoon powdered orris root for a longer-lasting scent. To fill out your sachet, add an unscented material, like cornstarch. Your sweet-smelling home should make you the envy of your neighbors.

Create your own potpourri. Sweeten the air in your home with homemade potpourri. Just gather your favorite herbs and spices and put them in a jar or basket. Or divide your potpourri into small bags, called sachets, and place them throughout your house.

Turn trash into treasure. It's easy to make loving keepsakes from old sewing scraps. Sew small pillows and fill them with potpourri. Sew quilt scraps into tea cozies, hot pads, or oven mitts. Piece small scraps into crazy quilt pillows or baby quilts. Make a wall hanging from your loved one's ties. Use round scraps to decorate homemade preserve jars. Create little gift bags using scraps, pinking shears, and ribbon. Or glue some scraps to blank cards to make stationery.

Make a potpourri pot. Fill a used jelly jar with some potpourri, punch a few holes in the lid, and you've got a sweet-smelling addition to an otherwise musty closet.

Scent your closet. Take a whole orange and cover it completely with cloves. Hang it in your closet for a fresh scent and to repel moths. It will dry and last for years.

Scavenge clothes before discarding. Before you toss that old dress that's falling apart, give it a good look. Does it have pretty buttons you could use to spruce up another outfit? Save anything of value, including the cloth, which might look nice in your next quilt.

Avert a sewing catastrophe. Do you remember the white socks — now pink — that accidentally got washed with your new red sweater? The same thing could happen to the quilt you spent weeks piecing together. To avoid ruining your project, wash the fabric before using it. Cloth straight off the bolt is not preshrunk and will leach dyes when washed for the first time. Washing and drying your fabric will remove the loose dye and shrink cotton to its normal size.

Use special thread for quilting. Making your first quilt? If you're using regular thread, you're probably having a rough time. Because quilts are heavy, quilters use waxed thread that glides easily through all the layers of material. Buy some waxed quilting thread and make your life a little easier.

The great put-up. Store antique fabrics and clothing flat if you possibly can. Quilts can easily be stored by laying them flat on a bed several quilts deep, if necessary. If items must be stored folded, take the time once a year or so to unfold them and re-fold them in a different place. Put acid-free tissue paper between the folds before you store them again.

Gentle dusting for hanging quilts. Antique quilts look beautiful as wall hangings, but they gather dust just like everything else on your walls. Gently clean off dust by vacuuming with a piece of nylon hosiery over the brush attachment. The top of the quilt will likely be dirtiest so focus your efforts there.

Dress up your phone book. Can't find a spot for that ugly, yellow phone book? Grab some leftover wallpaper and dress it up. Using the original cover as a guide, cut the wallpaper, glue it in place, and trim to fit. Be creative and make your book an object to display, not hide.

Preserve pictures of your ancestors. Passing down family portraits is a time-honored tradition, but sometimes there are more relatives than copies. When you need to reproduce a photo, don't photocopy it. The light from a copy machine can ruin the finish on a picture. Instead, have a professional photofinisher make a negative of your original and create copies from this negative.

Master scrapbooking basics. You don't need to invest in expensive accessories to make a keepsake album, just remember these basics. Stick to acid-free paper and pens, which will last forever. Clue others in to the subject of each page by providing a title. Write the names of the people in each photograph around the frame. Add some tidbit of history, a personal memory, or a poem and write it in your own handwriting for a personal touch. Remember, it's your thoughts that make an album something more than just a place to keep your photos.

Photocopy newspaper clippings. Mounting newspaper clippings in a photo album can be hazardous to your photos' health. The acid in newsprint causes the paper to yellow and may ruin your photos. To keep your pictures safe, make a photocopy of your clippings on acid-free paper and add it to your album. Hold on to the original clippings in a separate "brag book."

Ease photos off sticky paper. Magnetic photo albums have a reputation for not letting go of pictures. If you need to loosen the bond between photos and paper, use the lowest setting on your hair dryer to warm the adhesive. Just make sure you don't get too close to the pictures. When the paper is warm, gently lift off the photographs.

Move scenery photos to the sidelines. Boring pictures make a boring album. Use landscapes and crowd scenes to create a border around your best pictures. Trim the images so only the interesting features remain.

Travel proof your photo project. Make scrapbooking a lap craft you can take on vacations and doctors' visits. Keep photos, paper, scissors, punches, glue, and templates in the pockets of a diaper bag. Or use an old briefcase as a traveling workstation. It will keep things flat and clean and serve as a worktable in a pinch.

Be choosy when arranging photos. Deciding what goes in and what stays out is one of the hardest parts of scrapbooking. Look at your photos and plan what you can crop. Move a template over your picture until you find the perfect fit. Make sure the subject of your photograph dominates the final shape. Leave anything that may have historic significance, the name of a site, a skyline, or a temporary event or exhibit, in the picture.

Crop uninteresting elements, like the stranger waving in the background or the telephone pole in the foreground. Don't leave sharp corners. Round them with decorative scissors, a punch, or even a horizontal cut. Finally, arrange your photographs so the background space is attractively filled, and make sure you leave some room for journaling.

Photo realism. For every special event in your life, there are usually photos to be developed. When you pick up your photos, remember these money-saving tips: (1) Look through the photographs on the spot. Most developers will not charge you for the ones that didn't turn out, such as a photo of the ceiling or someone's feet. You can reject those photos and simply be charged for the ones you keep. (2) If the color processing is bad (for example, your friends have green faces), ask the photo lab to redo the photos. It will probably reprint them for free. (3) Avoid "one-hour" processing. It's the most expensive way to go.

Memories should be seen, not touched. Before you go dig out the old family photo albums or keepsake books to start preservation improvements, look at your hands. Visible dirt can do tremendous harm to paper items, but the invisible oils and acids on your skin can do even more. Always wash your hands well before handling your treasures and get some inexpensive white gloves from the local photo shop. They're made for handling photos and negatives, but they work well for any sensitive materials.

Extra! Extra! Newspaper clippings require special care. Newspapers were not designed to withstand the test of time, but most of us can't resist clipping something now and then, especially if it's about a friend or family member. The bad news is these clippings don't last when they're stored in the typical scrapbook or envelope. They can even damage other papers and photos they're stored with. To keep your clippings in tip-top shape, put them in mylar (polyester film) folders and put sheets of alkaline buffered paper behind each clipping. Store the film folders in acid-free boxes in a cool dry room away from direct light. Then someday your great-grandchildren can enjoy looking at them.

Keeping out dust is must. When framing precious documents, make sure they are completely sealed inside the frame. This will keep out pollutants and protect the paper from dust.

Frame it up for posterity. You might want to display some of your paper valuables in frames. This not only gets them out where they can be enjoyed but also gives you the chance to encase them in the proper materials to keep them safe. Acid-free boards can be used to mat and mount documents and artwork. You can even get special plexiglass or acrylic materials that filter UV (ultraviolet) light. Just make sure these materials don't touch the actual paper you are preserving. There should be small spacers between the paper and the glass. Ask the experts at a frame shop for the latest tools in paper preservation.

Give artwork the look of the masters. It's easy to take an inexpensive glossy picture and make it look like an oil painting worth hundreds of dollars. Simply cut a piece of nylon net slightly larger than the picture and tape it down tightly over it. Brush on a light coat of shellac. After just a few seconds, remove the net carefully and allow the picture to dry. You'll have a piece of art that will leave your friends guessing.

Neaten up your photos. Don't spend money on expensive photo organizers. Create your own from shoe boxes. Cover them with pretty wrapping, contact, or wallpaper. Stand your photos in order, separating them in groups with tabbed dividers. Put a date label on the front, and add an envelope for negatives.

Choose photo albums carefully. Don't feel guilty about those boxes of family photographs you never got around to putting into albums. Pat yourself on the back instead. Your photos are much better off in cardboard than they would be stored in most albums. Low-grade paper, acidic adhesives, and plastic dividers speed up the decay of your photos. Magnetic albums may be the worst of all. The plastic-coated cardboard pages give off peroxides and gases that stain and destroy images. To best protect your treasured pictures, use archival albums. They are made of non-polyvinyl materials and are worth the extra expense.

Stay in touch. Use a photo album for a more personal address book. Insert a picture of the family or friend to go with the address.

Preserve your newspaper clippings. Newsprint isn't designed to last a long time. But some of life's most special events — like weddings and births — are reported in the newspaper. So naturally you want to keep articles and pictures that are dear to you. To best protect your clippings, put them in polyester film folders with sheets of alkaline buffered paper behind them. Then place them in acid-free boxes, and store them in a cool, dry place away from direct light.

Safeguard your family photos. Use archival products to store your precious photos and documents. Archival products are made of acid-free paper or additive-free plastics that won't react chemically with the item you are storing. You can buy archival products from specialty mail-order houses, photographic supply stores, art supply stores, craft stores, and frame shops.

Keep important documents safe. A safe alternative to laminating your documents is to use two sheets of mylar (polyester film). Close the edges with double-sided tape, such as 3M's product number 415, taking care not to let the tape touch the document inside. Then it will be safe to display and handle the document.

Cut bias binding blunders. Finding a bias line is hard enough, but when all the stretching and tugging is done, it's difficult to hold the fabric in place. To simplify the process, use masking tape to mark the bias. And for straight strips, cut the fabric down both sides of the tape. Carefully remove the tape when you are ready to sew on your binding.

Store supplies in candy dispenser. Who said candy dispensers are only good for candy? Reuse flip-top breath mint boxes to store beads, needles, buttons, or nails. The clear plastic makes it easy to find what you need, and the flip top allows you to take out only what you want. You can even store these little boxes in hardware organizers for easy access. Best of all, they are portable, free, and still smell like refreshing mint when you open them.

Bag sewing patterns for safekeeping. Instead of squeezing pattern pieces back into the original envelope, store your favorites in individual, zip-lock bags. The plastic allows you to see the illustrations and keeps the delicate pattern pieces safe. Add a swatch of each sewing project to your bag for a quick record of your sewing history. You may be surprised how many memories these patterns bring back.

Give tired fingers some help. Don't give up on needle-work because your hands get tired. For a slip-free grip on smooth crochet hooks and knitting needles, wrap thick rubber bands around the needles where your fingers rest. If you have arthritis, this added padding can spell relief for your strained fingers.

Back your embroidery with dryer sheets. Used dryer sheets work perfectly for backing sewing and embroidery. They sew on smoothly and pull off easily when you're done.

Recycle the silver. Your heat-reflecting ironing board cover may be worn out, but it has life in it yet. Cut it up and use the less worn areas to make pot holders, hot pads for the table, or oven mitts. Just combine it with some fabric and batting to make items that can take the heat.

A stitch in time. Make yourself a good quality sewing kit so you'll be ready for those unexpected repairs. Cut a 3-inch by 10-inch strip of felt, heavy fabric, or paper and fold it in half to make a rectangle. Thread one needle with a length of white or ivory thread, another with dark gray or black thread, and another with light to medium brown thread. Knot the ends of each thread and wrap them around the cloth or paper rectangle, sticking the needles in last to hold the thread in place. Add four straight pins to the kit by threading them onto the cloth or paper. Put the kit in a top dresser drawer or on a closet shelf and store a pair of small scissors with it. Next time you need a quick repair, instead of rummaging around for matching thread and a needle, you can fix it in a couple of minutes and be on your way.

A measurable difference. Measure your fabric before you store it, and write the amount and width of the fabric on an index card, cut in half lengthwise. Tuck the card into the folds or roll of fabric. Next time you want to use a certain piece, you'll know whether you have enough yardage without opening the fabric and measuring it again.

On pins and needles. Save scraps of soap and wrap them in cloth for a pin cushion. The extra lubrication will help the pins slide more smoothly through your fabric.

Get to the point. Having trouble threading a needle? These two tips are for you: Spray a little hair spray on your fingers and smooth the cut end of the thread between your fingers. The hair spray will dry immediately and stiffen the thread enough to make a nice sharp point. Try holding the thread between your finger and thumb and bringing the needle's eye to the thread instead of putting the thread into the needle. This old embroiderer's trick allows you to hold the thread more firmly in place as it makes contact with the needle.

Shoulder to shoulder. You can recycle unneeded shoulder pads by putting them to good use. Fold one in half and stitch it along the curved edge to form a carrying case for small scissors or rotary cutters. Or make knee pads to use in your garden by sewing or safety-pinning both ends of a piece of narrow elastic to the sides of the shoulder pad.

Store scissors safely. Stick the ends of your scissors into a large cork. This eliminates accidents, especially with sewing scissors in a sewing box.

Stitch a strong hold. Heavy buttons won't come off coats as easily if you sew them on with dental floss. If you need a color to match the fabric, a colored marker should do the trick. The strength of dental floss is also a plus for repairing things made from heavy-duty fabrics, like tents, duffel bags, and convertible tops.

So easy sewing. Thread your needle and run it through a fabric softener sheet to prevent snarls and tangles.

Hem jeans. Usually hemming a pair of pants isn't a big deal, but hemming thick denim jeans can be a lot of trouble. You can make a "fake hem" by folding up the legs to the desired length, pressing, and taping in place with duct tape. The tape won't show, and it will last through several washings. When it comes off, you just replace it with more duct tape, and no one will ever know.

Make pinning hems a snap. Before you begin pinning a hem, slip a rubber band around your ruler at the measurement mark. You won't have to strain your eyes to see a faded number when the mark is clearly defined.

Sew sharp. A dull needle can slow your creative project. But you can sharpen a needle quickly without removing it from the sewing machine. Just stitch a few lines through a piece of sandpaper, and it's sharp as new. And you are back to work in no time.

Button up your sewing table. Plastic containers of all sizes can bring order to your sewing area. Margarine tubs are good for larger items, like spools of thread, while old pill bottles can help you keep track of little buttons and snaps.

Build an organizer for supplies. Don't pay high prices for desktop organizers. Make your own out of an empty tissue box and toilet paper rolls. Slit the cover of a tissue box from the opening to each of its four corners, fold the sides down, and glue them in place. Cut the toilet tissue rolls the height of the box and arrange them in rows inside. Glue the cardboard rolls in place and use them to hold brushes, pencils, markers, glue, scissors, and paper clips.

Brighten schoolbooks. Leftover wallpaper makes attractive and durable book covers.

Customize coffee cans for your kitchen. Transform old coffee cans into personalized kitchen counter canisters. Simply wrap the cans in contact paper that matches your kitchen wallpaper or paint. Then fill the cans with beans, rice, sugar, flour, or other kitchen essentials.

Decorate like a pro

Add a window without a carpenter. Want to make a room seem bigger with a unique decoration? Find an old, interesting window in a salvage yard or from someone remodeling. Remove the old glass, have mirrors cut to fit as panes, and glaze the mirrors into place just like you would a pane of glass. Paint the window an interesting color. Add a small flower box to the sill and fill it with silk flowers. Hang your creation on a bare-looking wall. The effect will be dramatic, and the mirrors will make your room appear more spacious.

Extend the enjoyment of candlelight. Candles will burn longer and drip less if you put them in the freezer for about an hour before lighting them.

Soak up carpet spills. Whenever you spill latex paint on your carpet, blend together one tablespoon of liquid dish detergent, one tablespoon of vinegar, and one quart of warm water. Sponge the spill away with this super paint remover.

Set a place for lace in your bedroom. Capture the elegant look of a cutwork or lace bed coverlet — for a fraction of the usual cost. Simply cover your bed with a lace tablecloth instead. For a full-size bed, use a 70-by-90-inch oblong tablecloth. You'll find it makes a charming substitute for the real thing.

Keep clouds away from your bouquet. Cloudy water in a clear vase can ruin the beauty of your cut flower arrangement. But a teaspoon of liquid bleach added to each quart of vase water will keep it clear and sparkling.

Discover the secret to drying flowers. You can dry flowers like a pro. The trick is to use borax and cornmeal. Make a mixture that's one part borax to two parts cornmeal and put some in an airtight container. Lay the flower on top of this layer and sprinkle more of the mixture over the flower. Do this gently so you don't crush or bend the flower. Close the container and let it sit at room temperature for a week to 10 days. Take out the flower and brush off the powder with a makeup brush or soft paintbrush.

Fill your room with foliage. Christmas isn't the only time you can bring a tree into your home. A tree or a large plant fills up space, looks great, and costs relatively little. You can find real or artificial trees and plants for less than $30. That's a cheaper way to fill a room than buying another sofa or chair.

Jazz up a dull dresser. Does your dresser put you in a gloomy mood? Add some cheer to your dark, boring dresser. Start by laying a bright table runner across the top. You could also set colorful vases, picture frames, candles, or other knick-knacks on top. Soon, your old dresser will be filled with new life.

Substitute a bottle for a costly vase. You don't need to spend a fortune on a fancy vase to display your flowers. Empty wine and olive oil bottles make wonderful — and inexpensive — vases. Save them, clean them out, and fill them with pretty flowers.

Branch out to brighten your home. Sticks and stones may break your bones, but they can also help spruce up a room. Pick some branches from a tree, spray paint them any color you like, and display them in a large vase on the floor. It will add a touch of outdoor charm to the inside of your home.

Top vase with tape for better arranging. For an attractive bouquet in a wide-mouth vase, place strips of green florist tape across the top, forming a grid. Insert stems of flowers in the openings. Flowers will stand up straight with balanced spacing, and the tape will blend with leaves and stems.

Chipped cup camouflage. A chipped china cup or coffee mug may no longer be nice enough to drink from, but it makes a pretty flowerpot for a small plant on your windowsill or table. Just turn the chipped area away from you and no one will see the flaw.

Dry but durable. Dried flowers can be so brittle and flaky that they are a mess to work with. Try giving them a light spritz of hairs pray before you start and leaves and petals should stay in place, instead of ending up on your floor.

Resize a vase. You've chosen the vase that has the look you want, but it's too large for your bouquet. No need to look for another container. Just put a slender olive jar inside the vase. It won't be noticed, even in a clear vase. And the flowers inside it will stand up instead of flopping over the sides.

New life for old vases. If you've got an old vase that has cracks or chips and no longer holds water, line it with a plastic grocery bag — but check the bag for holes first. Pour in some water, add flowers, and you can get many more years of enjoyment from an old treasure.

Decorate a bedroom fit for a king. For a dramatic look in a bedroom, use a section of tall, wrought iron fencing for a headboard. Use individual bars of wrought iron for curtain rods, and look in thrift stores for wall sconces that complement the look. Add several candles and some rich, floor-length curtains, and your room will take on the feeling of a stately castle.

Design your own conversation pieces

You don't have to pay a fortune to decorate your home with unique accent pieces. Go to yard sales, salvage yards, and thrift stores and use your imagination. An old stool would make a lovely plant stand. And a weathered, wooden gate could be painted and turned into a beautiful headboard for a child's bed. Treasure hunting can save you a bundle on decorating, and your home will be like no other.

Think 'out of the box' when decorating. Who says a piece of furniture must be used only in the room it was designed for? Move a mirrored dresser into the dining room and use it as a sideboard. Or maybe a small chest of drawers, painted to match your decor, is just what you need in the bathroom for your towels and personal items.

Throw new life over an old sofa. When your sofa has reached that worn and bedraggled stage, but your budget isn't ready for new furniture, pull out an extra bedspread or blanket. Use it as a loose "throw." Or, if it's big enough, tuck and pin it snugly, like new upholstery.

Change the scenery by moving your sofa. Maybe you don't need a new house. You just need a new outlook. Rearrange your furniture so you face the windows with the best view. Try this in the spring to bring you out of the winter doldrums.

Give an old lampshade a new life. Brighten up a tired lampshade with pretty ribbon in a contrasting color. Use a leather punch to make holes, evenly spaced, around the bottom and top of the lampshade. Run the ribbon through the holes, back and forth from bottom to top, making a crisscross pattern.

All that glitters. Don't throw out an old mirror just because of a few scratches in the silver backing. Get some metallic silver auto spray paint and give the scratches a couple of coats. Then seal with clear shellac spray.

Watch glasses glisten. If you have a display cabinet for your glassware, try lining the bottom and backs of the shelves with mirrors. The reflected light will make your stemware sparkle.

Mark paint level on the can. Before you close up that paint can for storage, check to see how much paint is left and mark how high it is on the outside of the can. When you need the paint a few months later, you'll know if you have enough for your new project.

Save leftovers for touchups. Always save paint, wallpaper, and fabric left over from your remodeling projects. When you need to do the unavoidable touchup, you'll be able to do it in a jiff.

Believe it or not. To prevent white paint from turning yellow, stir in a drop of black paint.

Storing leftover paint. When you finish painting a room, take an extra minute to label the side of the paint can. With a wide black permanent marker, write the room you painted and the date. If the color number is not on the top of the can, be sure to add it, too, in case you want to buy the same color again. Store paint cans with the labeled side showing. Next time you're cleaning out your paint supplies, you'll know at a glance whether the cans are keepers or not. And if your room needs a touch-up, you'll find the right paint quickly.

Not just grease paint. Consider donating leftover cans of paint (still usable, of course) to a high school drama or art department for painting scenery and art projects.

Tackle tiny paint jobs with tiny brush. The little brush that comes with eye shadow is great for painting tiny areas on your walls and window frames.

Flag the best brushes. When you're buying a new paint-brush, shop for quality with this simple tip. Look for bristles loaded with split ends. Professionals call these "flags," and they help spread paint evenly. Good brushes have half or more of their bristles flagged.

Swab away painting imperfections. Even if you've done a great paint job, you're likely to find spots that need touching up. Instead of using your big brush, use a cotton swab. You'll save a bucket load of effort and time on cleanup.

Make a paint holder from a laundry jug. A clean 100-ounce plastic laundry detergent jug can make a great paint holder. Just slice off the top two-thirds of the plastic jug and throw out the bottom part. Screw the cap on tightly, turn the jug upside down, and pour in the paint. The wide top makes it ideal for any size brush, while the handle makes carrying it easy. And when you're finished with the job, hold the spout over your paint can and unscrew the cap to return the paint to the can without a mess.

Paint tricky objects with a mitt. If you plan to paint a wrought-iron fence, a fancy stair railing, or some other detailed object, ignore your paintbrush and use a painting mitt. To make one, put your hand inside a plastic bag and wrap an old towel around it.

Keep hands clean with petroleum jelly. No matter how careful you are when rolling or brushing, paint somehow finds its way onto your hands. If you rub petroleum jelly on your hands before you start painting, the paint will come right off.

Carry touchup paint in a handy container. For those times you're doing detail work with a small brush, put your paint in an old coffee mug or a powdered laundry detergent measuring cup. The handle will make it easy to carry around, and it won't be as heavy or messy as a paint can.

Mix putty and paint for perfect match. If you need to reputty around your windowpanes, mix the putty with paint to match the windows so you won't have to paint over it.

Weigh differences before buying wood stains.
Before you buy a stain for your wood, learn the facts. Water-based stain is easy to clean up and isn't toxic, but it absorbs unevenly into the wood and might streak. Oil-based stain is easier to apply and will give you a smooth finish. Unfortunately, its fumes are toxic, and it's hard to clean up.

Shield your trim from paint. Try something new to keep your trim and molding free of paint. Instead of protecting them with tape, get out an old set of Venetian blinds. Cut a few slats free from the strings and fill in the string holes with tape so paint can't sneak through. Hold the slats against the wall where the trim and the wall meet. When too much paint builds up on the slat, toss it and use a fresh one.

Perk up dark paneling. Contrary to popular belief, your dark wooden paneling doesn't come with a life sentence. You can brighten your gloomy room with a simple paint job. Lightly sand the paneling and coat it with a primer before you paint the final layer. Choose soft colors, like beige or sand tones. You'll be surprised how much different — and how much friendlier — your room looks.

Revitalize stiff paintbrushes. Oops! Forget to wash your brushes last week after that paint job? If they're stiff, soften them up by washing them in a capful of fabric softener and water.

Sand before painting over glossy finish. Before you paint over a glossy finish, lightly sand the area, then wash off the dust with soapy water. Your new paint will stick much better.

ID that old paint. Before you paint old walls, rely on rubbing alcohol to determine what kind of paint is on them now. Dab the alcohol on the paint. If the old paint comes off, it's a latex-based paint. If it stays on, it's an oil-based paint. That's important because you don't want to put new latex on old oil paint.

Brighten a room for a few bucks. If your decorating budget is small, a fresh coat of paint may be the best way to achieve a dramatic new look. And you may not even need to paint the whole room. Sometimes just giving one wall a new color will make the whole space look more alive.

A sample in time saves nine. Each time you paint a room in your house, take a minute to brush a wide band of paint onto a plain index card. When the card is dry, label it with the room and the date, and keep it in an envelope in your car's glove compartment. When you are shopping for furniture, linens, or accessories for your home, you have an easy, instant way to make sure they will coordinate with the walls. To be even more accurate in your purchases, add a small swatch of the major fabrics you've used in the room. On ready-made or upholstered pieces, you can usually cut a little sliver of fabric from the inside of a seam allowance. Tape these to the card with the paint, and you'll save time and money by never having to return an accessory that doesn't match your room.

Scent-sational tip. Don't like the smell of oil-based paint? Give your nose a break. You'll improve the scent and make your painting job more enjoyable if you stir a spoonful of vanilla extract into the can of paint.

Handle your woes with a garden hose. Don't throw away that old garden hose! It can make carrying a paint can easier on the hands. Cut a small section the width of your hand and split it lengthwise on one side. Place the section of hose around the wire handle of the paint can, and you have an instant "comfort grip."

No drips allowed. Prevent paint spills and catch paint drippings at the same time. Trace the bottom of a paint can on the side of an old cereal box. Make a hole to fit the can by cutting out the circle on the side of the box. Place the paint can inside it. Any drips will be on the cereal box and not your floor.

Rim shot. Before you begin painting, punch a few holes in the inside rim of the paint can. When you dip your brush and wipe off the excess paint on the edge of the can, the paint will flow back into the can instead of dripping down the outside. Not only will the cleanup be easier, but you'll save paint as well. And without paint in the rim, the lid isn't as likely to stick when you close the can.

Wrap it up. You're in the middle of painting a room and suddenly there's a more pressing need elsewhere. No need to clean your brush or roller if you'll be ready to use it again shortly. Simply wrap it in aluminum foil or put it in a plastic bag and stick it in the freezer. It will stay moist while you take care of your other chores.

Foiled again. If you're using a paint tray, let aluminum foil help with the cleanup. Just line the tray with foil before you begin. When you finish painting you can pour any unused paint back into the can. Then toss the aluminum foil liner and your cleanup is done. When you are ready to start again, simply put in fresh foil.

Roll on. Here's a simple way to get more mileage from your paint roller sleeve. Just remove it from the frame from time to time and reverse the ends.

Under cover. Aluminum foil comes in handy for covering door knobs and thermostats while you paint the doors or walls. It's flexible and stays in place until you're ready to remove it.

Undercover stains. You thought you could cover that stain with fresh paint. But there it is again bleeding through. You should always wash off grease and hand prints with detergent and warm water before you paint a wall but sometimes that isn't enough. Professional painters put a stop to this problem by painting over the stains with pigmented white shellac before painting. If you can't find this product, you can use any spray or liquid shellac to seal the stains so you can paint over them without the stains bleeding through.

High plate dripper. Make a paint catcher from a paper plate or the plastic lid of a coffee can. Just cut a slit in the middle and push the paintbrush handle through it. Now you can even paint overhead without getting drips in your eyes.

A fan-cy cover. When you are ready to paint around the ceiling fan, here's a quick way to do it neatly without having to remove the blades. Save your plastic wrappers from your daily newspaper. Slip one over each blade and continue painting.

Go easy on yourself. Cooking oil, baby oil, shaving cream, or shampoo will soften and remove paint from your hands and face more pleasantly than harsh turpentine or mineral spirits. Did you forget to wear a cap while painting the ceiling? Baby oil is a good choice for removing the paint that dripped onto your hair.

Mess-free brush cleaning. Cleaning up after painting with an oil-based paint can get pretty messy. Make cleaning your paintbrush easier with the "bag method." Pour cleaning solvent into a large, strong, plastic bag and insert the brush handle end up. With one hand, hold the bag tightly closed and hold the brush by the handle. Use the other hand to swish and massage the bristles through the plastic bag. You'll clean your brush without getting your hands dirty.

Do-it-yourself hanger. When you have cleaned your brushes, hang them to dry with the bristles straight so they won't get bent and broken. Make a handy hanger for a couple of brushes from a coat hanger and two large paper clips. Bend the hanger corners down and push the bottom of the wire up in the center. Loop the paper clips over the corners, hook the brushes on the clips, and hang it all up to dry.

Tape it up. Before you use masking tape for protection when you paint, rub the edges of the roll of tape with a candle. The wax will make the tape easier to remove when you're finished, and it won't be as likely to pull off old paint with it.

Easy cleaning. To soak a paint brush, put water or paint thinner in a clean coffee can, and cut an "X" in the plastic lid. Push the handle of the brush through the "X," place the brush in the can, and snap on the lid.

No more new-paint smell. A freshly painted room is very satisfying — except for that lingering smell. One way to counteract those fumes is to chop up a large onion and put it in a bowl of water. Set it in the room for a few hours. Amazingly, it works.

Protect your chandelier. Cleaning paint off glass isn't fun, but cleaning it off a crystal chandelier is downright drudgery. To protect your chandelier from spatters when painting your ceiling, wrap a plastic garbage bag around it.

Color guide for painting. Whenever you paint the interior of your home, dip one end of a popsicle stick in the paint and let it dry. Using a permanent marker, write the name of the paint color and the room in which you used it on the other end of the stick. Save these sticks, and you'll never forget the name of the paint if you need to buy it again. You can also take the sticks with you when you shop for window treatments, wallpaper borders, or decorating accessories to help you coordinate colors.

Dripless painting. This tip will keep the rim of your paint can from overflowing with paint. Instead of wiping your paintbrush on the side of the can to remove the excess, stretch a large rubber band around the can so part of it is across the opening. Wipe your brush against the band, and the excess will drip right back into the can. No mess, no waste.

Salvage old paint. Got some old paint that's a little lumpy? Although you can't break up the lumps, you can still save the paint. Just strain it through an old piece of screen into a new container. The lumps will magically disappear.

No strain, no gain. You paint a room to make it pretty. But globs in your paint can become unattractive lumps on your wall. To solve this problem, stretch a piece of pantyhose across the mouth of an empty paint can, and pour the paint through it. You will catch all the lumps and guarantee a smooth paint job.

Brew up a natural deodorizer. Put a few handfuls of straw in a bucket. Cover it with warm water. Leave it in a freshly painted room overnight, and by morning any unpleasant paint odor should disappear.

Give holes a quick patch. Use equal parts salt and starch with just enough water to make a stiff putty for filling holes in your plaster walls before painting.

Cover spots on ceilings. Instead of trying to remove a small stain on a white ceiling, just cover it with a dab of white shoe polish. One quick swipe with the handy applicator and you are done.

Neat way to clean paint roller cover. Make a handy, disposable soaking bin for your paint roller cover. Just cut the top out of an empty milk carton, fill it with solution or water, and put your roller pad in to soak.

Remove hardened paint from a brush. To soften hardened paint on brushes, soak them in hot vinegar. Follow up by washing with warm soapy water.

Paint on extra protection. When you're painting windows, don't worry about getting paint on the glass. It will clean up easily with a razor scraper and some window cleaner. By painting along the edges between the wood and the glass, you're more likely to seal out moisture that could damage your windows over time.

Hang pictures without ugly nail holes. You want to hang a few pictures, but your landlord doesn't allow nail holes in the walls. Or perhaps you don't want nail holes in your own walls. No problem. Use sewing needles instead. They're surprisingly strong. In fact, they can support up to 30 pounds.

Hang in there. Hanging artwork in your home will be easy and fast if you use this terrific tip. For each painting or photo you want to hang, use newspaper or a brown paper bag to make a paper cutout. To do this, lay the item face down on the paper and draw around it, then cut out the shape. Use masking tape or transparent tape to stick the cutouts to the wall to see how the paintings will look. Change the arrangement as many times as you like until it's just the way you want it. Then nail your picture hangers in place right through the paper. The paper tears off easily and you haven't put any unnecessary holes in your wall.

Doily delights. You just couldn't throw away those crocheted doilies you inherited from Aunt Dorothy. So now what do you do with them? Put them to good use. A doily framed on a background that coordinates with your room becomes a piece of art. For a small, special gift, make a unique wrapper. Thread narrow ribbon through the edge of a large doily and pull it up to form a decorative pouch for your gift.

Display photos in jars. Apothecary jars and other clear glass containers make decorative picture frames. Just roll the picture slightly to get a curve and put it inside. Fill the jar with marbles, glass beads, shells, or other items that will hold the picture against the glass without damaging it.

Rehang pictures after a paint job. Don't worry about getting your pictures back in the right spot after painting a room. Stick a toothpick into the nail hole, and paint as usual. After the paint dries, remove the toothpicks and rehang your pictures.

Be bold with accessories

When decorating on a budget, choose neutral colors and avoid dramatic patterns for sofas and chairs. Enjoy bright colors or bold prints in accessories, like throw pillows or tablecloths. After a while, when you grow tired of these designs, you can replace them at little expense compared with the cost of new furniture.

Warm enamel paint for easier spreading. Sit your can of enamel paint in a pot of hot water before you use it. Just like butter, enamel paint spreads more smoothly when it's warm.

Brighten the insides of cupboards. Paint the insides of your cupboards a light color. They will reflect light, and you'll be able to see the contents more easily.

Mix a perfect match. Make sure you can re-mix a new batch of paint in just the right shade if you should run short. Put a piece of clear strapping tape over the coded mixing label on the can. That way, if it's accidentally painted over, you can clean it off and read it.

Step by step. When you're looking for a good way to display several potted plants together, consider a ladder. A small wooden step ladder from your local hardware or discount store makes an attractive movable shelf for plants. You can paint it to match your decor, stain it with wood stain, or leave it natural. Or you might find an old wooden or metal step ladder at a garage sale or in your basement. A ladder works especially well in the kitchen or on a patio or screened porch.

Hats off to hatboxes. Beautify a shelf or table with an unusual and charming design. Simply stack some hatboxes on top. You can find them in all sorts of pretty colors and patterns. Pick out a few different sizes for the best effect. Your guests will tip their hats to your creativity and good taste.

Frame doors and windows with books. You need a full wall of bookshelves, but you just don't have the space. Consider creating a border of books around doorways and windows instead.

Cheer up your shower curtain. Your shower might be hot, but your feelings for your shower curtain are probably lukewarm, at best. Warm up to it by adding a little more flair. Replace the rings that hold the shower curtain to the rod with pieces of bright ribbon. Then tie your shower curtain to the rod with big, bright bows. The new, cheerful look will let you shower in style.

Apply varnish perfectly. The key to a great varnish finish is the number three. That's the number of times you need to brush each coat. Brush once going along the grain of the wood. Then brush across the grain. Finish by going along the grain again. It might seem like triple the work, but you'll shine with pride when you see the results.

Remove old wallpaper with new trick. Your old wallpaper certainly doesn't have feelings — but it has become quite attached to the wall. Pry it loose with a simple, homemade mixture. Just fill a spray bottle with twice as much hot water as liquid fabric softener, and spray the wallpaper thoroughly. Focus on the top and along the seams. In about 20 minutes, the wallpaper should peel right off. If not, just keep spraying and try again.

Stretch your ceiling with stripes. Feeling cramped? Replace your current wallpaper with striped wallpaper. It will make your ceiling seem higher.

Color your way to a roomier home. Use the power of color to transform a small room into a big one. Choose mint green or pale blue wallpaper or paint to "enlarge" your room. Shades of white and beige also work well.

Flatten wallpaper bulges with easy trick. Next time you put up wallpaper, win the Battle of the Bulge. If an annoying bulge appears, slit it with a razor blade. With a knife, lift up the wallpaper to let the air out. Then smooth the wallpaper back down with a wet sponge.

Remove old wallpaper with a paint roller. Old wallpaper loosens up and peels off in seconds — almost effortlessly — with this amazing white vinegar tonic. Just mix equal parts white vinegar and hot water. Pour the solution into a wide pan. Apply with a paint roller, and the wallpaper should peel right off.

Lift out grease spots. To get grease stains out of wallpaper, first blot the spot with a paper towel to soak up what you can. Next, hold a piece of absorbent paper or a paper sack over the spot, and press down on it with a warm iron — not too hot and no steam. The stain should lift onto the sack. Repeat as necessary using a fresh sack.

Keep tabs on your curtain budget. Give your windows a stylish, modern look with tab curtains. Just don't give up your good, old-fashioned financial sense. Instead of buying an expensive wooden curtain rod, make your own. Buy long, 1 1/2 to 2-inch wooden dowels from your hardware store. Cut them to fit your windows, screw a drawer knob into each end, stain or paint the dowel, and hang your new curtains.

Get stained glass effect without the expense. Do you like the look of stained glass but can't afford an expensive panel? Get a similar effect by placing a variety of colored bottles in a sunny window. If you only have clear bottles, fill them with water tinted with a few drops of food coloring.

Table tired window treatments. For a fresh look to replace old curtains or draperies, experiment using table linens. Drape a tablecloth, for example, over a curtain rod and secure it with a large, decorative pin. Or hang overlapping cloth napkins diagonally on a rod. With all the creative possibilities, you can change your windows with the season — or your mood.

Fast and easy furniture fix-ups

Clean and restore wood with tea. Remember that old piece of furniture your Aunt Ethel gave you a million years ago — the one you keep hidden in the attic because you hate the color it's stained? You can easily re-stain it with an item that costs only pennies and is probably already in your kitchen — tea. With tea, you can remove old furniture polish, dirt, and grime and restore the original look to wood furniture. In a quart of water, toss in two tea bags and boil until the water is a brownish color you like. Let it cool, then test the back of the piece or another unseen area with a soft rag soaked in the solution. The first pass should remove old polish and strip the wood. Then you can apply some as stain. If you're pleased with the way it looks, finish the whole piece. But remember, tea is a permanent stain. When it's dry, buff it and follow up with polish if you want a finished look.

Uncover the beauty of old furniture. To clean an old, grimy piece of furniture, dip a cloth in pure ammonia, wring it dry, and give the piece a good rub down. Rinse the cloth with water as it gets dirty. Before long, you should see your furniture's original beauty.

Dress up your kitchen with a dresser. Who says bureaus have to stay in the bedroom? If your kitchen has an old-fashioned charm, use an antique bureau as a server. You can fill the drawers with napkins, tablecloths, and other kitchen supplies, and use the top when serving food buffet style. Not only will an antique bureau look classy, no one will see your clutter.

Originality counts. If you look at your antique furniture as an investment, the last thing you want to do is refinish it. Stripping off the original finish of an antique, no matter how scratched or cracked it is, can take away more than half of its value. To care for a piece of antique furniture that has scrapes, gouges, or other problems, use a thin coat of paste wax to even out the finish. You can always remove the wax later if you want to, and the original finish is not damaged or changed in any permanent way.

Dancing with Mr. Sandman. Who doesn't love the smell of cedar? Unfortunately, old chests and closets can lose some of their fresh scent as the wood ages and dries out. Bring back a bit of that great smell by giving your cedar furniture a light once-over with very fine sandpaper.

Table the issue. Garage sales are wonderful places to shop but sometimes you have to "think outside the box" to get what you want. If you're looking for a large, sturdy coffee table for a living room, den, or family room, you may not find the quality or size you want. Look instead for a sturdy, old dining room or kitchen table and cut off the legs to coffee-table height. You may even have an extra table in your attic that you had not thought of using this way. Try it, it works!

A quality that lasts

The best way to have furniture that lasts is to buy good quality pieces to begin with. When you're shopping for new furniture, take the time to test it out thoroughly for comfort and sturdiness. Sit on chairs and sofas; lie down on beds. Stay long enough to really get a feel for how comfortable it is. Here are some other key points to remember:

1. Look for furniture made of good quality wood. By reading the label carefully, you should be able to tell about the materials used. A label that says "cherry finish" is probably referring to the color or a simulated wood grain, not to a piece made of cherry wood.

2. Stay away from simulated wood, such as particle-board, unless you are looking for an inexpensive item to last for a short time. Keep such pieces away from dampness, or they can swell and warp.

3. Inspect the finish carefully. Make sure it is smooth and evenly applied.

4. Test doors and drawers to be sure they fit properly and glide easily, especially in a piece of furniture that will get a lot of use.

Heat your drawer to help it slide. A dresser drawer usually sticks because the wood has gotten wet and expanded. To fix it, you need to dry the wood. Empty the drawer and place a safety light containing a 60-watt incandescent bulb inside. Turn on the light and leave it in the drawer for about 20 minutes. The heat from the bulb will help it slide easily again.

Not just for chalkboards. When you are lining dresser drawers with shelf liner or contact paper, a chalkboard eraser is a handy tool for smoothing out the wrinkles and getting the paper to lie flat.

Don't push on plush. Always lift heavy furniture to move it across nylon carpet. If you push it, the weight and the friction can actually cause the carpet fibers to melt. This may leave permanent streaks.

Sock out scratches. Put thick socks over the legs of your furniture before moving it. This will prevent scratching your hardwood floors.

Lift flattened carpet. If you move a chair or table, you may find that the legs have left indentations in your carpet. To fluff it up again, hold a coin on its edge, and scrape it against the flattened pile. It should quickly pop back up. If the carpet is densely matted, try holding a steam iron a few inches above the affected spot until the area is slightly damp before fluffing with the coin.

Fluff up your carpet. If you've got areas of carpet mashed down from heavy furniture, you can also fluff them back up by placing an ice cube in each "dent." Let it melt, then come back with an old toothbrush, toothpick, coin, or just your fingers to perk up the nap.

No more carpet dents. Here's another way to remove those four little calling cards embedded in your carpet. Get rid of them quickly by laying a damp towel across the indentations and pressing lightly with an iron.

Chase blood from leather furniture. Did you get a gusher of a paper cut while sitting in your leather chair? Run for peroxide to clean off your finger. Now take the peroxide and a cotton ball back to the chair and pour a bit on the blood stain. As soon as it starts bubbling, wipe the spot with the cotton ball and watch it disappear.

Lather your leather. Sofas and chairs upholstered in leather are comfortable and durable but notoriously difficult and expensive to clean. Here's a simple method for cleaning your own leather furniture. Using warm water and a gentle bar soap, such as Ivory, make a lather on a soft cloth and clean a small area gently. Immediately rinse with another soft cloth dampened with clean water. With a third cloth, dry the cleaned area immediately.

Make your own furniture polish. Don't spend a bundle of money on expensive wood furniture polish. Make your own polish by mixing three parts olive oil to one part vinegar and start polishing. Or try this recipe. Mix one part lemon oil to three parts olive oil. Your furniture will look beautiful, and your house will smell great.

Prevent cracks in wood. Don't let the finish on your fine furniture crack. Clean it during early fall and late spring with naphtha, an oily liquid you can buy at most hardware stores. After cleaning with naphtha, treat your table to a coating of lemon oil. Let it soak in for about a week, wipe off, then polish as usual.

This is 'oil' you need. To shine the surface of your furniture, one of the best products is plain old mineral oil, the kind you can find in the pharmacy section of discount or grocery stores. It's the main ingredient in lemon-oil furniture polishes.

Say it, don't spray it. Be really careful when you use aerosol spray furniture polish. Overspray from this type of polish can create dangerously slick situations if it falls onto vinyl or hardwood floors where people walk. You can't really see it, but you can feel it when you slip and fall.

The care and feeding of furniture. Do you think your furniture needs expensive polish to "feed" the wood? If so, you're subscribing to an old myth that's just not true, says longtime woodworker and furniture maker Zach Etheridge. "The idea that applying a polish to the surface of furniture is 'feeding the wood' is a myth. If the surface of a piece of furniture is sealed by lacquer, varnish, paint, or polyurethane, polish cannot penetrate into the wood. It is only treating the finished surface." A furniture expert Zach has taught classes on furniture making, refinishing, and repair. He recommends using a small amount of mineral spirits on a clean, cotton cloth to clean the finish of your wood furniture. "This will not damage any 'sound' finish, which is one without deep cracks, gouges, or areas where the finish is completely gone. Don't buy 'paint thinner' but check the label for 100-percent mineral spirits. Wear rubber gloves when you use mineral spirits and work in a well-ventilated area."

Keep fingerprints off furniture. When your furniture is freshly polished, it's particularly prone to smudgy fingerprints. You can prevent this by sprinkling your furniture with cornstarch after you polish, then buffing with a soft cloth. The cornstarch will absorb excess polish and get rid of fingerprints.

Remove old furniture polish. Boil two tea bags in a quart of water and let cool. Soak a soft cloth in the tea and wring out. Wipe off dirt and old polish, let dry, buff, and then decide if you need to reapply polish.

Beware of potpourri. Potpourri smells great and looks pretty, but don't put it directly on your wood furniture. The ingredients in the mixture can take the finish off, even through a plastic bag. Put potpourri in a glass jar instead.

Make your own trivets. Large ceramic tiles — available at most home improvement stores — make great trivets for protecting your table. Best of all, they come in all sorts of colors and cost very little. Pick up a few in holiday colors, or colors that complement your china. Glue felt rounds onto the four bottom corners for added protection.

Tread softly with that sculpture. Decorative accessories of pottery, metal, and stone can be a lovely addition to your home decor. They can also scratch the living daylights out of your furniture if you aren't careful. Use inexpensive stick-on felt or cork pads on the bottom of each pot, bowl, or sculpture and save the finish of your furniture.

Give wood an extra coat of protection. When wiping down your wooden furniture, give it an extra boost of protection from the elements with a lemon solution. Start with one quart of mineral oil and add 10 drops of lemon extract. Don't use too much, and be sure to wipe the furniture down afterward with a soft cloth.

Touch up scratches with shoe polish. Don't spend a fortune having dings and scratches in your furniture repaired. You can use a variety of ordinary products to camouflage those scratches, but be sure to test a hidden area first. For scratches in dark wood, use shoe polish just a bit lighter than the finish. For light wood or cherry, use iodine diluted with denatured alcohol until the color matches. For a nick, use a matching crayon or marker.

Use ashes to erase water marks. If you follow this tip, you might have trouble explaining why you bought a pack of cigarettes, but it's all for a good cause — removing water marks from your table. Gently sand the rings with #000 steel wool pads. Next, mix some cigarette ashes with vegetable oil to make a dark paste and rub the paste into the rings. They should vanish quickly.

Attack water marks with toothpaste. When water damage leaves white spots on your furniture, try this simple solution before calling in the big guns. Mix equal amounts of toothpaste and baking soda to form a mildly abrasive paste. Dampen a cotton cloth with water and rub the paste into the spots. Now buff the area with a soft, dry cloth. If the damage is not too serious, this should restore your furniture.

Please pass the jelly. Remove imperfections in your wood furniture, like water spots and heat marks, by coating them with petroleum jelly and letting it stand overnight. Wipe clean in the morning.

Coffee cure. Hide small nicks in wood furniture with instant coffee! Make a thick paste with a little instant coffee and water and press into the blemishes with a clean, soft cloth. For longer-lasting coverage, mix the powdered coffee into a bit of beeswax or paste wax and apply to nicks and scratches. You can also buy an inexpensive wax crayon to match the color of the furniture and fill the scratch. Even a child's brown crayon may do the trick.

Padding along. For refinishing your furniture, a less-messy alternative to a steel wool pad is a plastic abrasive pad, such as Scotch-Brite, available at your local hardware store. These pads are washable and reusable, won't fall apart like steel wool, and avoid the problem of metal shavings that can go through rubber gloves and into your skin. If you can't find these pads, you can use the abrasive side of scrubber sponges from your local grocery, the kind that are cellulose on one side and plastic scrubber on the other.

Don't play with fire. Be extremely careful when you use the highly toxic and flammable chemicals associated with furniture care and refinishing. Always wear heavy-duty rubber gloves when using these chemicals and treat the rags you use properly. When rags are damp with mineral spirits, other solvents, or refinishing products, spread them out flat to dry somewhere away from your house. Do not wad them up; they can spontaneously burst into flame. Once the rags are completely dry, they are safe to throw in the garbage can.

Cover scratches in your furniture. Select a crayon that matches the color of your wood, soften it with a hair dryer, then rub it gently over the scratch. Take a dry rag, and wipe away any extra.

Pick up stuck-on paper. Scraping stuck-on paper off a wood surface really puts your finish at risk. Show a little patience. Put a few drops of salad oil on the paper, let it soak in, then rub the paper away. Keep adding drops as necessary, and before long, the problem's gone with no scratches left behind.

Remove water stains. To get water marks off your wood furniture, rub in mayonnaise. Let it sit all night, then wipe off.

Forget the flannel. If you used a flannel-backed cloth on your dining room table, and now you have fuzzy flannel stuck to the finish, don't despair. Try putting a generous amount of mayonnaise on the area, let it sit for about an hour, and then wipe off.

Remove candle wax from your sofa. All is not lost if you accidentally drip candle wax on your upholstered sofa or chair. Lay a brown paper bag over the hardened wax and slide a hot iron over the bag. The wax will soften and transfer itself to the bag.

Whip up a powerful cleaner. You can save the never-ending cost of upholstery cleaning by doing it yourself. Mix one-quarter cup hand dishwashing liquid in a cup of warm water. Use an egg beater to whip up lots of suds. To be sure the fabric is colorfast, rub a bit of the suds on a hidden part of the furniture and gently scrub with a soft brush. Let the upholstery dry. If it looks cleaner, but not as if the colors are running together, continue cleaning. Work on one small area at a time, being sure not to soak the fabric. Carefully remove dirty suds with a clean spatula. After you finish a small area, wipe it with a clean, damp cloth. Allow the furniture to dry completely before using it.

Toss on a throw in summer. Oils from skin and hair can cause dirt to build up on your upholstery. That's why some sofas and chairs come with extra coverings for arms and head-rests. You can take that idea one step further by covering your furniture with absorbent terry cloth throws in the summer.

You'll be amazed by how much dirt ends up on the terry cloth — and not on your furniture.

Give furniture a new lease on life. Your couch and chairs will last longer and wear more evenly if you regularly turn the cushions. And if you have matching chairs, switch their positions now and then if one gets more than the other.

Move furniture with the seasons. Notice how much sun falls on your upholstered furniture during different times of the year. Try to rearrange your pieces so no one chair or couch gets all the sun. If you don't, one piece of furniture will fade faster than the others, making your set look old before its time.

Whiten your dreary wicker. Has your white wicker furniture turned brown with grime from being outside? To make it look new again, vacuum it with a brush attachment to loosen the dirt. Then wash it with a few tablespoons of ammonia in a gallon of water. Scrub dirt out of crevices with an old toothbrush, then rinse with plenty of water. Let it dry in a shady place, and soon your wicker will again be an inviting place to relax and enjoy your yard.

Pay attention to patio furniture. Hose off washable patio furniture regularly to keep soil from building up. If dirt does accumulate, use a squirt of dishwashing liquid in a gallon of water to pretreat stains on cushions before rinsing with the hose. Use a brush on stubborn marks, but don't try any harsh chemical cleaners. These could ruin your furniture.

Perk up PVC furniture. If your outdoor furniture is made of PVC, you know how dirty it can get. So clean it regularly with one-quarter cup of bleach in one quart of water. Put the solution in a spray bottle, label it, and keep it out of the reach of children. To clean your PVC furniture, spray it on and let it soak in for about 10 minutes. Then wipe it off with paper towels.

Tighten sagging cane chairs. Do you have some old woven cane-seat chairs that you don't use because the cane is sagging? You can tighten up the seats with very little work. Start by pouring a cup of salt into a cup of boiling water. Let the solution cool, then sponge it onto the sagging seat, being careful not to get any on the wood. Place the chair in the sun to dry, and don't put any weight on it for a few days. The woven cane should tighten up nicely, and you'll have useful chairs again.

Get unsightly mildew out of wood. Your wooden patio furniture has seen better days, and now it's covered with mildew. Get rid of it quickly with this wonder wash. Mix one cup of ammonia with a half cup of vinegar, a quarter cup of baking soda, and one gallon of water.

Preserve your wicker's natural color. Scrub natural rattan and wicker furniture with a little warm water and Morton's salt to keep it from turning yellow.

Super gardening secrets

Reduce allergies with low-pollen posies. Perhaps you like to garden, but struggle with allergies during the growing season. If so, stick with plants that produce bright blossoms. Since they attract insects to spread their pollen, they need less of it. On the other hand, plants that depend on the wind for pollination produce a lot more of the stuff that makes you sneeze. Azalea, hibiscus, oleander, pyracantha, and yucca are some shrubs that shouldn't aggravate your allergies. Other plants you are likely to be comfortable with include cacti, chrysanthemums, crocus, daffodils, ferns, hyacinths, irises, lilies, orchids, roses, and tulips. If you have allergies, trees to avoid during pollen season include elm, sycamore, oak, walnut, maple, birch, ash, willow, and pecan. Some trees you won't need to avoid are fir, magnolia, palm, pear, redbud, and yew. Some other plants you may also want to watch out for are privet hedge, Bermuda grass, bluegrass, artemisia, amaranth, and sorrel.

Breathe easy in your garden

With a few precautions, gardening and lawn work don't have to be off limits even if you have allergies. Just cover your nose with a mask, wear long sleeves and pants, and wash your clothes right away when you come inside. Keep your grass short and your garden weed free. And stay indoors during early morning and late afternoon hours, when pollen counts are highest.

Store bulbs in oatmeal boxes. Save your oatmeal boxes to store bulbs over the winter. Punch a few holes in the sides and fill with dry peat moss and a few bulbs. Place them in a cool, dry place until spring. When storing different varieties, be sure to label them.

Double-duty dirt. When you have very little space to plant your tulips and crocuses, try planting them in the same space. Plant the tulip bulbs 8 inches deep and the crocus bulbs 4 inches deep above the tulips. The crocuses will come up as usual and a few weeks later so will the tulips keeping the garden colorful and thick with growth.

Protect your bulbs. Before planting bulbs, dust them with medicated baby powder to keep critters from munching on them.

Feed your ferns. Some plants just love eggs. Indulge them. A few days in advance, crush some calcium-rich eggshells into the water you plan to give your ferns or blooming perennials. Let the solution stand for a couple of days, shake well, then water as usual and watch your garden grow.

Fall storage for bulbs. Place bulbs inside the legs of pantyhose, label, close off the end, and hang for storage until next season.

Store bulbs safely. Daffodil and narcissus bulbs are poisonous. Don't store them in an area, like the root cellar or refrigerator, where they might be mistaken for onions. And it's best not to plant them in the same area as your vegetable garden.

Divide and conquer perennial problems

You'll have fewer pest and disease problems if you give your perennials plenty of room to grow. Fall is the best time to divide crowded plants. When you dig them up to separate them, be sure each clump has plenty of roots and one or more healthy growing tips. Give your transplants a boost with some rich compost in the soil, and you'll have beautiful, healthy plants come springtime.

Attract birds to your yard. Want to attract more birds to your yard? Don't get overzealous in your fall yard and garden cleanup. Be sure you leave plenty of plants — like thistle and milkweed — that provide flossy material for nests in the spring. One way to find out what the birds in your area like to use is to take apart a few of last year's nests and examine the building materials.

Encourage birds to take a bath. Birds won't take a dip in your birdbath if it's covered with green, slimy algae. To clean it, drain all the water. Soak paper towels with bleach and lay them on the bath. Wait about 30 minutes, then rinse and air dry. To prevent algae growth in the future, change the water and scrub your birdbath every week. Consider cleaning it every day if your birdbath is a bird hotspot.

Use scare tactics on invading birds. After a lot of hard work, you might think gardening is for the birds. But that doesn't mean you want the birds to eat all your crops. Take some precautions to scare birds out of your garden. It takes more than a simple scarecrow — unless it can sing and dance, like the one in "The Wizard of Oz." Try a variety of devices. Pinwheels, aluminum pie plates, balloons, and ribbons all work well. Stretch ribbons between two poles so they'll make a roaring noise when the wind blows. Make sure to alternate the devices and change their location every few days. And hide the devices that aren't being used. Otherwise, the birds will just get used to them. Keep things unpredictable. Start using the scary props about two weeks before your crop will start tempting the birds. If you start too soon, the birds will be too familiar with your props to be scared. If you start too late, the birds will be too familiar with the taste of your crops to be driven away.

Easy noisemaker. Keep the birds out of your garden with old tin cans and aluminum pie plates. If you hang them on copper wire stretched between two metal posts, you'll find your plants get greener after a storm. They'll attract more electricity, which helps turn oxygen into plant-enriching nitrogen.

Do the feathered folks a favor. The easiest bird feeder you'll ever make is the shell of your Christmas tree, laid on its side in an out-of-the-way corner of your yard. For a nice touch (festive for you, delicious for your guests), don't take off the cranberry and popcorn strings before putting it out.

Hang a birdhouse. Wire coat hangers make good, sturdy lines for hanging birdhouses outside. Attach them with any sort of wire, just don't use string. String and rope are no match for a squirrel's sharp teeth.

Feed the birds. A plastic milk jug makes a good bird feeder. Just cut a large hole in one side and hang the jug in your yard. You can add a perch by poking a chopstick through the bottle under the feeding hole.

This aquarium is for the birds. If you think you'd enjoy the birds outside more than you do the fish inside, make your fish tank into a bird feeder. Just turn it on its side — after removing water, fish, and whatever else may have been inside, of course. It will provide a protected place for birds to feed. And you can enjoy watching them from all sides.

Attract goldfinches to your yard. If you're particularly fond of goldfinches, here's a good way to attract them to your feeder. All finches love thistle seeds, but only goldfinches feed upside down. So put the opening for the seed beneath the perch. They'll be able to eat with no competition from other types of birds.

This box is for the birds. The next time you replace your mailbox, don't throw out that old battered one. It will make a perfect birdhouse. Just nail it to a tree or pole, or suspend it from branches, and leave it open.

Help birds build nests. An empty onion bag is ideal for hanging out nesting supplies for your backyard birds. Fill it with straw, bulrush down, cotton, feathers, animal hair, or small pieces of bark and wood. A "builder friendly" neighborhood will usually attract a good number of settlers.

Send bushy-tailed intruders slip-sliding away. Keep squirrels out of your bird feeder. Instead of hanging it from a tree or standing it on a wooden post, place it atop a section of PVC pipe. Let 'em try to climb up that.

Pickle your posies for more blooms. Give your sweet-smelling gardenias a sour treat, and watch for an astonishing increase in snow-white blossoms. When you finish a jar of pickles, just pour the liquid on the ground under the bush.

Nourish azaleas. Azaleas grow best in acidic soil, so for really beautiful plants, add some vinegar occasionally when watering them. Use two tablespoons of vinegar to one quart of water.

Learn the secret of drying hydrangeas. Blue, pink, or purple hydrangeas make attractive additions to your dried flower arrangements. For best results, pick them when their color peaks before the first frost. And use your parked car as a drying oven. On a sunny day, leave flowers inside with windows rolled up for 24 hours. You can tell they are dry enough when you rub the petals and they make the sound of rustling tissue paper.

Add pizzazz to your landscape

Annuals provide a lot of color in the garden. They show off their beauty best when planted in groups of the same kind, rather than interspersed with other colors and varieties. Some of the best bloomers that require the least amount of care are nasturtium, coleus, marigold, dusty miller, impatiens, periwinkle, zinnia, spider flower, sweet alyssum, and yellow cosmos.

Find free fertilizer in your fruit bowl. Whatever you want to grow — yummy vegetables or fabulous flowers — will thrive with hearty helpings of potassium and phosphorus. And you hold these minerals in your hand each time you eat a banana. So forget expensive fertilizers. Just save those peels, air dry them until crisp and crumbly, and store in an airtight container at room temperature. At planting time, mix the dried banana peels with garden soil and watch the prettiest plants in your neighborhood grow big and strong.

Let transplants rest on a bed of eggshells. You can add lime and provide drainage for your potted plants with eggshells. Wash the empty shells thoroughly and crush them. Then place the shells in the bottom of the pot before adding soil.

Hairy helper. Even better than manure, human hair is a rich source of nitrogen for your garden plants. If you have a friend in a barber shop or hair salon, see if she will collect hair trimmings for you. Spread them on loose garden dirt and work them well into the soil. This will also help keep deer from foraging in your garden.

Track your fertilizer. When fertilizing your lawn, if you mix a little flour in with the dry fertilizer, you'll be able to see exactly where you've spread it and identify any areas you missed. Use this tip when you're planting seeds, too, and you'll never overseed one particular area.

Mix up manure tea for your plants. Manure makes a great organic fertilizer. If you'd like to use it in liquid form, put a few scoops into a pantyhose leg, tie the top, and place in a bucket of water. (To make it easier to remove the pantyhose when it's done, tie the top to the bucket handle.) Let it brew for a few days. When you are ready to use it, dilute with plain water. For tender young plants, which can burn easily if it's too strong, mix three parts water to one part tea. It should look like weak iced tea.

Uncover robbers' favorite hiding places

Trees and shrubs add more than beauty to your home. They also give robbers a place to hide. That's why it's important to keep your shrubs trimmed below 3 feet, especially the ones around doors, windows, and walkways. It's also a good idea to trim trees so they don't block your neighbors' view of windows and doors. And trim limbs that could provide thieves easy access to your second-story windows.

Crush "dem" dry bones. What do you do with leftover chicken bones? They smell bad in the garbage, and you can't put them down the disposal. Instead, dry them in your microwave, put them in a strong paper bag, and crush them with a hammer. When you're finished, take them out to your garden and sprinkle them around the base of your plants. They'll thrive on the extra nutrients.

Clip, collect, and compost

Compost enriches and conditions your soil and gives you a great way to recycle some of your yard and kitchen waste. You can start a compost pile with a variety of different organic materials, like leaves, grass clippings, animal manure. You can buy a fancy composting bin but with just a pile of grass clippings and a pitchfork you can make all the compost you want. Simply add the tough outer leaves of lettuce and cabbage, those nectarines that spoiled in your vegetable bin, the dried-out carrots from your sack lunch. You can use an empty flower bed or any space in your yard where you can bury organic scraps. Set up a composting system and your yard and kitchen scraps will turn into "black gold" food for your flowers and vegetables.

Learn the secret to fabulous cut flowers. Don't throw out that flower arrangement before you have had time to enjoy it. A surprising sweet-and-sour combo will keep your bouquet looking absolutely gorgeous. To a quart of water, stir in two tablespoons of sugar for plant food and add two tablespoons of white vinegar to keep your flowers fresh.

Turn your flowers a different color. You can turn yellow daffodils green and white carnations blue. To work this magic, just place the stems in warm water and add a few drops of food coloring. Watch the flowers change color as they suck this solution up through their stems. Experiment with colors and different kinds of flowers for variety in your bouquets.

Clear the way for long-lasting blossoms. If your floral arrangement gets droopy too quickly, air bubbles in the stems could be preventing the flow of water to thirsty blossoms. To avoid this problem, hold the stems under cold water. Then, using sharp scissors, cut the stems at an angle. They're now ready to be placed in a vase.

Prolong the life of cut flowers. You can prolong the life of freshly cut flowers by adding a dash of salt to the water in the vase.

Dump water to deter bugs. Insects breed in stagnant water. Just don't give them a chance to do it in your house. When your fresh flowers die, make sure to dump out the water in the vase. Otherwise, the standing water will lure all sorts of critters.

Sweeten the pot for fresher flowers. The secret to cut flowers that last weeks longer is to drop a shiny copper penny and a cube of sugar into the vase of water.

Arrange some floral support. To arrange flowers in a vase with a wide mouth, you can cut strong twigs the diameter of the opening and wedge them horizontally in the vase just down from the top edge. Or you can use masking tape or green florist's tape to construct a grid across the opening of the vase. Either method supports the flower stems so the flowers can be arranged easily and will look pretty longer.

Don't be daffy with your daffodils. Cut flowers from your garden are a beautiful addition to your home. If you're lucky enough to have tulips and daffodils, here's a tip: don't bring them in from the garden and put them together in the same vase. The slime from daffodil stems can ruin cut tulips. So put the daffodils in a separate vase for about a day, then rinse off their stems, and you can safely add them to the tulips.

The last straw. If your cut flower needs a longer stem to go in the vase you've chosen, give it a little lift. Put the short stem into a plastic drinking straw cut to the length you want.

Perk up your posies. When you bring cut flowers into your home, there are certain things you can do to keep them fresh as long as possible. Before you put them into the vase, cut about an inch off the end of each flower stem at an angle. This will let the flower soak up as much water as it needs. When you fill the vase with water, add a dollop of 7-Up (regular not diet) to the water. The soft drink acts as "plant food" for the flowers. Every day pour out the old water in the vase and fill it with fresh water. Add a little fresh 7-Up as well. Finally, keep your vase of flowers out of direct sunlight if you can. These steps will prolong your enjoyment of the beautiful blossoms.

A penny for this thought. Put a penny in the bottom of your vase of cut tulips. It will help keep the tulips from opening up too fast.

Hold flowers in place. If you're making a flower arrangement in a bowl or basket, put a berry basket in the bottom and stick stems through the holes.

Transport cuttings without crushing. The next time you take cut flowers somewhere, don't lay them on your car seat without water. Instead, cut the top off a two-liter bottle, making sure it's tall enough for your flowers to completely fit inside. Add a few inches of water, stand your flowers inside, and cover the opening with plastic wrap and a rubber band.

Flowers stay fresh without a headache. You want your house guests to enjoy the cut flowers throughout their visit. Add an aspirin to the water, and your posies will stay fresh and lovely longer.

Fruit hazardous to cut flowers. Don't put cut flowers near a bowl of fruit. Apples, pears, and bananas give off an ethylene gas that can kill them.

Cushion your hands with handlebar covers. Don't let blisters from wooden wheelbarrow or rake handles spoil your fun in the garden. Head to the bicycle shop for some spongy handlebar covers. You may need to use a lubricant, like petroleum jelly or liquid dish soap, to get them to slide over the wooden handles. But once you get them in place, you'll love the way they protect your hands.

Clean and soften dirty hands naturally. Remove garden stains and soften your hands at the same time. Just rub them briskly with a paste of oatmeal and milk. If you don't have those ingredients on hand, try a mixture of two tablespoons of cornmeal, a tablespoon of water, and a little bit of apple cider vinegar.

Unstick sap with baking soda. To get tree sap off your hands, reach for baking soda instead of soap.

Bar dirt with a bar of soap. Scrape your fingernails over a bar of soap before heading to the garden. It will block most dirt from getting under your nails and make it easy to wash away any dirt that does.

Make outdoor cleanup a snap. After a hard day in the garden or garage, you may not be allowed back in the house without washing up at the outdoor faucet. You won't have to go hunting for soap if you slip a bar into the toe of an old stocking. Tie the end around the faucet and lather up right through the stocking.

Leave a shine on houseplant leaves. Clean most houseplants, except those with fuzzy leaves, like African violets, with a solution of one-half cup of baking soda to a gallon of cold water. To give them an even brighter shine, rub the leaves with a little bit of mayonnaise.

Water without making a mess. Are you tired of cleaning up puddles when the water runs straight through your houseplants? A neater way to water them is to toss a few ice cubes on top of the soil and let them dissolve slowly. Not only will it make less mess, the roots get a better chance to absorb the water.

Cut plant care time in half. You can dust your houseplants in half the time if you wear an old glove and wipe both sides at once.

Serve soda to your plants. Don't pour out club soda that has gone flat. Save it to water your plants. They thrive on the chemicals it contains.

Hang it high with lighter soil. When potting a new houseplant in a hanging container, begin by filling the bottom with pieces of Styrofoam. It won't be so heavy and will drain easily.

Group houseplants for higher humidity. Place several houseplants together to increase humidity. Or cover the bottom of a low pan with water, put in a layer of small stones, and place containers of plants on top. As the water evaporates, it will provide the extra moisture most plants love. If you have to be away for a few weeks, water the plants well, fill the pan with water, and slip it all inside a plastic dry cleaning bag. Your plants should be just fine when you return.

Water plants while you're away. With this practical tip, you won't have to worry about your plants drying out while you take a vacation. Just poke a small hole in the side of a plastic bottle, near the bottom, and fill it with water. Place it on the soil beside your plant. The slow drip will provide steady moisture while you're away. Use a 12-ounce bottle for small plants. For large houseplants or outdoor plants, use a 2-liter bottle.

Take a vacation from your plants. Going on a trip or just don't like to water your houseplants? Here's an easy way to ignore them. Run a soft cotton rope, a length of nylon hose, or a few strands of yarn from a large container of water to the soil around your plants. The water will move by capillary action from the container to the plant, providing a steady drink.

Soak houseplants in the shower. Put your houseplants outside on a rainy day, and let them enjoy a good soaking. When there isn't a cloud in the sky, use your bathroom shower instead. Make sure the water temperature isn't set on hot, and then give your dry plants a nice, gentle shower. When you turn off the water, close the door to hold in the remaining humidity as the plants drain.

Add a rusty nail for iron. African violets, just like people, need iron to be healthy. A simple way to be sure they get it is to push a couple of rusty nails into the soil beside them.

Check for dryness with a pencil. You know that over-watering can drown your plants. But how do you know how much is too much? Here's a simple test. Take a pencil and push it into the soil. When you pull it out, if there is dirt on it, don't water just yet. If it's soil free, go head and give it a good soaking.

Listen to your plants. If you listen to your potted plants, they will tell you when they need water. Just hold the container to your ear and thump it. If you hear a thud, the soil probably still holds some moisture. If it sounds hollow, it's time to get out the watering can.

Take control to keep plants pretty. To keep your houseplants from losing their pretty shape as they grow toward the light, rotate them one-quarter of a complete turn each time you water them. Pinch back new growth for a bushier plant, and prune any misshapen or straggly branches. Remove brown or discolored leaves. If only the tip of a leaf is brown, trim it at an angle with scissors.

Discourage gnats with dry soil. You might be doing too good a job watering your plants. If your plants are too wet between waterings, the damp soil invites fungus gnats. These pests need damp soil to breed. To counter fungus gnats, put some stones at the bottom of your plants' pots so the soil drains quicker. Another good strategy is to let your plants dry out completely between waterings.

Rub out mealybugs with magic wand. Find the ultimate weapon against mealybugs right in your bathroom's medicine cabinet. Just dip a cotton swab in rubbing alcohol, and you have a magic wand to make mealybugs disappear. Examine your plants for these pests, and touch each mealybug you find with the cotton swab. They will die and drop off the plant. When you're done, wash your plant with warm, soapy water and rinse.

Spray aphids with milk. Are aphids sucking the life out of your plants? Fight back with a simple and inexpensive solution. Mix powdered milk and warm water in a spray bottle. Spray your plants' leaves and let the mixture dry. As it dries, the milk will kill the aphids.

Nab gnats with sand. Your new plant might come with some uninvited guests. Fungus gnats love fresh potting soil and are more likely to breed in it than in older soil. But you can thwart these pests with a simple tactic. Just add a half-inch layer of sand to the top of your fresh potting soil. This dries out any fungus gnat eggs and prevents adult gnats from getting out.

Bag some moisture for your houseplant. Line the bottom of the container with used tea bags before potting a houseplant. It will help hold in moisture and add nourishment to the plant.

Let spuds do double duty. Potatoes boiled in their skins can provide a lot of nutrition, not only for you but for your houseplants, too. After boiling some potatoes, let the water cool and use it as a tonic for your plants. It's full of nitrogen, phosphorus, and potassium.

A clean plant is a happy plant. To keep your house-plants healthy, you need to give them an occasional bath to get rid of dust and spider webs. You can stand them in a shower and let the water douse the leaves, put them in the kitchen sink and use the sprayer, or take them outside and rinse them off with a hose. Just don't do this in bright sunlight or the leaves may burn. After a good bath, houseplants should be dusted regularly about as often as you dust your furniture. A soft dry cloth or a feather duster will do the trick. Then about once a month, wipe leaves clean with a damp cloth or sponge.

Off, off, darn bugs! To get rid of insects on your indoor plants, fill a quart-size spray bottle with water. Add two table-spoons of liquid soap and stir well to dissolve. Spray the leaves and stems of your plants and any bugs that you see hanging around.

Keep soil in its place. Houseplants need good drainage through the bottoms of their pots. It's common to use broken pieces of clay pots or rocks to block drain holes, but both can still let soil run through and out of the pot. Instead, try a piece of window screen over the drain holes. It's fine enough to keep in soil but let out water. Another idea is to reuse the plastic tops from milk or juice jugs. Cut small notches around the edge of the cap and put it over the drain holes. Or use the old-fashioned metal bottle caps (from beer or soft drinks) with ruffled edges. For hanging baskets, recycled pieces of Styrofoam will plug the drain hole and provide good drainage without any extra weight.

It's in the bag. Save those bags that cover your drycleaned clothes to cover houseplants when you go on vacation. They make a great mini-greenhouse that keep houseplants moist while you're gone. First, you'll need to put plastic or terra cotta saucers under your plants. Water as usual, letting some water overflow into the saucer. Then bend a wire coat hanger to make an arch, straighten the hook end, and stick it straight down into the soil near the pot's edge. Put the dry-cleaning bag over the hanger, trim off any excess, and tuck the ends under the saucer.

Gloss over it. To give your houseplants a healthy shine, wipe their leaves down with some glycerin on a soft cloth. It won't attract dust the way some "leaf glossing" products will.

Your plants need a treat, too

Everyday foods from your kitchen can give a real boost to your houseplants. Try these tips for healthier plants:

- A little bit of diced banana skin or ground-up eggshell is like a vitamin for your plants.

- A package of unflavored gelatin dissolved in a quart of water makes a plant food that is full of nitrogen, an important nutrient for plants.

- Ferns like a cup of tea as much as the rest of us do. Or mix wet tea leaves into their soil.

Drench sun-loving plants with light. For houseplants that need a lot of light, like geraniums and cacti, line a windowsill with aluminum foil. The reflection will increase the amount of light available to the plant.

Root for fresh water. When rooting plant cuttings, put a piece of charcoal in the water to keep it fresh.

Slice up some worm bait. Earthworms are good for the soil in your garden. Worms in your houseplants are another story. If you think your houseplant is suffering a worm attack, place a slice of potato on the soil. The worms will crawl out for a snack, and you can grab them.

Pour your own stepping stones. If you have some extra concrete mix and a 5-gallon bucket lying around, you can make your own stepping stones. First, cut off the top of the bucket above the handle. Place the bucket top on plywood and fill it with concrete mix. You can even get creative and set decorative objects in your steppingstones as they dry.

Age your garden with moss. You don't have to wait years for your new garden to acquire that mossy, old-fashioned look. You can quickly grow moss on patio surfaces, planters, and fountains. Just mix any amount of moss, buttermilk, and water in a blender, and apply it wherever you want moss to grow.

Place moisture-loving plants near puddles. Take advantage of those low areas in your lawn where water is slow to drain after a rain. Mint, lavender, hostas, and other plants that require a lot of moisture will be happy in those damp spots.

Think big. Many local nurseries will give you a sizable price break if you buy a large number of the same plant. Consider this before designing a garden full of individual specimens. It will also greatly simplify upkeep if you have large plantings of the same species.

Height does not make right. Don't waste your money choosing the wrong plants from the nursery. Though they might catch your eye first, tall "leggy" plants with flowers aren't the best choice. Instead look for plants with bushier, thicker growth and fewer flowers. The bushier ones will get established faster and will probably have more blooms later on.

Get help with your landscape design. Planning a new flower bed? Do like the pros and work with curved shapes instead of straight lines. Lay a garden hose out on your lawn and experiment with gentle curves and arcs. When you're happy with the design, secure the hose temporarily and use a spade to mark the edge of your new border. Remove the hose and get to work digging.

Make stepping stones for your garden. You can make attractive, inexpensive stepping stones for your yard or garden using plastic food containers, like margarine tubs. Choose different sizes and shapes for variety. Coat the inside of the container with petroleum jelly, mix up a bag of concrete following the directions on the bag, and put about 2 inches of the mixture in each plastic container. Stir gently to get rid of any air bubbles and smooth the top. After about an hour, add decorative touches, like trinkets, pebbles, writing, or leaf imprints if you desire. Let your stepping stones sit for a couple of days before removing them from the containers.

Aerate while you mow. How can you aerate your soil and cut the grass at the same time? Easy. Just wear your spiked golf shoes while you mow.

Recycle shells from seafood feast. Seafood shells — lobster, shrimp, and crabs — are full of calcium. Crush some up and sprinkle them over your lawn to feed the grass.

6 ways to deep-six weeds. (1) Maintain your lawn with regular feeding, watering, and mowing. (2) In flower beds, use a mulch that's 2 to 4 inches deep to help prevent weed seeds from germinating. (3) Plant shrubs in dense groupings and seed over your grass to choke out weeds. (4) Don't water too much; give just the amount needed according to what's planted. (5) Remove weeds from root balls of trees and potted plants that you bring into your yard. (6) When you see a weed, carefully take it out by hand, roots and all.

A 'mulch' better way to mow. If you use a "mulching mower," your mower is designed to pulverize the grass clippings and fallen leaves and spread them back over your yard to recycle nutrients. If you have a regular mower, you either use a bagger to catch the debris, or you may rake it up after mowing. Either way, yard wastes are a ready source of natural nutrients, like nitrogen, so don't throw those grass clippings away! Let the grass fall as you mow it, spread the clippings over your lawn, or let them become free fertilizer in your compost pile.

Make a seed sprinkler. If you need to scatter grass seed in small areas, you can make your own seed sprinkler from a coffee can. Poke holes in the lid large enough for the seeds to fall through, and sprinkle wherever you have a bald spot on your lawn. Keep an extra lid without holes on the bottom, and when you're through, just switch lids to make a handy storage container for your seed.

Kill unwanted grass. Do you have grass growing between the cracks in your sidewalk or other hard-to-reach places? If you hate using harsh chemicals, you can just pour a little white vinegar in the cracks, and it will kill that unwanted greenery.

Prevent weeds with a newspaper. Put layers of newspaper in your garden to block the sunlight so weeds can't grow. When you're ready to plant, just cut slits in the paper. It's porous enough for water to soak through, yet holds moisture in. For a more attractive appearance, you can cover it with mulch.

Much mulch for free. For free mulch, check your local landfill or a tree removal service. Many communities now have facilities that create mulch from yard debris and give it away. If yours doesn't, call a tree removal service. These companies have to pay to unload debris at dumps so they will be happy to let you have it. With a chipper/shredder machine, you can turn the stumps and branches into usable mulch. Even if you have to rent a chipper/shredder for the day, you can create a mountain of mulch for a fraction of the cost of mulch you buy in bags.

Become a collector. If you're aggravated by litter, pine cones, and other debris that gets in the way while you're mowing, don't just throw it out of the way. Instead, try this tip. Tie a heavy-duty garbage bag to the handle or push bar of your mower. Whenever you see a piece of trash or debris, just pick it up and pop it in the bag. It saves the time and trouble of going back to pick it up later.

Name that vegetable. A lot of plants look the same when they're small. To keep up with what you've planted, use a permanent marker to write the names on popsicle sticks. Place them in the proper rows as you plant. They will last a full season, and at harvest time, you can pull them up and toss them on the compost heap. They'll rot and become part of the soil for next year's garden.

Organize chores with a garden calendar

Keep a loose-leaf notebook that includes a calendar to record when planting, fertilizing, and other garden chores should be done. At the beginning of each month, copy what needs to be done that month on the family calendar and check things off as you do them. This keeps the master calendar clear for referral year after year. You may need to make some new pages in your master calendar from time to time, as you add or remove chores.

Mark your garden well. All those seedlings seem to look the same when they are only a few inches high. Remember what you planted with colorful seed packets as markers. First, staple the packet to the top of a popsicle stick. Then slip a plastic sandwich bag over it and staple again at the bottom. You'll have an attractive row marker that won't fade or fall apart when spring rains fall.

Tuck away your garden tools. Maybe your yard is too small for a toolshed. But you can still have your gardening hand tools close by. Just paint an old mailbox to fit your garden style, and install it. Keep gloves, a trowel, pruning shears, and other small tools neatly inside until you need them.

Solve pest problems naturally. Don't drown your garden vegetables in toxic pesticides. Instead, repel aphids, slugs, and other destructive pests simply and naturally with these solutions. To drive away aphids, combine two tablespoons of minced garlic, one-half cup of parsley flakes, and three cups of water. Boil it down to two cups, then strain the mixture and let it cool. Take one cup of the mixture, put it in a hose-end sprayer, and spray your plants. To stop slugs, fill a small bowl with half beer and half water and put it near plants the slugs enjoy eating. They will be attracted to the smell and fall in and drown. To kill a variety of bugs on your plants, mix a tablespoon of liquid dish detergent with a gallon of water.

Raise a stink over doggy-do. Doggy-do messing up your garden? Mix up a brew that will keep Fido and friends — with their sensitive noses — out of your yard for good. Chop up a clove of garlic and the most pungent onion you can find. Mix these and a teaspoon of Tabasco sauce, a tablespoon of cayenne pepper, four teaspoons of dried oregano, and a quart of warm water in a large pail. Let sit overnight, and then sprinkle in areas where dogs like to rest or dig. Once they smell this concoction, you won't see them in your yard again. If you think this mixture will be too strong for your human nose, here's an alternative. Brush or spray a mixture of two cups rubbing alcohol and a teaspoon of lemon grass on the areas you want treated. This also repels cats.

Outsmart cutworms. Sprinkle crushed eggshells on the ground around the stems of your tomato plants. Cutworms won't crawl across them, even for the most luscious tomatoes.

Banish ants with an orange smoothie. This powerful recipe will send ants scurrying out of your yard. In your blender, combine orange peels and water until smooth. Then pour this mixture on an anthill early in the morning, before the ants leave their nest. You can also use hot chili peppers instead of orange peels.

Shoo away pests and rust with mothballs. Make use of those old mothballs by scattering them around your garden and flower beds to keep rodents and cats away. On top of that, toss a few in your tool chest to prevent rust on your tools.

Keep bugs away with garlic. Bugs and worms will keep their distance if you bury a clove of garlic in the soil around your indoor and outdoor plants.

Chase caterpillars from cabbage patch. This smelly spray will send caterpillars crawling in the other direction. Just mix two shredded onions and their juices in a gallon of water. Let it sit overnight, strain, and spray the liquid on your cabbage plants. You might need to spray the plants twice.

Wipe out bugs with milk jug. Turn a harmless, plastic milk jug into a deadly bug killer. Just toss in a cup of sugar, a cup of vinegar, and a banana peel. Leave the jug open, and hang it from a tree or set it in your garden. All the bugs that have been munching on your fruits and vegetables will be lured to the milk jug — and their doom.

Evict raccoons from your garden. Raccoons sure are cute, but not in your garden. To keep them from eating your produce, spread dog hair around the edges. Raccoons will think a fearsome beast lives there and think better of eating his food.

Keep uninvited animals away. Don't let cats and squirrels trash your yard or garden. Fight back. In a large bowl, mix five tablespoons of flour, two tablespoons of cayenne pepper, and two tablespoons of powdered mustard. Slowly add five cups of water and five cups of vinegar and continue mixing. Use a funnel to pour the mixture into a spray bottle and label it. Squirt the mixture wherever animals are disturbing your yard. They won't be back for seconds.

Spoil the soil for moles. Whip up a concoction to put moles on the move. In a blender, mix 3 ounces of castor oil and three tablespoons of liquid dishwashing detergent until you get a frothy mixture. Throw in eight tablespoons of water and blend until it's frothy again. Put a cup of the potion into a 15-gallon hose-end sprayer. Fill the rest with water and spray the mixture on your yard and garden. Make sure you thoroughly soak the soil. This treatment won't harm the moles, but they'll look somewhere else to tunnel.

Use soap to cope with deer. Get the deer that are chomping at your garden to clean up their act. Hang a bar of deodorant soap in a pair of old pantyhose. That should discourage them from trespassing anymore.

Pepper your plants to stump squirrels. Turning squirrels away from your garden is a breeze. Make that a sneeze. Just sprinkle some cayenne or black pepper around anything the bushy-tailed pests might eat. They'll think twice about coming back.

Liquidate slugs with a beverage. Placing a dish of beer in your garden will take care of slugs. But you don't have to run out and buy beer or waste the beer you already have on a slug. You can use soda, fruit juice, or sugar water and get the same results. A more elaborate trap involves cutting off the upper part of a soda bottle, then sticking the section you just cut off back in the bottle, neck first. Tape the two parts together, fill half the bottle with one of the beverages mentioned earlier, and bury the bottle in your garden so the entrance is level with the ground. It should fill up quickly with dead slugs.

Try different tricks to frighten deer. When it comes to driving deer out of your garden, you have plenty of options. Everyday items you can use to deter deer include cayenne pepper, hot-pepper sauce, baby powder, dog hair, deodorant soap, and aluminum pie tins. You can also blare your radio or play a recording of a barking dog to frighten the deer away. The key is to use a variety of these tactics. Switch things around every now and then. Otherwise, the deer will catch on.

Mow down mosquitoes. Cutting down weeds and regularly mowing your lawn does more than improve the look of your property. It also lessens your chances of being bitten by mosquitoes. Mosquitoes love to rest atop weeds and in high vegetation. When you trim the weeds and the grass, you eliminate potential shelters for these pests.

Slay slugs with salt. Here's a simple way to get rid of slugs. Just sprinkle salt on them. When they come in contact with salt, slugs shrivel and die.

Steer deer clear of your garden. You like Bambi as much as the next fellow, but not when he's eating your crops. Spray your plants with a mixture of two raw eggs, a cup of milk, two tablespoons of liquid detergent, two tablespoons of cooking oil, and two gallons of water. Or protect up to a whole acre of land by mixing 18 raw eggs with five gallons of water. The scent will keep deer away, but it won't bother humans.

Give gophers bad vibes. Rid your yard of gophers with this unusual tactic. Put a large patio stone, at least a foot in diameter, in the middle of your lawn. Then, using a shovel with a straight wooden handle, pound on the stone two to three minutes a day for two to three days. The vibrations will drive the gophers away. Before you begin, you might want to explain your plan to your neighbors, who might otherwise be concerned about your bizarre behavior.

Attack gophers with ammonia. Are gophers ruining your lovely lawn? Go on the offensive with a mixture of ammonia and water. Add a cup of ammonia to two gallons of water, open a hole, and pour the mixture down into it. Then cover the hole with dirt. Repeat if necessary.

Discourage cats with pungent mixture. Cats won't treat your yard as an outdoor litter box if you spread a pungent mixture of orange peels and coffee grounds around your plants.

Repel rodents with Epsom salt. Keep nosy raccoons and woodchucks out of your garden or garbage can. Just sprinkle a few tablespoons of Epsom salt around those areas. The rodents hate the salt and will steer clear of it. Plus, the salt acts as food for your plants. Don't worry — it won't harm the animals, either. To make sure the Epsom salt trick keeps working, you'll have to replace it every time it rains.

It must be the lovely smell. Mothballs repel not only moths but lots of other bugs you don't want indoors with you. So put a mothball in your houseplants that you put outside in spring, and you won't have to bring the bugs with them when they come back inside in the fall.

Put the bite on slugs. Collect egg shells and crush them finely. Then sprinkle them on the ground near the base of the plants the slugs are attacking. They don't like the feel of the sharp, prickly shell fragments and will leave the area alone.

Get 'em with garlic. Repel aphids with this "terrible tea." Mince two cloves of garlic and put in a jar with a pint of boiling water. After cooling, strain out the garlic and put the remaining liquid in a spray bottle. Spray new shoots and flower buds to protect them from aphid assaults.

Sneaky snake trick. Discourage birds from taking up residence in your garden or yard by creating a "snake" with some garden hose. Cut a section about 6 feet long and paint it with a bright pattern and two beady eyes. Wrap it around a nearby fence post or lay it out on the open ground; they'll get the idea pretty quickly that it's not a friendly environment, and they'll move on.

Recycled repellent. Try this trick for getting rid of moles. Dig up one of their tunnels and plug it up with cat litter. Fresh litter will do the job, but used litter might make a more lasting impression.

Hit them with your best shot. A sure-fire way to shoo the neighbor's cat from your yard: Get one of the long-range water guns and fill it with a solution of water plus a tablespoon or so of vinegar. If the cat strays into your yard, spray him with the water gun. Most cats really don't like to get wet, and the smell of vinegar discourages them even more.

'Hot' dog repellent. Trouble with the neighbor's dog urinating on your lovely plants and shrubs? Keep him away by whipping up a batch of this naturally pungent brew. Drop a few cloves of garlic and hot peppers (the hotter the better) in a blender and puree them. Add a little water and pour this concoction around the edge of the area you want to protect. Dogs will get the message and stay away.

Scare deer away from your garden. Want to keep deer out of your garden without hurting them? Run a string around the perimeter, about 3 or 4 feet off the ground. Cut strips from a white sheet and tie them along the string every few feet. A flash of a white tail is a warning signal to deer. The white strips, hung about tail height, should frighten them away from your peas and corn.

Wash away garden pests. To keep aphids, spider mites, and other pests away from your garden, spray your plants with a mixture of four tablespoons of liquid dishwashing detergent and one gallon of water.

One more recipe to clear out bugs. Snails, caterpillars, and other rampaging pests don't like garlic. If you can't drive them out, try spraying this potent brew around the yard. Blend three garlic heads into six tablespoons of mineral oil and let the mixture sit, unrefrigerated, for two days. Add one pint of hot water and one tablespoon of oil-base soap and refrigerate. When you're ready to spray, combine just two tablespoons of this stinky mix with four pints of water, and watch those snails speed away.

Give plant lice a new 'do.' African violets are often attacked by little critters called plant lice. To get rid of them, gather up your spray and a plastic bag. Coat the inside of the bag with hair spray, then pop it over your plant and tie it shut. Leave it on for only a day.

Keep cats at bay. If you've got cats that love to lie in your flower beds, scatter lemon peels around their favorite plants. They don't like the smell of citrus.

Repel pests. Scatter mothballs around your garden and flower beds to keep rodents and even cats away.

Spray away unwanted guests. Black pepper may be nothing for garden pests to sneeze at, but a few cayenne peppers will really burn them. Ants, spiders, caterpillars, and cabbage worms are just a few of the bothersome friends that won't appreciate the extra spice in their lives. To make an effective spray, just blend a few dried cayennes with water in a blender. Or if ants are your problem, grind up a handful of dried cayenne peppers and dump the hot powder into the colony. They'll evacuate the premises in no time.

Deer cayenne't stand it. Bugs aren't the only creatures turned away by spicy peppers. Bigger pests cringe at the taste, too. Keep deer and other leaf-chewers away from your bushes by spraying them with a cayenne and water blend.

General Basil to the rescue. Tomato plants under insect siege? Drive away flies and worms with a little well-placed basil.

The great flood. Ant hills a problem? Send them a message of biblical proportion. A nice tidal wave of boiling water, right down the hatch, will make them think twice about putting up another condo in your yard.

Dress your deck for a beach party. Give your deck or porch a festive look by using a beach pail as a planter. Just put some rocks in the bottom and set a pot that's already planted inside. That way, you won't have to cut holes in the bucket for drainage, and you can still use it when you head to the beach.

Keep planters portable with cans. Large planters can be moved more easily if you reduce the amount of heavy soil inside. To make them lighter, fill one-third to one-half of the bottom with aluminum cans. Finish filling with soil and add your plants. The aluminum cans, which won't rust or decay, will also help your planters drain well.

Spruce up your patio with a recycled planter. A coat of paint and a few flowers or vines planted inside are all it takes to turn an old barbecue grill into an attractive planter for your patio.

Winterize terra cotta pots. Winter rain and freezing temperatures can destroy your pretty terra cotta flowerpots. That's why you should empty the contents and bring them inside, or at least find a dry place to store them. While you're at it, check for traces of white salts that have built up from fertilizer or water. Scrub these away with a wire brush and soak in a solution of one part bleach to 10 parts water to kill any organisms that might be harmful to your plants next season.

Help clay pots hold moisture. Terra cotta flowerpots have an appeal the plastic variety just can't match. Unfortunately, soil tends to dry out much faster in clay pots. You can slow the evaporation by lining the inside with newspaper before planting.

Portable planting. If you live in an apartment, you can still grow vegetables and herbs — just grow them in containers. Pie tins and other lightweight baking pans make simple, inexpensive planters for shallow-rooted plants, like herbs and strawberries. As the seasons go by and the sunlight changes on your patio or porch, you can move the containers to take best advantage of the light and warmth. Growing even a few vegetables and herbs will save you money and give you food of the highest quality.

Planters with pizzazz. Looking for inexpensive but creative garden planters? Try these creative substitutes: Cinder blocks laid on their sides. Tin cans with holes punched in the bottoms. An old bathtub with a working drain opening. A used wheelbarrow with a few rust holes. An old pair of shoes sprayed with outdoor paint.

Save your potting soil. Before potting your next container plant, lay a paper coffee filter in the bottom of the pot. This will keep all the potting soil from washing out the drainage holes.

A new way to start your cuttings. Give your geranium cuttings a better start in life with a potato. All you have to do is bore a hole in the potato, slip the geranium stem inside, and plant the potato.

Gardening on the go. If you have a small yard or even no yard at all, don't despair. You can still enjoy flowers and even some vegetables. Just prepare a wheelbarrow like you would any other container, and plant away. It's easy to move from sun to shade as needed, and when winter rolls around, you can dump it out and store as usual.

Grow a movable garden. Put an old wagon the kids have out-grown to good use. Drill holes in the bottom for drainage and fill with garden soil. Plant flowers, vegetables, or even a small strawberry bed in it. You can leave it in one spot, or move it during the day to take advantage of morning sun or afternoon shade.

Prune your trees with ease. Dead, damaged, and diseased branches should be the first to go when pruning trees and shrubs. Next, cut out the weak ones and those that cross each other, and your job is done.

Protect your hands from thorns. When pruning roses
or other thorny plants, wear oven mitts rather than regular gardening gloves.

Prune when the time is right. For the healthiest bushes
and shrubs, don't start pruning until late in the spring when
you see at least a few inches of new growth. You might even
want to wait until early summer. Evergreen bushes and shrubs
prefer a June pruning. In the fall, stop pruning at least six weeks
before the usual date of the first frost. Shrubs that bloom in the
fall like to be pruned in the spring. Likewise those that bloom
in the spring like to be pruned in the fall. Exceptions are those
plants that bloom on last year's growth, such as lilacs. Don't
prune your lilacs after the Fourth of July. By that time, they've
started forming flower heads for the next year. If you prune,
you'll cut them off and won't see any of next year's blooms.

Ship-shape shears. Always use freshly sharpened shears or
clippers when pruning hedges. Dull blades can lead to split or
broken branches and can open the door to diseases and pests.

Just a trim, please. Most hedges and shrubs should be
pruned about once a month. However, some appreciate even
more frequent shaping up. Privet hemlock, holly juniper, and
boxwoods can all be pruned more often with good results.

Slick, quick, pruning shears. Before you start pruning,
give your shears a spritz of vegetable oil spray. Plant sap will
wipe right off when you're finished pruning.

Infection protection. Just like people, plants can get infections that make them sick. It's especially easy to spread problems
from one plant to another when you're cutting into them with
pruning shears. Regularly clean your pruning shears with a solution of 10 parts water to one part bleach to prevent the spread
of disease.

Trim hedges straight. If your hedges usually look a little lopsided when you finish trimming, try this. Tie a string to a branch on one side of the hedge, and run it to the other side. Step back and eyeball it to make sure it looks straight, and then use it as a guide while you trim.

Take the pain out of pruning. When trimming roses and other thorny plants, protect your fingers by holding the branch you want to remove with barbecue tongs.

Give your roses a tea party. You don't have to read tea leaves for the secret to bigger, more beautiful roses. And you don't have to slave under the hot sun for hours either. Just sprinkle tea leaves on the ground beneath your rose bushes. The tannic acid is really their cup of tea, especially in midsummer when production starts to slow down. Ferns also like tea. You can water them occasionally with the beverage or mix wet tea leaves into the soil around them.

Fasten your climbing plants with floss. A good way to attach your climbing roses or other trailing plants to a trellis or fence is with mint-flavored dental floss. It's strong and weather resistant, and the green color will blend with the green vines and leaves.

Fertilize your plants with coffee grounds. After you make a pot of coffee, don't toss out the grounds. Save them to fertilize your roses, evergreens, azaleas, rhododendrons, and camellias.

Rose-saving secret. If you're tired of watching the Japanese beetles devour your lovely floribunda and grandiflora rosebuds in midsummer, try this trick. Go ahead and enjoy the first flush of late spring blossoms then give them a good trimming. Though you'll miss them for a couple of months, by September, they'll start blooming again without danger from the beetles. An added bonus: this technique also controls black spot disease, which also tends to strike at midsummer. But don't try this clever trick on roses that bloom on old wood, like climbers, because it will remove the very branches where blooms would form.

Pull up poison ivy. Don't take chances when removing poison ivy or other rash-inducing plants from your yard. Cover your hand and arm with a plastic garbage bag. Pull the plants up by the roots. With your other hand, carefully pull the bag off your arm and over the plants. The offending plants are bagged and ready to be disposed of.

Save money on seedling starters. Get an early start on your spring garden and save money, too, by using egg cartons as starter trays for your seedlings. Just fill the cups with soil, plant your seeds, and keep them in a sunny window. If you use cardboard cartons, you can separate the cups and plant them directly in the soil when the threat of frost has passed. If you use Styrofoam cartons, remove the seedlings from the cups before you transplant them. If your small plants or seedlings need protection from the weather, grab a plastic milk jug or soda bottle. Cut off the bottom and place it over your plant. Leave the top off for air and water.

Nurse your seedlings in a bottle. Create a mini greenhouse from a plastic 2-liter soft drink bottle to give your garden plants an early start. Cut a 3-inch-wide flap in one side of the bottle, beginning at the neck and stopping several inches from the bottom. Punch some drainage holes in the opposite side. With the bottle resting on its side, lift the flap and put in a few inches of potting soil. Plant and water your seeds, and place the bottle in a sunny window with the flap closed. Moisture held inside will help the seeds sprout, but you can open the flap to adjust the humidity as needed. If established plants grow too large before it's time to transplant them, you can cut the flap away to give them more room.

Soak seeds for speedier sprouting. Seeds will sprout twice as fast if you soak them overnight before planting. Mix the tiniest ones with sand, and they'll be easier to spread evenly.

Wait for seeds to mature. Don't rush to collect the seeds as soon as your flowers die. Wait until the capsules turn brown. You'll know then the seeds are fully ripened.

Baby your seedlings with baby shampoo. Plant your seeds and then water them with a mixture of one teaspoon of baby shampoo and a quart of water. Your seedlings will find it easy to burst through the moist, soft soil.

Egg-cellent seed starter. Another ideal seed starting container: empty egg shells. Put seed starting medium in half of an eggshell, plant your seed, and put the shell back in the carton. Place the carton in a sunny window. When the seedling is ready to plant, crack the shell in several places, and put it directly in the garden soil for a nutritional boost for the growing plant.

Kinder, gentler watering. Once your seedlings are up and growing, they may look vigorous, but they're really still fragile. Don't pour water from a pitcher or watering can directly on them. Instead, use the "bottom-up" method of watering. When planting seeds in individual planting cells, leave one cell empty near the center and always pour your water in it. It will slowly dispense the water into the tray underneath, and it will gradually spread throughout the soil to all the seedlings. If you're using a recycled food container without cells, just don't plant any seeds right in the center of the container and add water there.

A spot of tea. Recycle used tea bags as seed starters. Cut a tiny slit on one side, put in a seed, and "plant" the tea bag in a peat pot. Keep it moist until the seed sprouts and is ready to transplant. Then mix the leftover tea leaves from the bag into the soil of a houseplant or potted plant. Ferns especially love tea.

Protect seedlings. Push toilet paper tubes into the soil around seedlings that are susceptible to cutworms.

Pamper tender plants. Cut the bottoms out of coffee cans, and put them over newly planted seedlings in your spring garden.

At night, put the plastic lids on for protection. Take them off during sunny days. Remove the cans when the threat of frost damage has passed.

Empty gas from mower with kitchen tool. A turkey baster makes a simple tool for removing gasoline from your lawn mower at the end of the grass-cutting season. Buy one and keep it with your gardening tools.

Store tools for a round of gardening. An old golf bag makes a terrific caddy for your long-handled garden tools, like rakes and shovels. And your gloves and hand tools fit neatly in the side pockets.

Don't hose away your garden budget. Those plastic garden hose holders are nice but costly, especially when you can make one for free. Instead of giving away your tire rim (the metal part that holds the rubber tire) next time you get a new tire, save that rim! Your garden hose will curl up nicely around the rim and will unroll easily without tangling. Hang one on the wall near the spigot. You can even paint it to match your house. Your hose is easier to use and you can spend that money elsewhere. Another inexpensive way to store your garden hose is to use a sturdy metal five-gallon bucket. Mount the bottom securely to the side of your house or shed with the open end facing outward and wrap the hose around it. Use the inside of the bucket to store hose nozzles, fertilizer sprayers, and garden gloves.

The lawn ranger. Self-taught mechanic and lifelong tinker-er Bill Desch has owned the same lawnmower since 1985. And it still runs like new. His secret? He treats his mower right. "Preventive maintenance is the key to a long life for anything with a motor" says Bill. "If you take care of your tools, they'll take care of you." Babying your lawnmower is as simple as an annual check-up. Each spring, Bill changes his mower's oil, installs a new filter, and makes sure the plugs are still in good firing order. "And sharpen the blade" he adds. "It wears down just like anything else." Even if you don't have Bill's mechanical ability, you can always find a repair shop that will tune up your mower usually for about $25. And your mower will thank you for it — the engine will last longer and perform better.

Brighten it up. It's easy to misplace your small garden tools when you're working in the yard. Paint the handles of your garden tools a bright color, like yellow or hot pink, so they'll be easier to find if you lay them down in tall grass and shrubs. No more replacing lost tools!

Hold your hoses. If you bring your garden hoses in for the winter, here's a neat way to store them. Cut a plastic garbage can down until it's only a few feet high. Then simply coil your hoses inside, and store them in your basement, shed, or garage.

Don't fail to water in the fall

You would never neglect watering your hollies, magnolias, and other special deciduous trees during a hot, dry summer. But it's easy to forget their needs when temperatures cool down. Fall, however, is when roots grow the most. So your trees may need regular watering to keep them strong against winter damage, even after they drop their leaves. As the temperatures fall, you can water them less often.

Spread borax for abundant fruit. Fruit trees need a trace of boron. If yours are not producing fruit, this might be the reason. Correct it by sprinkling a pound of borax under each tree.

Stamp out small stumps. You cut down a small tree, but before you knew it, new growth appeared. If you want to get rid of it for good, you must kill the roots. For the stump of a tree no more than 2 inches in diameter, cut a deep cross with a saw or hatchet and fill the open space with baking soda. Leave it for 20 minutes and then pour vinegar into the space. This will destroy even a tough stump, like mesquite.

Plant more value into your landscape

Not only do the trees around your house add beauty and shade, they give your property more monetary value. One study found that people were willing to pay 15 percent more for a house with two red oaks, each just 2 inches in diameter.

Remove moss from tree trunks. Moss growing on trees won't hurt them. But if you don't like the way it looks, here's how to get rid of it. Mix half a cup each of bleach and liquid dishwashing soap in a gallon of warm water and pour over the moss. You may need to do this a few times to completely kill it.

The shade-tree gardener. Under most conditions, grass doesn't grow well under large trees. Instead of struggling with unwilling grass, try something different that will spruce up your yard and keep down your frustration level. Shade-tolerant plants like hostas, ferns, columbine, and impatiens, and vines like ivy and periwinkle will fill in those bare areas under your trees with color and texture that grass just can't match.

Put it to rest all over your home. With a couple quick chops, your used Christmas tree can find lots of little homes all around your house. Bushier branches can be snipped off and used to protect plants in your garden, the dried needles will be a welcome contribution to your compost pile, and the trunk can be easily transformed into a few logs for a warm January around the fireplace.

Save your saplings. Keep rodents from feeding on your young trees. Wrap a few strips of fiberglass insulation around the trunks. The critters won't find them so delicious anymore.

Stake your claim. Locate a local stand of bamboo and cut some stalks to use as stakes for tender, long-stemmed plants. The bamboo looks much better than metal poles or strings and is sturdy enough to last for several seasons.

'Hang' your flowers. Certain flowers, like gladiolas, tend to grow tall and spindly. To keep them from falling over, use a straightened coat hanger as a stake. If you form a loop at one end, the flower can grow right up through it.

Tie up plants. Use twist ties to fasten the stems of plants to stakes. Be sure you fasten them loosely so the twist tie doesn't injure the plant as it grows.

Make a trellis. You can make a unique and beautiful trellis for your morning glories or other climbing plants. Remove the fabric from an umbrella, and bury the handle in the ground.

Be kind to tomato plants. For a kinder, gentler way to stake tomato plants and other tender vines, cut the legs off old pantyhose and tie up the branches. The stretchable fabric will give as the plant grows and gets heavier with fruit or flowers.

Sow some seeds directly in the garden. While some plants grow best from transplants, others, like squash, pumpkin, melons, and carrots, do best when seeds are planted directly in the ground.

Pick pests off produce with vinegar. Growing your own produce often means picking off your own bugs. To get bugs off your fresh vegetables, rinse the vegetables well. Then soak them in a solution of one cup of vinegar and a gallon of water. Five minutes later, you'll be able to pick the bugs off much easier. And you won't ruin the taste of your produce.

Weed out worms with marigolds. Let marigolds protect your produce. Nematodes, a type of worm, and other insects love to munch on beans, spinach, tomatoes, and celery. But the roots of marigolds produce a chemical that kills nematodes. So plant some marigolds among your vegetables for a worm-free garden.

Guard your garden with garlic. Onions and garlic add flavor and aroma to many delicious meals. But these members of the leek family also deter Japanese beetles from munching on your garden. Make sure to plant plenty of onions and garlic for a zesty source of natural defense.

Bug-busting combinations

When you're planning your next garden, consider these "companion plantings" to help keep down the bug population:

- Plant radishes with your squash plants to keep away squash bugs.

- Marigolds repel aphids, Colorado potato beetles, whiteflies, and even rabbits.

- Grow basil around your eggplants and tomatoes to keep away pests.

- Try sage, rosemary, and thyme with cabbage to repel cabbage worms.

- Onions keep bugs away from beets.

- Borage will defend your tomatoes against the dreaded tomato horn worm.

- Garlic will keep aphids away from almost anything.

Nail those naughty cutworms. The hardware store has just what you need — ten-penny finishing nails — to keep cutworms from feasting on your prized tomatoes. Press a nail into the soil beside the stem of each tomato, leaving the head about an inch or so above ground. It will make it impossible for the cutworm to wrap around the stem and eat away at your tender plants.

Grow unmatchable peppers. For the best sweet peppers ever, bury a book of matches in the soil with each pepper plant. These acid-loving veggies will thrive on the sulfur that will be released. Peppers also need magnesium. When the first blossoms appear, dissolve two tablespoons Epsom salt in a gallon of water and give each plant a pint of this liquid.

Turn up the heat on garden pests. Teach rodents to stay out of your vegetable garden with a mixture of one gallon of water and 3 ounces of cayenne pepper. Mix it up and pour it over the plants you want to protect.

Foil an insect's plan for your garden. Use strips of aluminum foil as mulch in your garden around corn, cucumbers, and squash. The aluminum foil reflects light, which repels many insects.

Plant caffeinated carrots. Before sowing your carrot seeds, mix them with coffee grounds. Not only does this add bulk, making planting easier, but you'll increase your harvest as well. That's because coffee grounds will keep root maggots from munching on the carrots. As an extra bonus, the grounds will help add nutrients to the soil around the plant as they decompose.

Heat up your tomatoes. Cover the ground around your young tomato plants with black plastic trash bags to give them an extra boost. The extra heat collected by the black plastic will make the plants grow stronger and fuller.

Wash dirt from fresh produce. An old screen door placed over two sawhorses makes a great surface to wash, drain, and dry vegetables from your garden. Put it within reach of the water hose, but in the shade where the sun won't scorch the produce. And if you place it over a dry part of your garden, you can let the "wash water" do double duty and give your garden a drink.

Keep your kitchen clean at harvest time. Use a plastic laundry hamper to gather fresh vegetables from your garden. Then stop by the water hose and wash away the grit. Let it drain completely before taking it into the kitchen. Your housekeeper will thank you.

A match is made in gardening heaven. Get double duty from your limited garden space — plant tomatoes and potatoes together. When your tomato seedlings have grown two sets of leaves, scoop out the center of an Irish potato for each seedling. Fill the holes with potting soil and transplant the tomatoes. Place the tomato-holding potatoes in containers with a couple of inches of soil. When the soil is warm enough, plant them in the garden. The tomatoes will grow and produce fruits during the summer. In the fall, you can harvest the potatoes.

Become a topiary master. Wire hangers become garden art when you recycle them into beautiful topiary frames. Just bend the hanger into whatever shape you like, then unbend the hook and drive it into the ground. Plant dwarf ivy around the base and keep an eye on its vines, making sure they attach themselves to the wire. Before long, the ivy will have transformed your old hanger into a little green man or animal, or your favorite letter of the alphabet.

Soak dry roots in a tub. Just watering your hanging plants may not be enough during a hot, dry summer. If the water runs quickly through, that means the roots are too dry to take up enough moisture. You may need to immerse them — pot and all — in a tub of water for a few minutes to give the roots a good soaking.

Grow strong plants with Epsom salt. Get your garden off to a good start with a cup of Epsom salt mixed into every

100 square feet of soil. Stalks will be stronger and leaves greener. And to keep your vegetables and flowers healthy, give them another dose every two to four weeks. Feed individual tomato plants and rose bushes one teaspoon per foot of height, and sprinkle one tablespoon over each 9 square feet of the root zone of azaleas, rhododendrons, and evergreens. Lawns like Epsom salt, too. Apply 6 pounds per 2,500 square feet. Feed houseplants, as well, with one teaspoon per gallon of water.

Treat thirsty roots to a long drink. Newly planted trees and shrubs require lots of water. You can save time and water with a system that gets it right to the roots where it's needed. Just take an 18-inch length of PVC pipe and drill a number of half-inch holes about an inch apart. When planting, place the pipe in the hole near the root ball with the top even with the ground. Place the garden hose into the pipe and let water run slowly so it will be absorbed into the soil.

Fish for houseplant fertilizer. Are you searching for a good organic fertilizer for your houseplants? Look no further than the dirty water in your fish tank. Not only does this water contain nutrients that plants love, it is free of chlorine and other chemicals. So when it's time to clean the tank, dump the water on your plants, not down the drain.

Don't leave footprints in your grass. If you leave a path of footprints when you walk across your lawn, it's time to turn on the sprinkler. Dry turf doesn't bounce back the way grass that's had a good soaking does. And be especially careful not to walk on grass just before you mow it. You won't get an even cut if parts of it are flattened.

Visit the henhouse for houseplant helper. Every time you prepare boiled eggs, you make the perfect tonic to perk up your droopy or dying plants. The calcium that remains in the water is good for all kinds of plants, so when it's cool, give them a drink. A little milk also gives plants a boost. Rinse out your empty milk bottle or carton and use that water on your plants as well.

Make a handy rain gauge. After it rains, you may wonder if your garden got enough water or if you need to turn on the sprinkler. To solve the mystery, place empty coffee cans here and there in your garden. When the rain stops, just measure the depth of the water in the cans. If you have at least an inch, there's no need for additional watering.

Give your plants a squeeze. You can recycle a squeeze bottle from liquid detergent into a watering can just the right size for small plants. Or you can use it to mix and distribute your plant food.

Cap it off. To prevent dripping from hanging plants after you water them, cover the bottoms of the planters with old shower caps. Remove the caps after several hours, and your floors should stay dry.

Having a dry spell? Houseplants can get so dry sometimes that when you water it runs right through and doesn't soak the soil thoroughly. Try this technique to make sure they get a complete soaking. Set the plant in a medium-sized trash can or five-gallon bucket. Gradually add water until it flows over the lip of the pot and the soil is immersed. Let the plant sit in the water for about a half hour. Then carefully lift the pot, let the excess water drain out the bottom, and put it in a plant saucer or tray.

Pasta for your plants. Don't dump out that water from the pot when you cook noodles or potatoes. Instead, let it cool off, take it outside to the garden, and pour it on your plants. They'll love the starchy boost of nutrition.

Aid for failing ferns. Here's an inexpensive tonic for your ferns: mix one tablespoon of castor oil and one tablespoon of baby shampoo into two pints of lukewarm water. Give your fern about three tablespoons of tonic, then give it a drink of plain water. Your plant should be perky soon.

Smaller means drier. Remember that the smaller the flowerpot or planter, the more often you'll need to water your plants. It helps to use saucers underneath pots or gather several small pots together on a tray filled with pebbles. The tray or saucer should be able to hold an inch or so of water.

Feed your plants from afar. Going away for a few days? Keep your houseplants watered with this handy trick. Line the bottom of your tub with several thick layers of old towels, then soak them well with water. Put your houseplants in on top of them, and they'll have water when they need it.

Fertilize your garden. Sprinkle coffee grounds around the plants in your garden to give them a little nutrient boost. But be sure and use grounds from a drip coffeemaker, not boiled grounds from a percolator. The drip grounds are richer in nitrogen.

Give your outdoor decking new life. If you've got moss growing on your deck, pour apple cider vinegar on it, and let it sit for an hour. Rinse off and enjoy a like-new deck.

If you can't beat 'em, join 'em. Don't trash your garden hose just because it has a few holes. Instead, use an awl or screwdriver to punch a few extra, larger holes into it, then use the holey hose as a soaker for your flower beds or garden.

Smart and slow garden watering. It's always better to give your garden plants a slow, thorough watering. To make this job easier, take an empty gallon plastic milk jug or two-liter soda bottle and punch several small holes in the bottom. Bury it near your plants with the mouth above the soil line. Fill it with water and some slow-release fertilizer, and watch your garden grow.

Stop a leak. Make a quick, temporary repair to a leaky garden hose by pressing the point of a toothpick into the hole.

Water will cause the toothpick to swell, plugging the hole. Break off the rest of the toothpick, and wrap the area with duct tape.

Give plants a nutritious drink. Never waste water you used to cook vegetables. As long as you didn't add salt, you can use it again to water your plants. But first let it cool to room temperature.

Zap poison ivy with salt and soap. There's a natural way to get rid of the poison ivy that comes creeping around. Just stir 3 pounds of salt into a gallon of soapy water and spray it on the leaves and stems.

Hammer out weeds. A plain, old hammer can be a useful tool for weeding your garden. Slam it into the soil, catching the weed between the claws, and pull it up, just like you would with a nail.

Quick tips for using herbicides

The first step in fighting weeds is to know your enemy. Get a county extension agent to help you identify the weeds in your yard or get a field guide to common weeds and grasses and identify them yourself. Then follow these simple steps for killing weeds:

1. Pick an herbicide that is right for your particular weeds.

2. Always wear protective clothing, safety glasses, and gloves when you apply herbicides.

3. Use weed killers on days when the wind is not blowing.

4. Don't mow your lawn just before or just after applying herbicides.

Kill weeds with boiling water. Get rid of weeds that are ruining the appearance of your cement or flagstone walk by pouring boiling water on them. You may have to repeat the process from time to time.

Wipe out weeds without emptying your wallet. Kill bothersome weeds easily by pouring vinegar and salt directly on them. Your neighbors who pay an expensive lawn-care company for this service will be green with envy.

Countdown to a weed-free lawn. In spring, apply a pre-emergent herbicide, before weeds start to grow. It's time to do this when the dogwoods are in bloom. In summer, check to see what weeds survived your initial attack. Apply more or different herbicides on individual weeds or pull them by hand. In fall, after your final trip around the yard with the mower, do one more application of a general weed killer. Pull up by hand any weeds that slipped through your defenses. Next year, you should have a weed-free lawn!

Feel your best for less

Take two aspirin and gargle in the morning. A sore throat can be a real headache. So why not fight it with aspirin? Dissolve two aspirin tablets in warm water and gargle. You'll feel hours of soothing relief. Just make sure you don't use coated aspirin tablets or acetaminophen.

Sink headaches with limes. British sailors once used limes to ward off scurvy. But limes come in handy for more common ailments, too. If you have a throbbing headache, cut a lime in half and rub it on your forehead. You'll be ready to sail the seven seas in no time.

Sock pain with warm rice. Behold the amazing microwavable heat pad — its actually just a bag filled with uncooked rice. Make your own by filling a soft, cotton sock or a small pillowcase with rice and sewing it closed. Just pop it in the microwave for a minute or two. This warm pouch is perfect for soothing sore muscles at the end of the day or warming cold feet at night.

RICE is good advice. Remember the RICE technique for safe, effective relief of sprains and strains. Rest the injured limb. Ice the affected area for 10 to 20 minutes every couple of hours. Compress the area with a loosely applied compression bandage, wrapped around and slightly above and below the injury. Elevate the affected part. Keep it higher than heart level if possible.

Oh no, not a pimple! Try a small dab of toothpaste on a pimple before going to bed. It will help dry the pimple out overnight and make it less noticeable the next day. Or try dabbing a lemon on the blemish after washing your face. Citric acid also helps dry and heal pimples fast.

A mitey allergy aid. Do you or someone in your family suffer from asthma or allergies? If so, you know how miserable dust mite droppings in clothing and bedding can make you feel. You can get rid of both the droppings and the dust mites by adding eucalyptus oil to your wash. The Journal of Allergy and Clinical Immunology reported that this "recipe" can kill up to 95 percent of dust mites: 1 part detergent 3 to 5 parts eucalyptus oil Make sure the detergent dissolves in the oil. If not switch detergents. Add this mixture to the washer after it's filled with water. Put in the items to be washed and soak 30 minutes to an hour. Wash normally.

Ease asthma attacks. Don't waste money on costly spacer devices for your asthma inhaler. An empty cardboard toilet paper tube works just as well. Just hold the inhaler in one end of the tube, and place the other end against your mouth. This trick comes in handy in a pinch because even if you don't have a spacer, chances are you have some toilet paper.

Sweet way to relieve a cough. If you need some relief from coughing, try this simple remedy: a cup of warm milk with two teaspoons of honey. This relaxing beverage will soothe the throat, stop the cough, and help you sleep.

Rx for scratched glasses. Seeing the world through rose-colored glasses might be fun, but looking through scratched glasses is anything but. If your plastic lenses are scratched, make them like new again with Pledge furniture polish. Just spray the furniture polish on both sides of the lenses, gently rub it in, and wipe with a soft cloth.

When your face is dragging. If you wake up with puffy bags under your eyes, just brew yourself a pot of tea. If you make it chamomile and wear it instead of drink it, you'll be on your way to smoother skin. How? Chamomile is a naturally soothing herb that temporarily decreases puffiness. Just ice the tea, soak a couple of gauze pads, and place them over your eyes. Bye-bye bags!

Keep the crows away. Fight crow's feet with olive oil. Just dab a couple of drops around your eyes each night before bed.

Quick-fix eyeglasses. If you lose the tiny screw that holds the earpiece onto the rest of your eyeglasses, you can poke a twist tie through the hole. Twist the ends and cut off the excess. It should hold until you can get a new screw.

Brighten your complexion with salt. Rejuvenate your face with this combination of cupboard ingredients. Mix equal parts salt and olive oil and gently massage your face and throat for five minutes. Then wash your face with your favorite cleanser, and your skin will have a radiant, golden glow.

Smooth your skin with yogurt. Wake up to smoother skin when you use this homemade night cream. Simply squeeze half a lemon into a cup of plain yogurt and stir. Then raid the refrigerator each night for a dollop of this mixture. Rub it onto your face before bed, just like you would use your regular night cream. After three or four weeks, you'll notice healthier-looking skin.

KO dry skin with mayo. No more dry, flaky skin! Reach into your refrigerator for a peerless "smoothing cream" — mayonnaise. Spread some whole-egg mayonnaise on your face, and leave it there for 20 minutes. Then wipe it off and rinse with cool water. You'll never waste money on expensive facial creams again.

Smooth as a baby's bottom. If you're looking for cheap makeup removers, you'll find them right next to the diapers. How about baby wipes? They're loaded with soothing ingredients that will take off your makeup in a flash.

Mix a honey of a beauty mask. Combine honey, oatmeal, and lemon juice in a bowl. Use enough to make a good paste that will stick to your skin. Leave it on your face for about 10 minutes, then rinse. This mask is particularly good for oily skin.

Stop traveling rugs. If an area rug doesn't want to stay in place, use your glue gun to make a zigzag or other pattern on the bottom. Let it cool and turn it over. It should stay put. Out of glue? Sew a rubber jar ring to the bottom.

Knock out smelly socks. Sweeten smelly feet by washing your socks in a solution of one-quarter cup baking soda and a gallon of water. Dry without rinsing.

Rock and roll for relief. For cheap and effective relief of heel spurs, place your bare foot on an empty glass soft drink bottle and roll your foot back and forth. Before you begin, make sure the bottle doesn't have any chips or cracks that could cut you. Some people find a frozen can of fruit juice works even better because it offers the doubly helpful combination of cold therapy and stretching.

Tackle athlete's foot. The itch of athlete's foot can drive you crazy. You can cut down on this by soaking socks in a solution of one cup vinegar and four cups of water, then washing them as usual. Soaking your feet in full-strength apple cider vinegar may also help relieve the itching.

Pop a homemade ice pack in your freezer. You never know when an emergency might pop up. That's why you should always be ready with an ice pack. Luckily, you can make one easily. Just put unpopped popcorn kernels in a zip-lock bag and freeze.

Lick ticks with petroleum jelly. Ticked off because you can't get a tick off? Remove a tick from your body with petroleum jelly. Just put a big dollop of petroleum jelly on the tick and leave it there for about half an hour. You should be able to wipe the tick off with ease.

Kill germs and save money. Give germs some of their own medicine with this easy-to-make disinfectant. All you need are one cup of borax and one gallon of hot water. But remember — borax is toxic so handle and store carefully.

Cleanse your hair with baking soda. Your hair has become a gathering place for old hair spray, gel, and other residue. Strip away the film in your hair with baking soda. Just blend a little baking soda with your regular shampoo. You can also try mixing baking soda with water and massaging it into your hair before you shampoo. Just be careful not to get any baking soda in your eyes.

Revive your hair with beer. Your limp hair could use a lift, but who wants to spend money on expensive hair products? Flat beer strips away soapy film and brings new life and bounce to your hair. Just mix three tablespoons of flat beer in half a cup of warm water and pour it over your head during your shower. Finish your shower and rinse. The beer gets rid of the residue from commercial hair products that can leave your hair feeling heavy and lifeless.

Set your sights on great-looking hair. Style your hair with a gorgeous, expensive salon look. It's easier than you think. Just dissolve a teaspoon of unflavored gelatin in a cup of warm water. You'll create an instant setting lotion for your hair.

Hair spray haven. Step into the shower stall when you spray your hair. This way the floor and other stuff in the bathroom doesn't get sticky and the shower gets rinsed every day anyway. If your bathroom is carpeted, this is especially useful for preventing a damaging buildup of dust and dirt on the carpet.

The 'green' way to douse dandruff. A sure cure for dandruff is in the aloe vera plant on your windowsill. Break a branch off your plant and slit it open, scraping out the pulpy gel. Apply this soothing ointment to your scalp and leave it on for five minutes, then wash with your regular shampoo. Aloe vera gel is also available in health food stores. Just be sure it's the real thing.

For blondes only. Here's how to remove that greenish tint you sometimes get from the chlorine in swimming pools. Dissolve an aspirin in a cup of water and pour it over your hair, from roots to ends. Massage well into hair, then rinse.

Deep condition hair. Hot oil treatments can be expensive at a salon, but you can do your own at home. Just warm up some olive oil, massage into your hair and scalp, and wrap your head in a warm towel. Wait about 20 minutes, then wash your hair as usual.

Lose the dandruff. Scrub away dandruff with everyday table salt. Just shake a tablespoon or so into your hair while dry. Rub it through your hair, massaging your scalp, then shampoo as usual.

Shine your hair. Put an apple-fresh shine in your hair with an apple cider vinegar rinse. Mix a half cup of apple cider vinegar with two cups of warm water, and pour over your freshly washed hair.

Stretch your shampoo. Don't throw out a shampoo bottle when it's hard to squeeze out the last bit. Just before it's empty, add water until the bottle is about one-third full. You'll be able to use almost every drop.

Quick-dry nails. If you always seem to mess up your nail polish about 10 seconds after you finish polishing, you may be tempted to buy one of those quick-dry sprays. Try this instead. Immediately after polishing, dip your fingers into a container of ice-cold water, being careful not to touch the sides of the container. Your nails will be dry in no time.

Face it — hemorrhoid cream works. You know certain creams can help relieve the itching, burning, and swelling of hemorrhoids. But hemorrhoid cream can also be used on your face to fight wrinkles, puffy eyes, and a saggy jaw line. Give this unusual treatment a try. Just be careful not to get any in your eyes.

Rub out mosquito bites. Next time you get bitten by a mosquito, rub some rubbing alcohol on the bite. It will stop the itching and virtually make the bite disappear. If you want to be even more prepared, splash some rubbing alcohol on yourself and let it dry before you go outside. This will stop mosquitoes from biting you in the first place.

Poultices from your pantry. Feeling the sting of an angry bee? For instant relief, mash some fresh papaya and apply it to the site of the sting. If you don't have any papaya handy, a paste of meat tenderizer and water will offer similar relief. If you don't have any meat tenderizer either, it's probably a good bet you do have baking soda. A paste of baking soda and water will also soothe stings. All of the above will also reduce swelling and relieve pain and itching.

Give bugs the spray. If you don't have bug spray handy when a pest starts buzzing around your head, use hair spray. It will make the bug's wings stiff and sticky. He'll drop like a stone and then you can swat him.

Smell swell to repel bugs. Sometimes avoiding bug bites is a matter of common "scents." Apply some lavender oil, just like you would perfume. People will think you smell great, but insects won't agree — and they'll leave you alone.

Relieve nausea with lemons. Lemons may make you pucker up, but they're also an astonishing remedy for motion sickness. If you feel queasy while riding in a car or boat, try sucking on a lemon wedge. It should help relieve the nausea. Another natural remedy for queasiness is ginger. You can buy ginger supplements at health food stores. Powdered, grated, and whole ginger are also widely available. One cup of boiling water poured over two teaspoons of powdered ginger and steeped for 10 minutes makes a soothing tea.

Ease acid indigestion. Baking soda helps neutralize stomach acid, which can cause indigestion and heartburn. For quick relief, drink a half glass of water mixed with a half teaspoon of baking soda.

Batten down your throw rugs. Make throw rugs less of an obstacle for your feet by sewing rubber jar seals underneath. The jar seals will keep the rugs — and you — from slipping and sliding. These rubber seals are easy to find in kitchen supply stores.

Make muggers think twice. Split your valuables between your two front pockets. In one, hold your cash. In the other, keep your credit cards and identification card. If you are mugged, hand over the cash.

Scare burglars with vegetables. For a homemade security alarm, line up food cans along the insides of your doors and windows. If someone tries to break in, they'll make a racket knocking over the cans. That will give you time to escape, and it might even scare off the burglars.

Soothe your skin with oatmeal. Your skin is irritated —
but, thanks to this common breakfast food, you don't have to
be. Soothe itchy skin rashes, sunburn, poison ivy, and even
chicken pox with oatmeal. Cut the foot off a pantyhose leg and
fill it with rolled oats. Then, tie the end and hold it under the
faucet as you run a bath. The soothing oatmeal bath will ease
your discomfort. Plus, you can save the homemade oatmeal bag
for next time.

Take the itch out of poison ivy. To relieve the burning
and itching of poison ivy or oak, make a paste of baking soda and
water. Gently spread the thick mixture over the affected area.

Polish off an irritation. If your wristwatch makes your
skin break out in a rash, paint the back of the watch with clear
nail polish, and you'll be able to wear it again. Repaint it from
time to time as the polish wears off.

Unwrap the power of soap. Put a new bar of soap to
work right away. As soon as you get home from the store,
unwrap the bar of soap and put it in your linen closet. Your
soap will do double duty. First, it will give your closet a pleasant
scent. At the same time, it will harden, making it last longer
when you move it into the bathroom.

And two shall become one. When you're down to that
last sliver of bar soap and ready to start a new one, moisten
them both. Then work up a bit of lather on the new one and
stick the sliver on it. It will soon become one with the new bar
of soap and there's no waste.

It beats yelling and pounding your fists. Caught in
the middle of rush hour and feeling stressed out? Try a quick
breathing exercise. Put one hand on your stomach, then inhale
slowly and deeply while counting from one to four. Exhale as
you count backward from four to one. According to Dr. Alice
Domar of the Mind/Body Center at Beth Israel Deaconess

Hospital in Boston, this mini meditation reduces stress, blood pressure, and heart rate.

Give cold sores a 'pep' talk. Think pink the next time you get a cold sore. Bismuth subsalicylate (Pepto Bismol), known for coating your stomach to relieve indigestion, works the same way on pesky cold sores. Just apply some to the affected area. It will coat and contain the cold sore virus.

Get more mileage out of your toothbrush. Would you like a clean, fresh toothbrush without buying a new one? How about throwing your old one in the dishwasher? It might sound strange, but the high heat and detergent that kills bacteria on your dishes can do wonders for personal hygiene items. So while you're at it, throw in your nail brushes, loofahs, or other sponges and give them all a new lease on life.

Prevent vaginal yeast infections. A bacteria called Candida albicans can cause annoying yeast infections, but yogurt contains a "good" bacteria called Lactobacillus acidophilus that can help fight yeast infections. Medical research finds that eating yogurt regularly can greatly reduce your risk of yeast infections. Applying yogurt directly on the inflamed area can also relieve a vaginal yeast infection.

Insider's guide to home improvement

Personalize your putty. For your next woodworking project, make wood putty that will match the particular wood you're using. Take a spare piece of wood and sand off a pile of the finest sawdust you can manage. Then whip the sawdust into clear epoxy. You'll have personal putty that could make any carpenter envious.

You talk the talk, but can you caulk the caulk? You want your house to be snug and warm in the winter and cool in the summer. You also want to pay as little as possible in energy bills. One way to help accomplish these goals is to make sure your house is tightly sealed. Caulking around windows doors siding and trim will help. Here's how to caulk your home: Before adding new caulk remove as much of the old caulk as possible. Wash the area with soap and water. Use chlorine bleach if mildew is present. Rinse and let dry thoroughly. The caulk will stick much better to a clean dry surface. Stuff some scraps of insulation into wide or deep cracks before caulking. Check the weather forecast before starting. If it rains within 24 hours after you caulk, all your hard work may be washed away. Cut the nozzle of your caulking tube off at a 45-degree angle and use a coat hanger or nail to pierce the seal. Apply steady pressure holding the caulking gun at a 45-degree angle to your work surface. Smooth the caulk down with a wet finger or damp sponge, but don't push it in too far. That might cause it to shrink too much as it dries and not fill the crack.

Say 'adios' to concrete stains. Mix one cup of ammonia with one gallon of water and you'll be able to deal with any concrete stain. Just scrub the solution into the stain and rinse off with a hose.

Banish damp smells with cat litter. Next to a haunted basement, a dank, smelly cellar can be a homeowner's biggest nightmare. To scare away moisture and odor, mix 10 pounds of cat litter with 5 pounds of baking soda. Every week, put about 2 inches of litter in shallow pans and place them around your basement.

Drill a hole-in-one. Next time you're drilling into sheet metal, make sure to hit your mark. Press on a strip of masking tape where you plan to put the hole. The tape will keep the drill bit from slipping and damaging the metal.

Help your drill see in the dark. Strap a penlight onto your drill using rubber bands or tape. Wherever you drill, you'll be able to see exactly what you're doing.

Homemade depth stops. You want to drill holes to a certain depth, but how do you know when you've gone deep enough? If you're a clever craftsman, you use a depth stop, and if you're a really clever craftsman, you use a cheap depth stop made of cork. Simply drill a hole smaller than the bit you will be using through a regular cork, then screw the cork onto the drill bit to the appropriate depth. The cork must be tight on the bit so it won't budge when it hits the wood.

Organize projects with an egg carton. It doesn't do any good to take something apart and fix it if you can't put it back together. An empty egg carton provides an egg-cellent solution to this problem. Just number each of the 12 compartments. When you take something apart piece by piece, put each screw, bolt, or part in the matching egg compartment. Place the first set of screws in compartment one, the next group in compartment two, and so on. When you want to put everything back together, start with the compartment you filled last and work your way back to number one.

Skip a trip on electrical cords. Keep electrical cords out of your way by taping them to the walls or floor. It's a bad idea to run them under carpets, where they're likely to get worn and short out. Stapling or nailing cords along your wall is also dangerous since you can damage the cords' insulation. Tape is the safest bet.

Tame those tangled cables. If your computer or stereo cables are out of control, try this handy tip for getting them neat and organized. Buy a coiled telephone cord in the length you need or cut an old one to the right size. Then gather the unruly wires together and wrap the phone cord around them.

Battery power. To prolong the life of a battery, lightly file both ends of the battery with an emery board or some fine-grit sandpaper.

Remove a broken light bulb. A raw potato makes a handy tool for removing the end of a broken light bulb from its socket. Make sure the switch is turned off, push the potato into the socket, and turn.

Camouflage floor flaws with a crayon. Fixing a scratch on a wood or vinyl floor is as easy as coloring between the lines.

First, match the floor's color with a crayon from your child's collection and melt it in the microwave. Next, pour the liquid wax into the scratch until it blends in smoothly. When the crayon hardens, wax the floor. Nobody will ever know the difference.

Repair vinyl floor with a food grater. To repair a gash in your vinyl floor, find an old scrap piece. Rub it against a food grater until you have a pile of fine dust. Stir this into clear nail polish and use it to fill the hole. You'll be surprised how well it blends in when it dries.

Quiet a squeaky floor. If your hardwood floor squeaks whenever you step in a certain spot, try sprinkling a little cornstarch or baby powder between the boards.

Nix the nicks. Clear nail polish can fill in small nicks and scratches on varnished wood floors and glass or Plexiglas surfaces — and no one will ever know.

Hush that squeak. Chances are, that squeaky floor is telling you the sub-flooring boards are rubbing against joists that have dried and shrunk. You can easily fix that problem with a drill and a number eight wood screw that's one-and-a-half inches long. First, locate the floor joists near the squeak. They are usually laid in the direction of front to back of the house, 16 inches apart. Next, drill the screw through the carpet and into the joist where the squeak occurs. Now you can make a midnight raid on the refrigerator without a squeaky floor giving you away.

Lay a lasting shelf liner. Leftover pieces of vinyl flooring make sturdy liners for your kitchen shelves and drawers. It's easy to cut to fit, you can remove it quickly to clean, and it lasts longer than paper.

Stop a squeak with a candle. Tired of sliding doors that squeak or drawers that don't budge? Rub the runners with a candle for a smooth and silent solution. The same trick works for stubborn windows with aluminum casings. As an added bonus, you can still use the candle when you're done.

Tighten sagging chair bottoms. Cane chair bottoms can lose their charm when they sag. To make them taut again, soak two cloths in a solution of hot water and baking soda. Coat the entire surface from the top with one cloth, while pushing up from the underside with the other. Use a clean cloth to absorb excess moisture and put the chair in the sun to finish drying.

Mend rug's braids with hot trick. Your braided rug might be falling apart, but that doesn't mean it's ready for the junkyard. Use your hot glue gun to repair it. Seal the gaps by putting hot glue on the edges of the braids and pushing them together. It's a quick and easy way to save money and extend the life of your rug. Be sure to put some wax paper down to protect your floor while you make your repairs.

Glue wood projects like a professional. When gluing something together, don't make the embarrassing mistake of gluing your project to your workbench. Instead, before you start, slip sheets of wax paper between the project and your bench.

No more sticky lids. Spread petroleum jelly on the inside of your glue lid, and it will never get stuck again.

Keep glue soft. You can still use all those hardened bits of glue in the bottom of the container by mixing in a bit of vinegar. If your glue is too thick, just put a few drops of vinegar in the container and shake it, and it will turn soft and easy to work with.

Uncover the secret to cleaner hands. Before you start your next project, apply a light coating of shaving cream to your hands. When it's time to clean up, dirt and grime will slide right off.

Beware of treated wood. Wear gloves whenever you are working with treated wood. After following that safety precaution, it's still important to wash up with soap and water before eating and drinking and after you are finished for the day. Your work clothes also need to be washed before you wear them again. To be on the safe side, wash them separately from other clothes.

Save yourself from sawdust. Always saw, sand, and drill treated wood outside. That way, you'll inhale as little of the potentially harmful sawdust as possible, and none of it will build up in your house. If you can't avoid working indoors, at least wear a dust mask.

Keep your footing when climbing a ladder. Feel safe the next time you climb up your ladder. Attach burlap to the bottom rung and wipe your feet on the way up. You'll be much less likely to slip.

Figure out ladder safety. Remember this formula if you want to be safe next time you're up on a ladder. Divide the ladder's height by four to figure the farthest distance you can stand your ladder from a wall. So, for instance, you would need to place a 12-foot ladder 3 feet or closer to the wall.

Tighten knobs with nail polish. Loose knob on your dresser or cabinet? Take the knob off and dip the screws in nail polish. After you screw the knob back on, the nail polish will dry, and the knob won't be loose anymore.

Loosen a rusty screw with vinegar. If you have a rusty screw or nut that needs loosening, call on one of these household super heroes — vinegar or hydrogen peroxide. A shot of either one will get the job done.

Repair screw holes with tees. If you have screw holes that are too large to hold screws, dip wooden golf tees into carpenter's glue and bang them into the holes. After the glue dries, saw off the part of the tee that's sticking out of the wall.

Pop open a lock with Coke. If you're having a hard time opening a rusty lock, don't throw away hundreds of dollars calling a locksmith. Fix it yourself with a Coca-Cola bubble bath. Just pour Coke or any carbonated drink on the lock, screw, or bolt, and the carbonation will loosen it for you.

When things get a little screwy. One of the hardest things for the amateur woodworker to do is get a screw to go in straight. Fortunately, one of the handyman's oldest tricks takes care of this problem. Before applying the screw, rub the threads with a bar of soap. The soap helps the screw go into the wood more smoothly and, hopefully, in a straighter line.

Bang the lid slowly. Tired of putting dents or holes in your wall because you missed a nail with your hammer? Never again. Instead of panicking over the condition of your wall, get yourself a plastic lid off a coffee can or an old Tupperware bowl. Drill a hole in the center that's large enough for your nails to go through, then place this guard around the nails as you pound them home. Now if your aim misses the mark, the plastic shield takes the blow, not your wall.

Survival tactics for fingers. Little nails can mean big pain for large fingers. To keep from hammering your fingers when dealing with a small nail, stick the nail through a small piece of thin cardboard first. Holding the cardboard by an edge, pound the nail home. Now tear away the cardboard, and you're all set safe and sound. Another way to handle small nails and tacks is with a comb. Put the nail in position between two of the comb's teeth. The plastic should serve the double purpose of holding the nail in place and protecting both the wall and your fingertips from unfortunate swings of the hammer.

Don't get stuck by drywall. If you're surrounded by drywall, try this to keep the drywall plaster from chipping away when you nail into it. Place a little bit of masking tape or cellophane tape on the spot where you're going to put the nail. After your nail is in, just peel away the tape from around it. But go slowly. Tape can get a pretty sticky grip, and you could peel away some of the paint if you're not careful.

Got a screw loose? Here's an easy fix for a loose screw. Get yourself a "twist-tie" or two, the kind used to keep bread fresh. Cut the ties or fold them over so they are about as long as the hole is deep. Next, take the screw out of the wall and insert the twist ties into the hole. When you put the screw back in, it should mash into the twist-ties and the extra width created should make the screw fit tightly.

Organize nuts and bolts. An old muffin pan makes a perfect organizer for odd-sized nuts, bolts, screws, and nails. You can even mount it under a shelf or bench top by securing it with a screw on one end. Use a washer as a spacer, and you'll be able to swing the muffin pan out to find that perfect fastener, then swing it back under when you're finished.

Tighten a screw hole. Holes sometimes get too large to hold in a screw. Here's the solution. Soak a cotton ball in ordinary white glue, stuff it into the hole, and let it dry for 24 hours. Then try your screw.

Wrap up loose screws. Wrap a piece of thin string or thread around the screw threads before inserting it into a hole, and you'll have a tighter fit.

Repair shower curtains. You can repair torn ring holes in your shower curtain. Just put a piece of duct tape or heavy plastic tape on either side of the hole, and use a hole puncher to poke a new hole through the tape.

Drive away oil spills with cat litter. To make grease spots disappear from your driveway, cover them with cat litter. If the spots are fresh, the cat litter will soak up most of the oil right away. If the stains are old, pour some paint thinner on the stain and toss on the cat litter. Wait 12 hours then sweep your driveway clean.

Easier locking. Make your key work more smoothly by spraying it with cooking spray.

Get rid of stains on concrete. Need to lift a nasty grease stain off your patio? Dump a generous amount of dishwashing detergent over the spot and let it sit. After a while, rinse it away with boiling water, then repeat the process.

The stay-put solution. If you're taking apart something with lots of tiny parts — a watch, for instance, or a model — stick a piece of double-sided tape to your work table and place the pieces on it as you remove them. This way, they won't go wandering off, and you'll know just where they are when you need to put them back in place.

Make changing outdoor light bulbs a snap. Weather, dirt, pollen, and dust can all make outdoor light bulbs seem welded into the fixture. Here's a bright idea. Smear a thin layer of petroleum jelly on the base of the bulb before you screw it in. When it's time to change the bulb, you'll be done in a flash.

Leave a trail of breadcrumbs. Whenever your fix-it project involves taking something apart, it's also going to involve putting it back together. Make this process easier by lining up each part in order as you remove it. It's also a good idea to jot down the order on a slip of paper, just in case you knock the assembly line out of whack.

Hide your home's imperfections. White liquid correction fluid, the stuff that's helped hide typos for years, can also make your house free of blemishes. Dab a little on white tiles or appliances that are dinged up. Or touch up your white molding. Follow with a coat of clear nail polish if you want a shiny finish.

Deter deck decay. Clean and reseal your deck at least every other year to keep it protected from the elements. If your deck isn't mildewed, you can just use a mild detergent. To get rid of mildew, use a water and bleach solution or a commercial deck wash. Be sure to rinse thoroughly and let the deck dry completely before sealing the wood.

Add an extra 'room' to your house. Turning a closet into a laundry room is like adding an extra room to your house. Just follow these five easy solutions, and you'll have an organized laundry room at little or no cost. First, make sure to keep the original closet shelves above the washer and dryer. They can hold detergents and stain removers. Set up a rod or dowel to hang clothes that need to be ironed or pre-treated. Next, install towel racks on the back of the closet door to hang clothes that need drying. For clothes that need to dry flat, like sweaters and knits, set up wire shelves. And for a convenient spot to iron, hang a drop-down ironing board on a side wall.

Mend a burned carpet. To repair a cigarette burn in carpet, cut out the blackened fibers using small scissors. Fill this indentation with some liquid glue and carpet fibers cut from a remnant of your carpet.

Demolish corrosion with club soda. Fizzle away corrosion with club soda or scour it away with baking soda and water.

Don't toss a rusty tool. Before you decide to throw away that rusty trowel or other gardening tool, try soaking it overnight in cider vinegar. Wipe away the residue with a cloth, and you may find it's as good as new.

Save your tool collection. Place a few mothballs in your toolbox to prevent rust.

A salty-sour solution. If your household tools are rusty from disuse, get them back in tiptop shape with a little salt and lemon juice. Mix enough salt into a tablespoon of lemon juice to make a paste, apply to rusted areas with a dry cloth, and rub.

Keep rust in check. If you find rust on your tools, don't panic. Remove the rust by rubbing it down with sandpaper. Start with the finest grade you have and work up to coarser grades if the finer ones don't work. Steel wool will also work for certain types of rust. Make sure you get every last bit of rust — don't be afraid to sand all the way down to the metal. It's better to remove a little of the surface with sanding than to leave even a small trace of rust, which will continue to spread and cause deterioration.

Take a step toward better traction. Give your outside concrete steps traction as well as a new color. Mix a handful of clean sand into your paint before you brush it on the stairs. The sand will give your feet the grip they need to keep from slipping.

Step up to safer steps. Paint your outside steps white so you'll have no trouble seeing them at night, no matter how poor the lighting is.

Add traction to ice with cornmeal. When your outside deck turns into an ice skating rink, sprinkle cornmeal for traction. And don't worry — the cornmeal won't damage the wood or your yard, and you can easily sweep it away once the ice melts.

Head off stair climbing injuries. If the low overhang of a staircase is a hazard in your house, attach a mirror to the front of it. When people see their reflection coming at them, they'll know to duck.

Help prowlers to see the light. Darkened yards are an open invitation to intruders. No ne'er-do-well wants to commit a break-in on a brightly lit stage. A few well-placed exterior lights can do wonders for correcting this problem. Many stores sell reasonably priced outdoor lights that are activated by motion. These light up your yard when something is moving but keep you from having to live in the spotlight.

Help the police help you. Your address numbers should be visible day and night so police, firemen, or ambulance drivers can locate your house quickly in an emergency. Small digits on your mailbox are not enough. Almost any hardware store carries a full line of reflective address numbers which are inexpensive and easy to install. Place your house number in a visible location. It's for your own protection.

Lights, camera, crime! Don't turn out all the lights when you go on vacation. A house that is dark for several nights in a row is a pretty attractive lure for thieves. For a few dollars, you can pick up a timer device that turns lights on and off for you while you are away. Plug a few well-chosen lights into your timer and set it for an irregular pattern. This should keep any sinister watchers guessing.

Tool insurance. If your workshop has a concrete floor, it's a good idea to put down some carpet remnants, at least in the areas closest to your work bench. Your feet might not notice the difference, but tools and containers that get knocked off the bench will be much less likely to break.

Cap broom handles. Cut a finger off an old rubber glove and slip it over the end of your broom. Then when you have to prop it against a wall, the rubber will keep it from sliding, and you'll be protecting your wall from scratches at the same time. This tip also works well on outdoor utensils, like hoes and shovels.

Rub small jobs the right way. Sandpaper can be too clumsy when you need to work on something small or hard to reach. Try using an emery board to get the job done.

Grate expectations. Sharpen a dull pair of scissors quickly and easily by cutting through a folded piece of fine-grade sandpaper several times. Be sure to have the rough side on the outside of the fold.

Happy sandings. Wrapping sandpaper around a small block of wood gives you something more substantial to hold onto while you're sanding large objects. If you practice this common technique, be sure to dampen the back of the paper before you wrap it. This will help keep the paper from tearing so it will work better and last longer.

Extend the life of your vacuum. Keep your workshop vacuum running smoothly by keeping the filter clean with the help of an old pair of pantyhose. All you need to do is cut off one leg of the pantyhose, wrap the open end over the filter, and secure it with a large rubber band. Then trim off the extra fabric and tie the end closed. Save the other leg as a replacement for the first one when it gets dirty.

Keep your shop vac in one piece. There's no need to hunt for your shop vacuum cleaner attachments anymore. Apply a piece of Velcro to the attachment and a piece to the vacuum. Put the two together, and they'll always be there when you need them.

Make your grout like new. The grout between floor tiles can get pretty grimy, especially in the bathroom. Return it to its original, bright color by gently rubbing it with folded sandpaper. To keep your grout looking like new, apply a coat of tile sealer.

Hide that burn. Your kitchen countertop looks great except for that ugly burned spot beside the stove. No need to replace the countertop. Just glue a decorative tile over the damaged area. You'll save yourself some money and add a permanent hot pad.

Take a bite out of tool grime. Toothpaste makes a great cleaner for hand tools. Just rub on the paste with a damp rag. It won't damage cutting edges or leave deposits on the tools. For really heavy grime, like caked-on gels and grease, wear a pair of gloves and use a spray-on cleaner.

Protect your tools from damage. It sounds like something you'd read in Poor Richard's Almanac. You store your tools carefully so they'll be in tiptop shape when you need them. Then just when you least expect it, you damage a tool as you're using it. To prevent this from happening, lay a foam mat or a carpet remnant on your workbench for added protection.

Give your tools a home. Keep track of your hand tools by storing them on a pegboard on the wall. Around each one, draw an outline with chalk or a marker. That way, you'll know where each tool goes and which ones are missing.

Wax your saw's teeth. Paste wax can make a handsaw easier to use. Just rub on a light coat before using your saw, and it will slide right through wood. On top of that, the wax will protect your saw's teeth.

Hammer together a hammer holder. Make yourself the handiest hammer storage rack on the block. Hammer 2-inch drywall nails into a board and hang it on your shop wall. Use as many nails as you have hammers. Then rest the claw of each hammer on a nail as if you were going to try and pull the nail out. This V-notch will fit onto the nail snugly so you won't have to worry about falling hammers. Plus, your hammers will stick out at easy-to-grab angles.

Rough up your hammer. Don't let wood and metal residue build up on the head of your hammer. Every once in a while, rub it with fine sandpaper. Now your hammer will hit nails head-on, instead of slipping and hurting the wood or the nail.

Zap sap from your shears. After trimming trees and bushes all day, it's no wonder your pruning shears are covered with sap. To clean them, dip an old toothbrush in vinegar and scrub the sap away.

Slick snow removal. To make snow shoveling easier, coat your snow shovel with car wax. Snow slides right off. If you don't have any wax handy, try using nonstick cooking spray.

Laying rust to rest. If you'll be storing a particular tool for a while, spray it with WD-40 before putting it away. A very fine coating will help protect the metal from moisture. If you have a tool that is frequently exposed to water (especially salt water) or is constantly used in harsh conditions, coat its metal parts with petroleum jelly before storing.

The rent is overdue. If you are planning to do a project that will require expensive tools, consider renting instead of buying. Estimate how long you'll need to rent a tool and how much the rental is per day. If this is less than the cost of the tools, you'll do better renting. Or rent for a day to see how you like the process and then decide whether to buy.

Keep a screwdriver from slipping. It seems like it takes you forever to fix anything because your screwdriver keeps slipping off. But if you rub a little chalk on the blade of the screwdriver, it will hold better to most surfaces.

Reject rust in your toolshed. Drop a couple of charcoal briquettes in your toolbox to keep your metal tools from rusting.

Locate wall studs with electric razor. You need to know where the studs are if you're going to hang something on your wall. If you don't have a stud finder, turn on your electric razor and run it over the wall. When it passes over a stud, its tone will change.

Plaster in a jiff. A few small cracks in the ceiling don't have to mean a whole new plaster job. Just mix a little white glue with baking soda, and use the paste to cover the small cracks. If the ceiling isn't white, use food coloring to match the color of the plaster.

Don't buy a hole new screen. Don't trash that window screen yet. Here are two quick fixes: Small holes in a screen can easily be patched using a few thin coats of clear nail polish. Dab it on lightly, letting it dry between coats. This will prevent clumping and dripping and make the repair job almost invisible. If you have some extra screening on hand, you can repair a small hole in a screen by gluing a small piece of screening over the hole. Use a permanent waterproof glue that dries clear.

Unsqueak door hinges. That squeaky door hinge is driving you crazy, but you don't have anything to oil it with. Check your cupboards before you drive to the hardware store. Cooking spray will eliminate that annoying squeak. Or try shaving cream — it should work just as well.

Loosen locks. If you have trouble opening a lock, rub the edges of your key with a soft lead pencil. The graphite in the pencil lead will soon have it turning smoothly.

Don't be a sore head. You keep bumping your head on a cabinet door that swings open when it should be closed. Glue a piece of magnetic tape to the inside edge of the door. And glue another to the spot where the first one touches the cabinet. It will stay shut until you want it open.

Saw without splitting. Don't let splintered plywood spoil your project. Before you cut, put a strip of masking tape over the starting point. It won't split when you start to saw.

Make your workshop seem bigger. If you want an extra countertop in your workshop but don't think you have enough space, think again. Just attach a fold-down table to the wall. When not in use, you won't even notice it. But in a jiffy, it becomes an additional workspace.

Create workspace storage. Empty coffee cans make great storage cubbies in the toolshed or garage. Nail them to shelves or the wall, either standing up or lying down. If they're on their side, label the plastic lid to make hardware easier to find.

Keep string at your fingertips. For handy string storage, take a clean two- or three-liter plastic bottle and cut off the bottom. Nail the bottle upside down into the wall and place a roll of string inside. Feed the end of the string through the bottle's neck. For even more convenience, attach a pair of scissors to the bottle with a separate length of string.

Make a handy scooper. Clean, plastic milk jugs can be turned into great scoopers. Here's how. Hold the jug so the handle is on top. Use a marker to draw a wedge on the diagonal and cut out this section. You now have a great way to dispense things like cat litter, birdseed, and sand. You can take the cap off for filling small spaces, like bird feeders. It will also do double duty as a funnel.

Attract scattered screws. Keep a magnet on your workbench. It will be handy for a quick pickup if you spill a jar of small items like nails, tacks, or washers.

Entertain with style

Punch up your holiday party. Make a splash at your next party with an eye-catching bowl of punch. Find a fancy punch bowl and ladle, and use your favorite punch recipe. But forget those little ice cubes that water down drinks way too fast. Fill muffin tins with some punch and toss a maraschino cherry into each one. You'll have classy ice cubes that will keep the punch cold instead of diluting it.

Defeat dripping candles with salt. Avoid the annoyance of cleaning up runaway candle wax. Stop your candles from dripping by soaking them in a very salty solution for a few hours. Dry them thoroughly, then light your amazing drip-free candles.

Don't be a drip. To keep dripping wax from running all over your candlesticks, refrigerate your candles for several hours before lighting them.

Make a pretty centerpiece. Decorate your table or mantle with apples. It's easy. Core several large apples and insert candles of different heights. Add some greenery and you've got a terrific country look.

Light your sidewalk with a gift from the East.
Contact your local Chinese restaurant and ask where you can buy a supply of take-out containers. Punch designs in the sides, add some sand and a candle, and you've got a new twist on the plain old luminary.

Foil sticky candles. Place a bit of aluminum foil around the bottom of each candle to go in your menorah or kinara. You'll be able to remove and replace the burned-down candles more easily.

Light up your holiday. Make inexpensive candle holders for any holiday season by decorating clean baby food jars to match your theme and setting a tealight inside.

Zap sticky tree sap. You finally got the Christmas tree to stand up straight in the tree stand, and it looks great. But your hands are another story. You can get that sticky sap off your fingers by rubbing shortening on them and wiping it off with a paper towel. Now wash your hands with soap and water, and you can get back to admiring your tree.

Take the hassle out of hanging lights. Every year you spend a frustrating hour or two untangling the Christmas lights before you can hang them. Save yourself the hassle next time by wrapping each strand in heavy-duty aluminum foil before putting them away. Crunch the foil around the bulbs, and you'll prevent tangling and broken bulbs. Next year, you'll be whistling carols while you decorate.

Avoid being 'needled' by your tree. If the Christmas tree you picked out this year is particularly prickly, use giant paper clips to hang your ornaments. Twist the clip open in the shape of an "S," and fasten the ornament to the smaller end. Holding the paper clip in the middle, carefully hook each ornament on a branch.

Play Santa to a child

Did you know that many post offices keep letters written to Santa? This year, ask for a few from a low-income neighborhood. You can buy gifts from a child's wish list and include some extra toys in case there are other children in the home. Purchase a gift certificate from a local grocery store and tuck it in a card with an encouraging message. Send the package anonymously and enjoy your secret all year.

String lights on your palm tree. Ho, ho, hold on a minute. How are you supposed to decorate for Christmas now that you live in a year-round warm climate? Don't sweat it. Gather up leaves of citrus and eucalyptus trees and place them on mantles and tables. You can even fashion a wreath of the leaves and add a big holiday bow. Use your imagination to turn local flora into holiday decorations, and you'll have a holly, jolly Christmas after all.

Here comes the gingerbread man. Take a gingerbread man cookie cutter and use it to trace shapes from brown paper bags. Decorate with paint, fabric, markers, or sewing notions. Hang them throughout your house or on your tree. Let your imagination run wild.

Give your decorations the look of snow. Use pieces of baby's breath or small branches painted white to fill in gaps in your Christmas tree, wreaths, garlands, or swags — a very inexpensive way to give everything the look of snowflakes.

Let it snow, let it snow. To create a winter landscape for your miniature village, buy quilt batting. Cut it to fit your display area, then arrange your village on this fresh layer of "snow." For even more country charm, nestle a small mirror in the snow to create a pond.

Make your own Christmas tree snow. Gather two-thirds cup liquid starch, two cups soap flakes, two to four tablespoons water, and blue food coloring. Mix together the liquid starch and soap flakes in a bowl. Add the water and beat with a rotary egg beater until the mixture becomes thick and stiff. Add the food coloring a drop at a time, while beating, until the snow becomes an icy-white color. Paint this on your Christmas tree branches. For a sparkling touch, sprinkle some glitter on the "snow" while it's still wet.

Spice up your Christmas tree. Cut netting into 12-inch squares. Place a handful of pine scent or apple cinnamon spice potpourri in the center of each square. Bring the corners together, tie tightly with gold ribbon, and place these "potpourri balls" in your tree.

Get the best of both worlds. If you have an artificial tree but miss the smell of real pine, here's an inexpensive way to have both. Visit your local tree seller and ask to collect greenery off the ground. Or better yet, ask your friends who still get real trees to save the branches and bits they cut off. Place these in baskets around your house, on your mantel, or tie them together for a garland.

Change your decorations to match the holiday. It's easy to convert your traditional Christmas decorations into beautiful ornaments for other holidays, like Valentine's Day, Easter, July 4th, or Halloween. Simply take your wreaths, candles, and table settings and add ribbons that are more appropriate to your new holiday theme.

Entertain the easy way. For a more relaxed way to serve a large number of guests, try a buffet. You can serve anything from finger sandwiches, chips, and drinks to a variety of fancy foods. Decorate the buffet table according to the season, and place utensils, plates, and napkins before the food. Your guests will appreciate the casual atmosphere, and you'll feel free to mingle and enjoy yourself.

Here's the scoop. For ease in serving ice cream at your child's birthday party, prepare ice cream servings ahead of time. Simply scoop the ice cream into paper muffin cups, place them on a cookie sheet, and return them to the freezer. When it's time to serve the cake, take out the ice cream all ready to serve. No mess no delay!

Color 'egg-citing' Easter eggs. Do your grand kids love to dye eggs for Easter? Try this fun way to make really unique designs. Save all sorts of rubber bands — wide ones, thin ones — and cut some of the thicker ones into wavy or v-shaped patterns. Cut small ovals into a thick band by pinching the elastic at intervals and cutting half circles. Once you have a variety of shapes and sizes, dress up your eggs with the rubber bands and toss them into the dye. When you pull the bands off, you'll have plenty of interesting designs. For a two-toned effect, dye plain eggs a pastel color, then put the bands on and dye a darker shade.

Save money sending flowers. You can arrange to have pretty flowers delivered monthly to a friend or relative, but it'll cost you a pretty penny. If the person lives within driving distance, why not give the gift of flowers and a visit from you? On your way to visit each month, stop at the grocery store, where flowers are inexpensive, and buy a new bunch. Your special someone will feel even more special when you visit, and you'll save on the high cost of delivery.

Vase the facts. Here's a great way to recycle and save money, too. Buy inexpensive vases from garage sales; you can often get them for about 25 cents. Then provide your own vase the next time you go to the florist to buy flowers as a gift. You'll save as much as $3 depending on the size of the arrangement.

Unstick tape with a button. Wrapping gifts wouldn't be so bothersome if you could only find the end of your roll of tape. Here's a simple way to do just that — stick a button on it. As you use the tape, keep moving the button.

It's a wrap. Get more creative with wrapping paper and save money to boot. Use the pages of fancy gardening magazines for small gifts or the cartoon section of the newspaper for a wrap with a different look. Old posters are another good substitute for more expensive wrapping paper.

Bow beauty. If you recycle bows for your holiday gifts, you may find them a little squashed when you take them out of the storage box. A hand-held hair dryer set on high heat can perk them up and make them usable again.

Wrap up a 'kiss.' You can wrap a special gift to look like a giant chocolate kiss. Place the gift on a paper plate or circular piece of cardboard. Starting underneath the plate, wrap aluminum foil up around the item to form the "kiss" shape. Make the gift tag out of a long piece of white paper and stick it in the top.

Dispense wrapping paper like a pro. Are you tired of trying to keep your wrapping paper stored neatly? Are the ends always unrolling? Then take an empty wrapping paper tube and slit it lengthwise. Slide it on top of a new roll, leaving the edge of paper hanging slightly through the slit. Not only will your paper stay neatly rolled, it will make wrapping your next gift a snap.

Make a gift tag that really shines. Take an extra large Christmas light bulb and write "To" and "From" on it using a permanent marker. Tie it onto your package's bow for a unique gift tag.

Make emergency kits for gifts. If you're tired of ties, scarves, and fruitcakes for Christmas, try giving practical gifts this year. Make emergency kits for your loved ones to keep in their cars. Fill a plastic storage box with a first-aid kit, a flashlight, a flare, and an insulated blanket. Add some bottled water, a can opener, and packages of factory-sealed and canned foods to feed someone for several days. Your gift could come in very handy someday.

A gift of romance. If you have a person on your gift list who is really hard to buy for, or a gift to buy for an upcoming wedding, consider an "evening in a basket." Start with an inexpensive basket purchased at a garage sale and one of your favorite main-dish recipes. Line the basket with pretty paper or leftover fabric and add all the nonperishable ingredients in your recipe. Finish with something to drink such as exotic tea, fruit juice, or a bottle of wine and a small box of chocolates for dessert.

Recycle presents. Everyone gets "white elephant" gifts from time to time — nice things that you have absolutely no use for. Save them in their original packages and attach notes saying who gave them to you. Then when one of your white elephants turns out to be just the right gift for someone else, it's still fresh and new and ready to go.

Create your own Christmas cards. Make your own Christmas cards using a photograph of your family at a holiday dinner, your home blanketed with snow, or a beloved pet surrounded by holiday decorations. Have copies made of your favorite photo, and use spray adhesive to glue the pictures to the front of blank cards. Use a fine-tip marker to write a message inside. Far-flung friends and relatives will treasure their holiday "visit" to your home.

Carve spooky jack-o'-lanterns. Don't pay a lot of money for ceramic jack-o'-lanterns. You can make Halloween decorations out of real ones. Working from underneath, hollow out tiny pumpkins and gourds. Then carve scary faces on them with a small, sharp knife. Using a string of battery-operated Christmas tree lights, tuck one light under each little face. Arrange the spooky heads on a tray of fall leaves and dim the overhead lights for extra drama.

Try this homemade face paint. Need a safe, easy-to-make face paint for your Halloween costume? Mix one teaspoon cornstarch, a half teaspoon water, a half teaspoon cold cream, and two drops food coloring. It's that easy.

Make cute, edible Halloween decorations. Fill small, clear jars (recycled from pickles, olives, etc.) with inexpensive candy corn. Then buy a half-yard or more of Halloween-theme fabric at your local craft or fabric store. Cover each jar top with a square or circle of fabric, held in place with a rubber band or some coordinating ribbon or yarn. "Scrunch up" the remaining fabric in the center of your table, raw ends folded under, and hold the fabric in place with the jars of candy corn to complete your centerpiece.

Carve a better pumpkin. This year, set tradition on its ear by carving your jack-o'-lantern a bit differently. Instead of cutting a lid on the top of the pumpkin, make a hole in the bottom. Not only will this make old jack more stable, it allows you to position and light your candle more easily.

Be prepared for Halloween. Take a large box or trunk and throughout the year drop in unusual clothes or accessories you'd otherwise toss out, or add pieces you find at garage sales or thrift stores. When Halloween rolls around, you'll have a wonderful assortment of items that only need a bit of imagination to create inexpensive costumes.

Take the stress out of holiday baking. Make baking for the holidays effortless this year. Beginning in September, start freezing half a dozen cookies every time you bake. Do the same with candies and any other treat you create. When your holiday guests arrive, you'll have a wide variety of goodies to serve them, and you won't be stressed by last-minute baking.

Make a cake plate. If you're worried about breaking or losing your good china when you take your homemade cakes to picnics, bake sales, or school functions, try this. Make a disposable cake plate by covering a sturdy piece of cardboard with aluminum foil.

Let the children create fun memories. If you've got a crowd coming this Thanksgiving, set up a separate table for the kids. Cover the table with brightly colored paper or an inexpensive tablecloth. Buy laundry markers so the kids can write what they're thankful for on the cloth or just decorate it during the meal. Each year bring out the old tablecloth to reminisce, then set out a new one.

Recycle glass ornaments. Here's a great way to give new life to scratched glass ornaments. Take out the metal neck and hanger, and soak the ornament in bleach for about 10 to 15 minutes. Clean the inside carefully, using a cotton swab. Rinse the ornament and let it dry. Once the ornament is completely dry, use your imagination and fill it with potpourri, dried flowers, tinsel, glitter, colored paper, or lace.

Shoo fly. Don't let a party on your deck or patio be ruined by pesky flies, gnats, or mosquitoes. Borrow or invest in a portable electric fan. Aimed at the center of the party action, a fan will cool the area while it discourages flying insects. A second fan aimed at the same area from another direction will help even more.

Help your guests find their place. Instead of traditional place cards on your table, personalize individual flower arrangements beside each plate by writing the guest's name in gold ink on a leaf. This can work for any holiday from July 4th to New Year's.

Picture this at your party. Give your party guests a lovely memento to take home — a snapshot. Use an instant camera to take photos of each guest near a special decoration, such as a Christmas tree or chatting with other partygoers. Hand the pictures out during the festivities, and they'll also spark conversation. Your guests will remember your party for years to come, and they'll appreciate your thoughtful touch.

Here comes the bride.   To save money on a wedding cake, have one layer of real cake and the rest decorated Styrofoam. After cutting the cake for the traditional photographs, ask the servers to roll it back into the kitchen. Have sheet cakes waiting to be cut and served. Sheet cakes are much less expensive than tiered cakes and will serve a crowd neatly and easily.

Recycle old holiday tins.   The tin you got as a holiday present was great when it was filled with popcorn. But now that the snack is gone, don't just throw it out. Since most of these tins come decorated in a holiday theme, it could make a pretty and easy-to-find storage bin for your ornaments.

Toast a classy centerpiece.   With a little know-how, four wine glasses can make a classy holiday centerpiece for your table. Here's how. Fill the glasses half full with red or green dry gelatin. Next, place short, red votive candles in each glass. Use transparent tape to secure holly cuttings around the glass stems. When your guests arrive, light the candles, stand back, and enjoy the compliments.

Bargain bandannas.   To brighten your table and give it a Southwestern flair, use inexpensive bandannas as napkins. You'll find them in a rainbow of colors in craft stores or the scarf department of discount stores. If you choose the polyester/cotton kind rather than all cotton, you'll never need to iron. You can also sew bandannas together to make an easy, inexpensive tablecloth.

Set a festive fall table.   Hollow out miniature pumpkins and squash to make serving bowls and containers for cranberry sauces, relishes, dips, soups, or individual desserts. Cut a thin slice off the bottom so the pumpkin or squash will stand firm.

Set a pretty table. For casual dining, use pretty kitchen towels as place mats. They are durable and will absorb spills — great for kids. And cleanup is a snap. Just throw them in the washer.

Give a personalized wreath. Find out what special hobby or interest the recipient has, like sewing, gardening, dogs, or fishing. Buy small articles representing that interest and hot glue them onto a ready-made wreath. Add coordinating ribbon, fabric, or a bow.

Heard it through the grapevine? Grapevine wreaths are great for any holiday. Go to your local craft store and buy small ornaments and flower picks, like wooden eggs and bunnies, hearts and roses, pumpkins, witches, four-leaf clovers, flags, snowmen, Santas, packages, dreidels, and gold coins. Hot glue them on, then wrap with coordinating ribbon and add a bow. These are inexpensive enough to have one for every holiday.

Wage war on dirty laundry

Unstick gum with egg whites. There is more than one way to remove chewing gum from fabric. Try using a toothbrush to scrub the gum with egg whites. Leave it for 15 minutes, and then wipe away remaining traces and launder as usual. Or cover it with wax paper and press it with a warm iron. Just peel off the paper, and the gum should come off with it. You can also remove gum by soaking it in warm vinegar.

Squeeze a lemon to loosen adhesive. The next time adhesive tape or gum sticks to your clothes, grab a lemon and squeeze some juice on the sticky spot. Wait a few minutes while the lemon juice does its thing. Then rinse with warm water.

Do away with melted decals. Don't let heat melt the decals on T-shirts or other clothing. Wash them inside out in cold or lukewarm water, and line dry or use the dryer's air-only setting.

Remove gum from clothing. Every time this happens, you swear your children will never get chewing gum again. But right now, you need to get the stuck-on gum out of your daughter's Sunday dress. Rub an ice cube over the gum to harden it. Then you can scrape it off with a spoon or other utensil, and wash as usual.

Air dry a sweater faster. If you want to shorten a sweater's drying time, stuff it with a paper bag before you spread it out to dry.

Quick-dry your lingerie. In a hurry to dry a delicate item? Use your hair dryer. It will dry even faster if you slip a dry cleaner bag over the item and trap the hot air inside.

Hang up your clothes with paper clips. What should you do if you want to hang up small items to dry, but don't have any clothespins? Try using paper clips, bobby pins, pen caps with pocket clasps, or clip-on earrings. To prevent rust from the metal, put wax paper or plastic wrap between the clip and the cloth.

Hang a rain-or-shine drying rack. Your garage is a good place to dry clothes, no matter what the weather. Suspend an old refrigerator rack or oven rack from the ceiling, and hang your wet clothes on hangers from the rack.

Stuff your sneakers. Fabric tennis shoes will hold their shape better if you fill them with paper towels and air dry them after washing.

Clean and fluff blankets easily. If your woolen blankets need refreshing but you don't want to dry clean them, use your washer's gentle cycle and a mild dishwashing soap. Then dry them using the air-only setting on your dryer. They'll come out nice and fluffy.

Best place to hang a clothesline. Place your clothesline where the prevailing wind will blow across the wires, not from post to post. If possible, place it where part of the line is in the shade during the middle of the day. You can hang bright colors out of direct sun where they'll fade less. But avoid putting it directly under trees where bird droppings might mess up a line of clean clothes. And locate it where garments blowing in the wind won't get caught on branches or a fence.

Restore the color in faded cotton. Black cotton garments and lingerie look sharp when they are new. But it doesn't take long for them to look dull and brownish. Restore that shiny black sheen by adding two cups of strong black coffee to the rinse water.

Neon know-how. It's fun to perk up a tired wardrobe with some of those really bright colors — hot pinks, neon oranges, and electric blues. But they may not be colorfast, so wash each color alone the first time following the instructions on the label. They'll probably lose some of their brightness with each washing for a while. If you get a stain, you may need to treat the whole article so the color will be uniform.

Cover bleach spots. You can recolor spots on fabric that got splashed with bleach. Choose a crayon that matches the color. Heat the area to be repaired by ironing it. Color in the spot while it's warm. Then cover with waxed paper, and iron again to set the color.

Balance bulky items in your washer. If the label says it's safe to machine wash your pillows or stuffed toys, go ahead. But wash two at a time and place them on opposite sides of the agitator for balance. To clean your nonwashable "cuddly" things, shake them in a closed pillowcase containing some baking soda.

Handle 'down' with care. Before washing a down-filled garment, check to be sure the outer material is washable. Then make a bag twice as big as the garment from tightly woven, white fabric and put the item securely inside. Close the bag using strong thread and stitches small enough to assure no feathers will escape if there is a loose seam in the garment. Always machine dry down-filled pieces. Use a low-temperature setting, and toss in a few clean tennis balls to fluff the garment and make sure it dries evenly.

Hope for the shrunken sweater. Read the care instruction tag on sweaters carefully before laundering. They are made of a variety of fibers from cotton to wool. And they sometimes have delicate decorative parts that require special care to keep them looking their best. If you wash a wool sweater and it shrinks, try this: Soak it in lukewarm water with some good hair shampoo mixed in. This may soften it enough for you to be able to reshape it. Dry it flat on a sweater rack or on a clean, dry folded towel.

A warm, relaxing bath — for your blanket. Many blankets, even some woolen ones, can be machine washed and dried. But different fabrics and kinds of construction call for different temperatures and cycles. Others require dry cleaning. So always check the label and follow instructions carefully. Machine wash only one large woolen blanket at a time. And measure it first so it can be stretched to the same size after washing. Fill the tub with cold or warm water and dissolve the detergent in the water. Stop the machine before adding the blanket. Place it loosely around the agitator. Let it soak for 10 to 15 minutes. Advance the dial so that the water will drain out. Let it spin for about a minute and stop it again. Advance it to the final rinse cycle and let it continue through the final spin.

Pull a clean punch for pillows. If the label says they are washable, you can launder feather or polyester-filled pillows in the washing machine. You can wash two pillows at a time or balance one in the washer with some large towels. If they are particularly soiled, let them soak for 15 minutes before washing. Using a front-loading washer for this job is better. It allows them to move more freely and results in less lumping. And there will be less rub so pillows washed this way should last longer. If you use a top-loading machine, pillows will tend to float to the surface. It helps to push them under until they fill with water. Stop the machine and turn them over and punch them back under again once or twice while washing. Wash for four to eight minutes on the regular wash cycle. Rinse three times.

The case for a delicate wash. To wash an antique or delicate item that's heavily soiled, place it in a pillowcase and use long running stitches to close the top. Wash in the washing machine with other clothes of similar color using mild soap. Then take out the stitches from the top of the pillowcase and air dry the delicate piece.

Be fair with fine fabrics. Silks, woolens, and some man-made fibers require special care. The label may say you can hand wash or use the gentle machine cycle. (Fine wool clothing is generally best washed by hand.) Wash in warm or cold water and rinse in cold. Dissolve powdered or liquid detergent completely before putting delicate articles in the water.

Stiffen delicate fabrics. One packet of unflavored gelatin dissolved in two quarts of hot water makes a good substitute for starch on delicate fabrics, like batiste and organdy.

Give beloved stuffed animals new life. Favorite toys never look the same after they've been through the washer, but Teddy has to have an occasional bath. To get your stuffed friends nice and clean, put them inside a clean pillowcase, close the top using some string, and wash and dry as usual. You and your child will be pleased with the results.

Wash two loads in one. To save water and energy, make double use of a tub of water. While your washing machine is filling, add soap and wash items you need to do by hand. You can probably finish before the tub fills up. If not, stop the machine until you're done. Then add your regular load of laundry and turn the washer back on.

Beware blanket fuzz. Soak your blankets in water and detergent for 10 minutes, then wash them on the shortest wash cycle. This will reduce pilling, and they'll last longer, too.

Rejuvenate a woolen blanket. If your woolen blanket can be machine dried, toss it with two or three dry towels at high heat for 10 to 20 minutes. Warm the towels in the dryer for a few minutes before you add the blanket. They will absorb the moisture much faster this way. Remove the blanket before it is completely dry to avoid wrinkles and shrinkage. Finish drying flat or suspended over two clotheslines. If any shrinking has occurred, stretch to original shape and size.

Wash delicates. You don't have to buy a special bag for washing your delicate lingerie. Just put them in a large pillow-case, tie the top shut, and wash on the delicate cycle.

Don't let detergent fade your duds. Did you know that if detergent comes in direct contact with fabric it can cause it to fade? That's why it's a good idea to add it as the washer is filling with water and wait until it is dissolved before adding your clothes.

Get the scoop on soap. Soap and detergent aren't the same thing. If the label says use soap, be sure that's what you choose. Ivory liquid, for example, is a soap, while most dish-washing liquids are detergents.

Chase away overflowing suds. Too much laundry detergent can cause your washer to overflow. Counteract the excess suds with two tablespoons of white vinegar or a capful of fabric softener.

Increase your towels' drying power. If you want towels that really soak up moisture, it's important to get out all the laundry detergent. Just put a cup of white vinegar in the rinse water about once a month.

Know your soaps. Soap and detergent both help clean clothes by removing soil and suspending it in the wash water so it doesn't settle back into the fabric. Soaps are made from fat, lye, and a few other ingredients. Laundry soaps generally come in boxes of flakes or granules. They are used mainly for washing baby clothes, lingerie, or other gentle-wash items. Soap should only be used with soft water. In hard water, it can form a scum that remains on clothing. It may build up and make them look gray, dingy, and greasy. It sometimes remains on surfaces of the washing machine as well. Detergents are used for most of today's laundry chores, machine and hand washing alike. They have ingredients that quickly penetrate and loosen the soil and keep it suspended in the wash water until it's rinsed away. They are available in liquid or powder forms. The liquid is especially good for use in cold water since it dissolves more easily. And you can choose either heavy-duty or light-duty detergent. The light-duty type is good for hand washing delicate fabrics.

The scoop on detergent. The detergent container gives a recommended amount. But that's based on an average load of five to seven pounds of fairly soiled clothes, using moderately hard water. Use more detergent if the clothes are heavily soiled, your water is hard, or you are doing a bigger than average load in a large-capacity washer. If, on the other hand, your water is soft, your clothes are lightly soiled, or you are doing a smaller load, you can cut back on the amount of soap or detergent you use.

A hot tip for saving cold cash. Detergents dissolve best in warm or hot water. But some clothes are more likely to shrink or fade in hot water. And using cold water saves energy. One compromise is to put in the detergent and run enough hot water to dissolve it. Then switch the dial setting to cold water and begin adding the clothes as you finish filling the tub. Rinsing with cold water is almost always a good idea. Not only does it save energy, it keeps permanent press articles from wrinkling and makes others easier to iron.

Mind the mild label. If the care label says "Use a mild detergent," be sure you really do use a light-duty one. Otherwise, you may wind up with light spots on the garment. If this occurs, try soaking the entire article in a strong solution of regular detergent and water. This will lighten the garment, but the color should even out.

Stretch the soap. You have one more load of wash to do and your laundry soap is almost gone. Make it stretch by adding a quarter cup of baking soda. As a bonus, your clothes will smell fresh and feel soft as well.

Add suds control. If you put too much detergent in the washing machine, over-sudsing can make it overflow. Stop the foaming action by adding half a cup of salt to the wash.

Bleach acts faster than you think. Don't leave clothes soaking in bleach overnight. Soaking for 15 minutes is just as effective. Bleach can damage clothing if it soaks too long.

More is not always better. Always follow the directions on laundry products. Using more or less than recommended can damage your clothes or leave them dirty.

Don't burn rubber on your tiles. Next time you pull a rug out of your dryer, don't place it on your tile floor until it cools. The rubber bottom gets very hot in the dryer, which can cause it to melt onto the floor or discolor it. Try laying the rug upside down at first.

Don't set fire to your dryer. Never put fabric that has come in contact with paint, machine oil, gasoline, or any other flammable liquid or solid in your dryer. Their fumes can catch fire.

Save $$$ in your dryer. Whenever you use your dryer, try to run it more than once. By the second time, the dryer will already be heated up from the first load, and it won't have to work so hard to dry the clothes. You get the most efficiency by drying several loads in a row. You'll save money on both electricity and your clothes budget if you don't overdry fabrics. Unless you need to wear a garment immediately, take it out of the dryer while it's still slightly damp, especially in thicker areas such as pockets or waistbands. You'll find less shrinking, wrinkling, and static buildup. But to prevent the danger of mildew, let damp items dry completely in an open area before hanging them in the closet or putting them in drawers. Make sure you don't overload the dryer. Clothes that tumble freely will have fewer wrinkles so you may not have to heat up the energy-burning iron. And use the permanent press cycle with its cooling down period. That will also reduce wrinkles.

Size up fabric finishes. In doubt about which fabric finish to use? Starches work best on cottons and cotton blends. Save fabric finishes and sizings for synthetic fabrics.

Give droopy permanent press a boost. Over time, permanent press items can become limp and shapeless. Give them body again by adding a cup of powdered milk to the final wash and wear rinse cycle.

Earth-friendly spray starch. Mix two tablespoons of cornstarch with one pint of cold water, and put it in a clean spray bottle. The next time your clothes need a bit of stiffening, shake the bottle, spritz on, and iron as usual.

Crisper curtains. When you wash sheer curtains, do they come out limp and wrinkled? Instead of starching and ironing them, dissolve a packet of plain gelatin in hot water and add to your final rinse. You'll have crisp, wrinkle-free curtains.

Bring back the sheen to polished cotton. Polished cotton will look shiny again, and have more body, if you put a packet of plain gelatin in the final rinse cycle.

Spray inside. Spray starch on the inside of clothes, not the outside. This eliminates a slick look on your ironed clothes.

Soften clothes at a great price. With a few inexpensive items from your kitchen cabinet, you can make a fabric softener to rival the popular brands. All it takes is two cups white vinegar and two cups baking soda. Slowly stir these into four cups of water. Be sure to mix it in a container in the sink because it will fizz. Store in a plastic bottle, and shake well before adding one-quarter cup to the final rinse. These same ingredients may also do the job when used individually. Try adding half a cup of white vinegar or one-quarter cup of baking soda to the last rinse.

Make your own fabric softener sheets. You can replace expensive fabric softener sheets with a homemade version. Just mix a cup of liquid fabric softener with two cups of water. Keep a bottle of the solution in your laundry room. When it's time to dry your clothes, dampen an old washcloth with a small amount and toss it into the dryer with your wet clothes.

Get terrific dust cloths for free. Don't throw away used fabric softener sheets when you're unloading your dryer. Recycle them. They make great dust cloths.

Soften without spotting. When using liquid fabric softener in the washer, dilute it before adding it to the rinse. Never pour it full strength onto clothes. It can leave spots that look greasy. If you do make that mistake, here's how to get rid of the spots. Moisten them if they have dried. Rub with bar soap, rinse, and wash as usual. If they still remain, sponge them with rubbing alcohol, rinse thoroughly, and wash again.

Save cents on softeners. Fabric softener sheets can pull double duty. Use them twice, once in the dryer and again in the rinse cycle of the next wash load.

Soften your clothes with vinegar. For a natural fabric softener and static cling remover, try adding about a cup of white vinegar to the final rinse cycle of your wash. It is mild enough not to harm your clothes. But it's strong enough to dissolve alkalis in soaps and detergents. Vinegar gets rid of extra suds and soap deposits and leaves your clothes soft and fresh. Vinegar even breaks down uric acid, a plus if you're washing baby clothes. Add two cups of vinegar to a full tub of rinse water, and you'll have soft, fluffy blankets and sleepers for the little one.

Oil your woolen sweaters. When hand washing wool or cashmere sweaters, add a tiny drop of bath oil to the final rinse. The fabric will be easier to smooth into its original shape, and your sweater will keep just a hint of the fragrance.

Make a case for less fuzz. To keep sweaters from pilling, wash them in a pillowcase that's tied closed with string.

Control corduroy's lint and wrinkles. Clothing made from corduroy should be washed inside out so it doesn't pick up lint. Wash it in warm water and dry on a normal setting, but take it out of the dryer before it's completely dry. Smooth the pockets and seams by hand, and hang to finish drying.

Pin down delicate lace. To keep fragile lace from getting tangled when you wash it, pin it to a clean, white cloth. Gently hand wash in cool or lukewarm water using a soap or detergent designed for delicate fabrics. Squeeze out excess water — don't rub, wring, or twist. Then spread it on a towel to dry. Baste a large item, like a tablecloth, to a white sheet. Wait until both are dry to separate.

Rid hand washables of soap residue. When hand washing any fabric except silk, remove the residue of soap or detergent by adding a capful of white vinegar to the next to last rinse.

Use your bed as an ironing board. Use your bed as an ironing board the next time you iron a large tablecloth. You won't have to worry about keeping it off the floor as you iron. An extra-firm mattress works best.

Cool way to prevent mildew. When damp clothes must be kept for a while before ironing, prevent mildew by keeping them in your refrigerator.

Get a leg up on lint. A leg from an old pair of pantyhose, tied up in a knot, makes a great lint catcher in your dryer.

Toss off wet tissue. You make it a point to empty pockets before you do the laundry, but every now and then a tissue slips through unnoticed until you're ready to empty the dryer. It's hard to miss that white lint on your clean, dark clothes. You can solve this problem quickly. Just put a little fabric softener on a handkerchief and toss it in with the load for about five minutes on the delicate cycle.

Save money by drying at night. Do you wait all day to call your loved ones during the cheaper evening hours? Use the same logic to time your dryer cycles. Electricity is cheaper in off-peak hours, so plan to load your dryer between 10 p.m. and 9 a.m. Don't forget to clean out your filter before flipping the switch. Your clothes will dry faster, and you won't have to battle lint.

A mutual attraction. Load "linty" items together — things like fuzzy sweatshirts, flannels, terry cloth towels (especially new ones), and chenille bedspreads and bathrobes. Keep these away from permanent press and corduroy items which are magnets for hard-to-remove lint.

Forget the fuzzy stuff. It's best to wash clothes right side out to discourage lint from hanging on. Also, dry them right side out in the dryer to prevent lint settling in the creases. When drying them on the clothesline, this isn't a problem. So you can hang them inside out to prevent fading.

How to repel lint. If you're having a problem with lint on your laundry, consider what things you're washing together. Man-made fabrics, such as polyester, nylon, and acrylic, tend to attract lint. Avoid washing clothes made of these fibers with lint-producing items made of terry cloth or other fuzzy fabrics.

Save wear 'n tear on your wash 'n wear. Keep several threaded needles handy in your laundry room. Mend holes, rips, and weak seams to prevent additional wear and tear in your washing machine. If you don't have time for on-the-spot repairs, use safety pins to control the damage. If an article is too far gone to be saved by repairs, hand washing may give you a few more wearings before tossing it in the rag bag.

Arm yourself against mildew. You forgot to open a bag of dirty, damp clothes right after your camping trip, and now they are mildewed. You may be able to save them if you apply a paste of vinegar and baking soda, and then wash as usual. Or moisten the mildewed areas with lemon juice and salt and place in the sun to dry.

Plumper pillows. Pillows can be dried outside in the sunshine on a windy day. Or dry them on a low setting in the dryer. They take a long time to dry thoroughly, but mildew can be a problem if they are left damp. Shake and fluff them a few times for more even drying and to make them plumper.

Freshen your clothes with ease. Your clothes smell great when they come out of the dryer. Preserve that fresh scent by placing unused dryer sheets in your dresser drawers and closets.

Chase away cat odor. If your slip covers or throw rugs are soiled with cat urine, add a cup of vinegar to the wash cycle to get rid of the odor. In addition, vinegar in the rinse cycle reduces lint — another major benefit, especially if you have a Persian or other long-haired cat.

Neutralize sour baby odors. The sweet smell of a baby is quickly replaced by an unpleasant odor if he spits up on his clothes after feeding. Just sprinkle some baking soda on a moistened cloth, and dab away at the sour spot until the odor is gone.

Hang it up to air

Washing clothes as soon after wearing them as possible helps get out odors and stains before they set. But if washing has to wait, turn the items inside out and put them on hangers. This allows the perspiration to dry and prevents mildew and the permanent mingling of odors that can occur in laundry hampers.

Oust tobacco odors and stains. The best way to rid your clothes of odors and stains from cigars and cigarettes is to add some baking soda, along with your regular detergent, to the wash cycle.

Douse diaper pail smells. No need to hold your breath each time you open the diaper pail. Just pour in half a cup of vinegar to each gallon of water. Not only will the urine smell disappear, the vinegar will reduce stains as well.

Refresh your wash (along with your memory). Oh no! You forgot about that load of clothes you washed a couple of days ago. Now they smell sour. Quick! Wash them again with a little ammonia added to the water. Your wash should be "sweet" again.

Keep laundry bags and hampers fresh. Tuck a fabric softener sheet into anything that's smelly for gentle, long-lasting deodorizing.

Dispose of doodads in your dryer. Nickels and dimes rattling around in your dryer. Lint building up in the filter. Dollar bills hiding in pockets. Take care of these annoying problems with a plastic newspaper bag. Clip it to the side of your dryer with a magnet. Then dump the lint, coins, and other laundry leftovers into it.

Protect your duds in the suds. Be sure to empty the pockets of every article you put in the washing machine. And here are some more things you can do to protect your clothes from washday woes. (1) Close zippers and any other closures, such as hooks and eyes and belt buckles that might catch on fabric. (2) If there are any small rips or tears in your clothes, sew them up before you wash them. They may turn into bigger holes during washing. (3) Brush off loose dirt or dried mud from your clothes before putting them in the washer. Otherwise the dirt may get deposited on the other clothes in the wash. (4) Don't overload the washer. Clothes need room to circulate freely. If you didn't catch a small hole or tear or there was one that couldn't be mended, it is more likely to get bigger in an overloaded tub.

Lost and found in the laundry room. If you're forever finding odds and ends in pockets just before an item goes into the washer, keep a clean coffee can nearby. Drop the "lost" articles in the can, and wait for them to be "found."

Organize pocket 'treasures'. Although you stress the importance of emptying pockets before putting articles in the dirty clothes hamper, people will still forget sometimes. So keep two containers handy, one for trash and one for valuables that get left in pockets. You'll know where to look for extra change or that missing pocket knife without having to sift through lint and wads of tissue.

A little salt on that shirt, please. Color safe bleaches are designed to keep colors bright. But there's no need to spend money on those products unnecessarily. Try adding a couple of pinches of salt to the wash water. Your clothes should keep their vivid colors. And they'll wear longer, too. That's because bleach is harder on the fabric than salt is.

Lay your money on the line. Most folks these days don't think they have the time to hang loads of wash out to dry. But if you want to save money or just enjoy fresh air and fresh-smelling clothes, then it's time to string up a clothesline. If you are serious about regularly drying your clothes outside, you'll want to put up a permanent set of lines on metal poles that are sunk into the ground with concrete. You can find the materials you need and probably instructions for making your clothesline support at a well-stocked hardware store. You can find cotton rope or plastic cord at a pretty cheap price, but they will sag under the weight of a heavy load of wash. For better support, purchase more expensive but longer lasting 12-gauge galvanized wire.

Whiten your socks. To make those athletic socks look new again, hot foot it to your kitchen cabinet. Get out the baking soda and mix some with water to presoak your socks. It will loosen the soil, so when you throw them in the wash, they'll come out clean.

Slip on a damp slipcover. To prevent shrinking, remove slipcovers from the dryer while still damp. And if you put them back on your couch or chairs immediately, they'll dry smoothly and won't need ironing.

Make a tiny sweater big again. If you wash a woolen sweater and it shrinks, soak it in the same kind of cream rinse you use for your hair. By relaxing the fibers, you might be able to carefully stretch it back to its former size.

Simple way to sort socks. If you have trouble deciding which socks are dad's and which belong to your teenage son, here's a simple solution. Buy a zippered mesh bag for each member of your family. Ask them to put their dirty socks in the bag. Tie a different colored yarn on each zipper pull so it will be easy to identify whose socks are in which bag. When it's time to wash, just toss the zipped bags into the washer and then the drier. No more lost or mismatched socks.

Avoid the washday blues. It's a good idea to wash new blue jeans by themselves to avoid staining other garments. And after you dry them, check inside the dryer for dye that could ruin your next load of clothes. If you do find traces of dye, wipe out the drum with soapy water. Then swab it again with a clean, wet cloth to remove any soap residue.

Secrets of sorting. Remember when you went away to college and did your own wash for the first time? Everything turned that drab-looking gray color. But somewhere along the way you figured out that if you kept the light and dark clothes separate your wardrobe could look as bright as your future. But separating the laundry by colors is just the beginning. It's also a good idea to wash articles together that need similar soap or detergent wash cycles and water temperatures.

Make a note of it. You were really tired when you did that last load of clothes just before bedtime last night. Unfortunately, you forgot about your delicate blouse and tossed everything into the dryer this morning. Too late to save it now. But for future use, put a pad and pencil in the laundry room. Next time, make it a written reminder, and leave it on the washer where you won't miss it, no matter how rushed or sleepy you are.

Separate the heavyweights. Dry lightweight and heavy clothes in separate loads. Lighter weight items dry faster. And heavy items like blue jeans can damage delicate nylons and such.

Clip for a quick pick. Keep a bag of clothespins in the laundry room. When you have an item that needs special attention before it's washed, clip a clothespin to it. That way, if you forget, you'll be reminded as you start to put it in the washer.

Save sorting time. Have separate laundry baskets for every type of load you wash — like light, dark, and delicate. When you take off your clothes, put them in the proper basket. Then, when it's time to wash, the clothes are already sorted.

Learn the best way to sort. Separate the wash by how soiled the items are. Lightly soiled items can actually pick up soil from the wash water. Light items will get grayer or yellower and colors will be duller if regularly put in with heavily soiled articles. Also sort by fabric type. Loosely knit fabrics and delicate items can go together in a gentle wash cycle. Select a variety of sizes and weights to wash together, like king-size sheets with blouses or hand towels. Bigger items can move freely so you get a cleaner wash.

Dab away deodorant stains. To remove a deodorant stain from a washable shirt or dress, dab it with white vinegar. If that doesn't do the trick, sponge it with denatured alcohol and wash it in the hottest water the fabric can stand.

Squirt away stains with vinegar. Those fruit, beverage, and grass stains in your washable clothes won't stand a chance against a mixture of equal parts white vinegar, dishwashing liquid, and water. Squeeze on this solution from a plastic squirt bottle and work it in. Let it stand for a few minutes, rinse, and say good-bye to stains.

Remove spots right before your eyes. For a general, all-purpose stain remover, add one-quarter cup of borax to two cups of cold water. Soak the stained garment in the mixture before washing with laundry detergent and cold water.

Do away with costly stain removers. You don't have to use a costly commercial stain remover. Just keep a spray bottle filled with equal amounts of white vinegar and water in your laundry room. Spray spots on clothes right before adding them to the wash.

Pretreat problems away from home. Dealing quickly with stains is the key to removing them, but when you are away from home, this can be hard to do. If you keep a small stain stick with you to treat a new spot immediately and launder it as soon as you get home, chances are good the stain will disappear.

Remove mystery spots with soda. When you have no idea where a strange stain came from, club soda or seltzer is probably your best shot at getting it out.

Keep up a stain-free tradition

Your grandmothers knew the secret to getting out stains — Fels Naptha Soap. This 100-year-old laundry product is still doing the trick today, especially on oil-based stains. It's also good for getting makeup, baby formula, and even poison ivy resin out of your clothes. Just wet the bar, rub the stain, let it sit for a bit, then wash as usual.

Tenderize a tough blood stain. Like all stains, blood comes out better if you treat it while it's fresh. Soak it in cold water, changing the water frequently as it turns pink. To get out the tougher stains, mix unseasoned meat tenderizer with cold water to form a thick paste. Using a damp sponge, apply it to the stain. Let the garment dry for about 30 minutes, and rinse with cold water.

Cover a coffee stain with coffee. Can't remove that stubborn coffee stain from your white tablecloth? Soak it in a bucket of strong, black coffee to transform it into a lovely earth tone tablecloth instead.

Rub out red stains with alcohol. Stains from red drinks, ices, or berry juices can be removed with rubbing alcohol. Just pour it over the stain before laundering.

Wash away ink spots. You just discovered ink stains on your favorite shirt. Don't write it off as a lost cause just yet. Wet the stain with cold water, and work in a mixture of cream of tartar and lemon juice. Leave it for one hour, and launder as usual.

Scrub away spaghetti stains. Getting spaghetti stains out of your clothes can be almost as tricky as trying to eat this popular pasta gracefully. But here's a method that's worth a try. Wet the fabric, cover the stain with powdered automatic dishwashing detergent, and brush it in with an old toothbrush. Rinse away the powder and wash as usual.

Get the red out of your blues. You can't believe your eyes. Your new red flannel shirt bled on your jeans in the wash. Should you just throw them in the dryer, assuming they'll be your painting or gardening pants from now on? Not yet. The heat will set the stains permanently. Try soaking them in rubbing alcohol. You may have to soak and wash them a few times before the dye comes out, but don't throw them in the dryer until the stain is gone.

Wash out coffee spills. Coffee can leave some tough stains on your clothes. Fortunately, you can get it out. Using a white cloth, work in either beaten egg yolk or denatured alcohol, and then rinse with clear water. Or stir a half teaspoon mild detergent into two cups of water. Dab it on the stain and blot with a white towel. If the stain still isn't gone, apply a mixture of equal amounts of water and white vinegar.

Take a bite out of food stains. Denture tablets are a natural choice for removing stains from false teeth. But did your ever think of using them on your clothes? You might be surprised by the results. Just put the stained item in a container of warm water and plop in several denture tablets. Let soak for the amount of time recommended on the package for dentures, and then wash as usual.

Make grease disappear like magic. If you get a grease spot on your favorite blouse while cooking, quickly open your pantry and get out some baking soda, cornmeal, or cornstarch. Rub it into the spot to absorb the grease. Then let it dry, brush away the remaining powder, and wash the item as soon as possible.

Attack stubborn stains from behind. When you're trying to remove a stain, avoid working it deeper into the fabric. Here's how. Place the item, stained side down, on a white cloth or paper towel. Apply the stain remover and push the stain out from the back. With a particularly resistant spot, you may have to replace the cloth or towel several times.

Face the truth about cosmetic stains. A makeup stain might be easier to remove than you thought. Dip the spot in cool water, rub on some white bar soap, rinse, and wash as usual.

Create your own stain removal kit

Save money by creating a do-it-yourself stain removal kit for your laundry room. Include some baking soda, lemon juice, vinegar, and hair spray. Add a few clean, white cloths; a roll of white paper towel, and a toothbrush.

Move quickly to remove paint. If you act fast, acrylic, latex, and other water-based paints can be washed out of fabric with warm water. But if you let them dry, you'll probably find them impossible to remove.

Give shoe polish problems the boot. If you get shoe polish on a colored fabric, treat it with a mixture of one part rubbing alcohol to two parts water. If the fabric is white, use only alcohol.

Conquer tough iodine stains. Removing brown iodine stains can be tough, but you might be successful using a water and baking soda paste. Work it in, wait 30 minutes, rub gently, and wash as usual.

Remove rust or tea stains. To get rid of tea or rust stains, treat the fabric with lemon juice, then with salt. Let the fabric dry in the sun, and then wash as usual. A paste of lemon juice and cream of tartar may also do the trick. And here's another good idea. Check the drum of your washer to be sure that's not where the rust came from.

Pre-spot grease stains with dish detergent. Keep a bottle of liquid dish detergent in your laundry room for pre-spotting grease stains before washing. The degreaser in the formula makes it an effective greasy stain remover.

Wash away suntan oil. If you get suntan oil on your clothes, gently work in some liquid detergent and rinse under cold water at full force.

Work magic on wine spills. As you watch spilled wine spreading across your white tablecloth, all you can think of is a big cleaning bill. But if you act fast, dry cleaning won't be necessary. Grab enough salt to cover the stain and soak up the liquid. Place the cloth in cold water for 30 minutes and wash as usual.

Cut grass stains easily. Get those grass stains out of your favorite white shorts with bar soap. Wet the stain, lather with soap, and give it a brisk rubbing. Repeat if necessary. Apply soap once more before you add it to the normal wash.Another solution for grass stains is a few drops of household ammonia mixed with a teaspoon of 3 percent hydrogen peroxide. Apply to the stain and when the green is gone, rinse with plain water. You can also remove grass stains with toothpaste, and the ideal tool for rubbing it in is a toothbrush. Or soak the stain in molasses, leave it overnight, then hand wash using dishwashing liquid.

Ready, aim, paint. Pretreating heavily soiled parts of clothing with liquid laundry detergent is a good idea. But it can be messy and sometimes wasteful if your aim isn't exactly on target. Instead of pouring it on, use an old paintbrush (about one-and-a-half to two-inches wide). Just dip it into the liquid and "paint" it onto the dirty spot, without the mess and waste.

Reach for the right bleach

Bleach works with water and detergent to remove soil and stains and can help restore brightness and whiteness to some fabrics. It also deodorizes and disinfects. If used correctly, bleach will not break down fibers or cause fading. But read labels carefully. There are two kinds of bleach — chlorine and oxygen. The chlorine type comes in liquid and dry form. Don't use it on spandex, wool, silk, or fibers like mohair, angora, and cashmere. It is safe to use on other colorfast fabrics.

If you aren't sure about an article, test a hidden area, like a seam allowance or facing. Mix one tablespoon of bleach with one-fourth cup of water. Put a drop on the spot you are testing. If there is no color change, the fabric should be safe with chlorine bleach added to the wash water. But if the label says not to bleach, then don't.

Oxygen bleach is not as strong as chlorine bleach and works better when used on a regular basis as a preventative. It usually comes mixed with a water conditioner and brightener. Both the liquid and the powdered forms are generally safe for all fabrics. When using bleach, put it and the water in the washer tub before adding the clothes.

Fight to the finish. Launder the complete garment after treating it for stains. Check it to be sure the stains are completely gone. If not, repeat the treatment, then wash it again. While you're at it, check the rest of your clothes to see if you spot any stains you hadn't noticed before. You can treat them and wash them again before putting them into the dryer where they might get permanently set.

Quick (and cheap) stain removers. For a general stain remover for washable items, try one of these: Apply a paste made from a powdered laundry detergent and a little water. Soak in cornmeal and water, club soda, or lemon juice. For tougher stains, mix dry dishwasher soap in a bucket of water. Immerse the item in the soapy solution. If it floats, weight it down with something heavy, like a plastic bottle filled with water.

Clear your table toppers. After you use table linens, always check them carefully for spots and stains. Treat them as quickly as possible. If allowed to set, they'll be harder to remove completely. Soak protein food stains, like eggs, meat, and fish, in cold water. (Hot or warm water will set stains.) If it needs something more, try a paste of meat tenderizer and water. Dab it on, let it set for 15 to 30 minutes, and wash in cold water.

The real remover. Did you find a cola stain on a favorite sport shirt the morning after a fun night out? Maybe in the excitement of a fast-paced basketball game, you didn't even notice spilling it. Is it too late to get it out? Not if you apply full-strength white vinegar directly to the spot within 24 hours, then wash as usual. It should be spotless for the next time out.

It must be mustard. Your hot dog from lunch has left its mark — you've got a bright yellow stain right on the front of your shirt. As with all stains, act as quickly as possible to remove it. Mix a solution of one quart warm water, one-half teaspoon liquid handwashing detergent, and one tablespoon vinegar. Sponge it on the stain and let it air dry. Then do one of the following: Apply liquid detergent directly to the spot or dampen the spot with a wet sponge and apply a paste of water and powdered detergent. Launder as usual using bleach if it's safe for the fabric.

Don't come unglued. Do your kids come home from day camp with more glue on their clothes than they used on their creative art projects? Never fear. Just soak the clothing in warm water with three tablespoons of vinegar. Rinse well and all signs of the glue should disappear.

Run rings around an oily collar. Your bathroom has the answer for removal of oily collar "rings." Shampoo dissolves body oils so it's a natural for this job. Pour the shampoo into a squeeze bottle if it didn't come in one. Apply directly to the stain, let it stand, and then wash it.

If you find yourself wearing your coffee. If you spill tea or coffee on a favorite shirt or tablecloth, put it in this solution to soak for 15 minutes or so: one quart warm water, one teaspoon detergent, and one tablespoon white vinegar. Rinse. If the stain remains, sponge it with alcohol, rinse, and wash using chlorine bleach if the fabric can take it.

What did you say that stain was? It's best to deal with urine, vomit, and mucous stains right away, so don't be tempted to put it off. Sponge or soak these types of stains in cold water. Then apply laundry detergent directly to the stain and wash. If a change in color occurs, it may be possible to restore it by sponging ammonia on new stains or vinegar on old ones.

No crying over crayons. You always check your kids' pockets before you throw the clothes in the washer. But what happens if you forget? You could wind up with a whole load of wash spotted with crayon wax. Your best bet in this case is to scrape off the excess with a dull knife and head for the dry cleaners. Explain what happened and request bulk cleaning. Or you might try doing it yourself at a coin operated cleaner. If the stains don't come out with dry cleaning, wash them for 10 minutes in hot water. Use the amount of soap, not detergent, for a regular load and one cup of baking soda. If you have hard water, use a water softener as well. If stains still remain, work a soap paste into the stains, return to the hot water solution for five more minutes, then launder as usual.

A simple strategy

If you could just prevent stains from happening, life would be simpler. Unfortunately, accidents happen. So here are some basic rules for dealing with stains before you attempt to clean them. But be sure you read the garment label first and pay attention to any warnings from the manufacturer.

- Act fast. The quicker you deal with a stain, the more likely you are to remove it completely without damaging the fabric. That's because oxidation (the process that makes the cut surface of a banana or an apple turn brown) causes the staining substance to interact with the fibers of the fabric.

- Identify the stain. This is easy when you notice it immediately. But sometimes you find a spot you can't identify. If you're not sure what it is, rinse or soak washable items in cold water before treating or washing them. But keep an eye on them. Soaking too long can affect the color of the fabric.

- Test the stain removing substance. Apply it on a hidden place first — perhaps a seam allowance — before using it on the stain. Leave it for two to five minutes and rinse. If it damages the fabric or changes the color, do not use it on the rest of the garment. And never mix stain removers. If you try one that doesn't work, rinse the garment thoroughly before you try another.

Show shoe polish who's boss. If you spill liquid shoe polish on your clothes, pre-treat the spots with a paste of water and dry detergent. Then wash as usual. If it's a paste polish spoiling your attire, first scrape off as much of the residue as possible with a dull knife. Then pretreat with cleaning fluid or a prewash stain remover. Then rinse and apply detergent to the spots while it's still damp. Wash with chlorine bleach if the fabric can take it. Otherwise, wash using the milder oxygen bleach.

Don't muddy the waters. Southern gardeners who do a lot of digging in Georgia (or Alabama) red clay have learned not to spoil a load of clothes with the red stuff. When they've spent the morning digging in the garden and have some heavy-duty mud on their jeans, they hose them off with the garden hose before putting them in the wash. This is a good idea no matter which region your mud comes from.

Paint stains are a pain. You're always careful when you're painting, but somehow you dripped paint on your clothes. Don't take time to fret about it now. You need to act quickly before the paint dries. If the paint is water-based, sponge or soak it in cool water. Put detergent directly on the stain, then launder it as usual. You might want to add some chlorine bleach if the material can stand it. If it is oil-based paint, sponge it with turpentine and then rinse. Work some detergent into the stain. Wash it in hot water, using chlorine bleach, unless the clothing label warns against it.

The 'resin'able way to clean clothes. Climbing trees can be fun for kids unless they slip and skin their knees. But it's getting pine resin out of their clothes that causes the pain for the adult who does the laundry. It isn't easy, but it can be done. Dissolve the resin with turpentine, paint thinner, or mineral spirits. Rinse thoroughly and launder as usual.

Spot blotter. Grease spot on your favorite cotton dress or shirt? Take a clean powder puff or cotton ball and dip it in baby powder or cornstarch. Rub it into the stain. Brush off the excess powder when the stain disappears. For stubborn stains, repeat the process.

Remove stains from washable fabrics. Ammonia will help remove nonoily stains — like those from blood, milk, perspiration and urine — from most washable fabrics. Make a mixture of equal parts ammonia, dishwashing liquid, and water. Shake it together in a plastic squeeze bottle. Apply it directly to the stain, rub it in gently, let it stand for a few minutes, then rinse. This should not be used on acetate, acrylic, silk, spandex, or wool. For fragile fabrics, do not apply ammonia directly. Instead, hold the stain over the mouth of an open bottle of ammonia, and let the fumes permeate it. Then gently wash.

Wipe away lipstick. Use a slice of white bread to remove lipstick stains from fabric, or try a nongel toothpaste instead.

Get rid of ring around the collar. This common stain on your shirts is caused by oils from your skin. If you rub the stain heavily with white chalk, the chalk will absorb that oil, and the stain should then wash out more easily.

Get the gravy out. To pick up a gravy stain, cover the spill with cornstarch. The starch will absorb a good deal of the grease, making it much easier for you to wash. You can also use salt or talcum powder.

A gentle solution for strong fabrics. If a heavy fabric, like canvas or sailcloth, gets dirty marks on it, try removing them with a gum eraser.

Wash away oily fabric stains. Glycerin is a grease cutter that can usually be found with laundry products at the supermarket. It works well to remove oily stains on most washable fabrics except acetate, triacetate, and rayon. Make a solution of one tablespoon each of glycerin and liquid dishwashing detergent and eight tablespoons of water. Shake these together in a squeeze bottle, then apply directly to the stain. Let it work for several minutes before rinsing.

Out of bleach? No worries. Do you have stains? Clean them naturally with lemon juice. Cut a lemon in half, and rub it on a fruit juice stain. And get rid of rust or tea stains on fabric by applying lemon juice, then salt. Let the item dry in the sun, then wash normally.

Easy gum removal. Remove gum from leather by placing a small amount of peanut butter on the gum. Wait a few minutes, then peel it off. If removing gum from fabric has left a stain behind, rub some peanut butter into the stain, wipe off, then rinse before washing the fabric as usual.

Salty solution. If you get a grease stain but can't treat it immediately, pour on a generous amount of salt. It should absorb the grease. Out of salt? Try cornmeal or cornstarch.

Be gentle. When treating a stain that has soaked into the fibers, use a soft-bristled nylon toothbrush to dab at the stain, gently working the stain removing agent — bleach, alcohol, vinegar, or whatever you are using — into the fabric.

Remember vinegar. Vinegar is good for removing fruit, beverage, and grass stains from most washable fabrics. Mix it in equal parts with dishwashing liquid and water in a plastic squirt bottle. Squeeze it onto the stain and work it in. Leave it for several minutes and then rinse.

Squeeze away stains. Keep a plastic mustard or ketchup dispenser filled with liquid detergent in the laundry room. Squirt some directly on soiled collars and other extra-dirty spots to pretreat them before washing.

Don't make it worse. Always use a white cloth or towel when trying to remove fabric stains. Using a colored cloth may result in additional stains, since the color can bleed from one fabric to the other.

Rub out a spot. One of the main ingredients in many store-bought spot removers is — you guessed it — rubbing alcohol.

Can't remove it? Cover it. If you stain a blouse you can't bear to part with, try adding an applique to cover the stain.

Secret to cleaner clothes. To remove grease or food stains from your laundry, mix together one-half cup Wisk, one-half cup water, one-half cup vinegar, and one-half cup ammonia. Use this mixture to pretreat the stains, then wash as usual.

Scorch out under the sun. Sunlight may be the best whitener for old linens with scorch marks. Moisten them first, then put them in bright sunshine. You may need to repeat this a few times. For fabrics that aren't so delicate, bleach may reduce the scorch stain. This, too, may require repeating.

Lipstick gets the kiss of death. Rub lipstick stains with petroleum jelly, and launder the item by itself in hot water.

Work from the outside in. When removing a stain, start at the outer edge instead of the center. This method will help prevent rings forming around the stain.

Don't rub it in. Stains on cloth need to be blotted. Rubbing can damage the fabric.

Clobber 'sugar' stains. Other soft drinks and alcoholic beverages contain sugar that will caramelize and become difficult to remove if not handled at once. Mix one quart warm water, one teaspoon detergent, and one tablespoon white vinegar. Soak the garment in this solution for 15 minutes. Rinse with cool water. If the stain isn't gone, sponge with isopropyl rubbing (denatured) alcohol. Rinse thoroughly and wash using chlorine bleach if it's safe for the fabric.

Keep it on the driveway where it belongs. Scrape away tar or asphalt residue from clothing with a dull knife.

Saturate the stain with salad oil and let it sit for 24 hours. Pour some liquid laundry detergent on the stain. Wait a few minutes and launder as usual. If this doesn't get rid of all the stain, work petroleum jelly into the stain. Let stand for half an hour and wash in hot soapy water. Be sure to wash the item by itself.

Brighten dark colors with salt. If you buy brightly colored towels to perk up a dull bathroom, you don't want them fading after just a few uses. So add a cup of salt to the water the first time you wash them. It will set the color, and they'll stay pretty longer. Salt in the wash also helps dark clothes retain their deep colors, and it perks them up again when they start to fade.

Throw in the towel. Bath towels, especially new ones, shed a lot of lint that can cling to other clothes, so wash them by themselves. And they'll stay fresher later when they are damp from use if you add a quarter cup of baking soda with the detergent.

'Pin' socks with a plastic top. Don't pin socks together before you wash them. Pins can rust or come open in the washer and get too hot in the dryer. The plastic top of a milk jug offers a better alternative. With a sharp knife cut an X in the middle of the top — just big enough to push a bit of the two socks through for a snug hold.

Save water when you wash. If you don't have a full load of dirty clothes, adjust the water level appropriately or wait until you have more. Also, if you presoak heavily soiled clothes, you won't need to rewash them. This will save even more water.

Overloaded with temptation. It can be so tempting to add just one more towel or a couple of shirts to an already full washing machine. But to get clothes really clean, don't overload the washer. You need to allow lots of room for items to move. And they need plenty of water to carry away the dirt, so choose the appropriate water level for the amount of clothing. When washing large articles, like sheets, check from time to time to be sure they haven't wrapped around the agitator post.

Get white socks dazzlingly clean. Even those dingy sweat socks come out white when you soak them in a solution of a half cup lemon juice or two tablespoons automatic dishwasher detergent in a gallon of super-hot water. Soak for 30 minutes, or overnight if they are very dirty.

Brighten your whites. You won't believe how bright your white clothes will be when you add a bit of cream of tartar to the wash water.

Boost your bleach. Use half the bleach you've been using, and still make your favorite white clothes bright again. Just add half a cup of baking soda, a time-tested whitening agent, to a regular wash load to give your bleach a boost.

Unbeatable whitener. Keep a spray bottle of a bleach and water mixture (at least four parts water to one part bleach) handy in the laundry. Spray it directly on heavily soiled spots on white washables that can take bleach. Read the label if you aren't sure. Be careful to keep it away from colored and dark items, including any you might be wearing.

Get the yellow out. When washable items made of wool or silk have yellowed with age, try whitening them with this solution. Mix a tablespoon of white vinegar with a pint of water. Sponge it on the yellowed areas and then rinse. Wash as suggested.

Hot tips for chocolate. Got a chocolate drink stain on a white T-shirt? Dab on ammonia and wash as usual. Or maybe a little person enjoyed a big slice of chocolate cake, but his sticky hands found their way to your shirt. Take the stains out by soaking with club soda before washing.

Age-defying solution. When white cotton or linen fabrics get yellow with age, use hot water with twice as much detergent as usual. Wash on the regular wash cycle for four minutes then stop the washer and let items soak for 15 minutes. Restart the machine, agitate for 15 more minutes, and complete the wash cycle. Repeat if necessary. For yellowed nylon, soak the article overnight in a solution of water and oxygen bleach. Then wash in hot water, using oxygen bleach and twice as much detergent as usual.

The sun is the oldest bleach around. For whiter clothes, spread them on a white sheet and leave them on the ground in the sunshine all day. Better still, get up early and place them directly on wet grass. According to legend, dew has the magical ability to whiten.

Stop ironing your curtains. You can save money, energy, and time if you hang curtains while they are still damp. If you like, toss them in the dryer for a few minutes to shake out the wrinkles. But in most cases, the weight of the fabric will straighten them out just fine.

Make post-wash wrinkles vanish. If you interrupt the cycle to take slightly damp clothes out of your dryer and hang them up immediately, they shouldn't need ironing. But what if you can't get to them in time and wrinkles set in? Hang them up anyway and mist them lightly with water from a spray bottle. Or hang them in the bathroom while you take a shower. The wrinkles should disappear as your clothes dry.

Always rinse in cold. Save energy and prevent wrinkles by using a cold water rinse regardless of what you are washing.

Spend less time ironing. If you're always at the ironing board, try these tips to cut down on your workload. (1) Shake out each item as you remove it from the washer. (2) Don't overload the dryer. (3) Remove clothes at the end of the drying cycle before wrinkles have a chance to set. (4) Hang them up or smooth and fold them right away. These steps will cut down on wrinkles, but they won't give your clothes a pressed look. For that, you'll have to pull out the trusty iron and ironing board.

Expert advice for cutting clutter

Reuse the containers. When all the baby wipes are gone, those sturdy plastic containers make handy, stackable boxes for audio cassette tapes, pens and pencils, and small tools. They can also be used to store sewing supplies, first-aid gear, or makeup in your car. Use one to make a fishing tackle box, or cut a hole in the top and use it for a coin bank.

Beat bath-time cleanup blues. If you have little ones at home or visiting on weekends, you know that bath time means lots of toys in the tub. To make cleanup and storage hassle-free, buy a mesh bag with a drawstring top. Load up all the bath toys when the bath is done. Give them a quick rinse under the faucet, then hang the bag from the shower head to drip dry.

Hang onto hair care products. Don't let scattered toiletries turn you into a basket case. Buy one of those three-tiered, hanging basket sets that people usually fill with fruits and veg-etables. Hang it in the bathroom and use it to hold your hair supplies. Put your sprays and styling gels in one basket, your brushes and picks in another, and your hair dryer and curlers in the third.

Provide a place for toilet paper. Pedestal sinks are both trendy and classic, but they don't come with a cabinet to store toilet paper. If you have a pedestal sink, keep toilet paper rolls in a decorative basket in the bathroom.

Jot down ideas in the john. Experts say the bathroom is one of the top 10 places to think. Keep a pad of paper and pen there just in case you feel inspired.

A tisket a tasket. If you don't have any cabinet space in your bathroom to store towels, use a small basket on the count-er for hand towels and a larger basket on the floor to hold bath towels. You can fit more towels in the baskets if you roll each towel up and stand it on its end.

Hook up your towels. Does your bathroom floor or laun-dry basket seem to stay full of damp bath towels? Your family members are more likely to hang and reuse towels if you make your bathroom more functional. Take down the towel bar, and put up several hooks instead. Assign each family member a hook to hang his towel on.

Prevent rust rings. The lids from potato chip cans fit snugly on the bottoms of some shaving cream containers. Snapping them on is simple — especially when compared to removing rust circles from bathtubs and countertops.

Help your books find their way home. Place an address label on the inside cover of all your books. That way, when you lend books to friends and family, they'll always remember to return them to you.

Free yourself from a book bind. When your private library outgrows your bookshelves, start double-parking your books. Stack one row of paperbacks in front of another, placing your favorite books in the front row. If you're a real book hound, you can even stack books on top of each other to quadruple your shelf space. Organize your books by subject, author, title, or even cover color — whichever way is easiest for you.

Store magazines in a cereal box. Looking for a neat way to store your magazines? Look no further than your breakfast cereal. Simply cut off a corner of the cereal box, and slide your magazines inside. It also works as a storage box for random papers or a holding tank for coupons that need to be clipped. Spruce up the cereal box with wrapping paper, newspaper, or drawings by your grandkids.

Be seasonal about magazines. If you save your home and garden magazines, store them by seasons instead of titles. In springtime, you'll likely be looking for articles about starting your garden. In winter, you'll want to find recipes for hearty winter meals or articles on holiday decorating. So putting them together this way is more useful.

Freeze odors away. That book you picked up from an estate sale is beautiful, but the musty odor is straight from someone's basement. And the Tupperware that went on the fishing trip says trout every time you open it. Don't despair. Place these — and other items with odors — in a frost-free freezer. Leave them overnight, and by morning they'll be smelling fresh once more.

Create containers for your candles. You can never have too many candles, but you do need somewhere to stash them. For your long candles, try a cleaned-out potato chip can. If your candles are too long for that, put them in a paper towel roll. Seal the ends by taping paper over them.

Save your teapot spout. If you have a favorite china teapot, don't risk chipping the spout during storage or a move. Slip a toilet paper tube over it.

Protect dishes. You can protect your good china in storage by putting a coffee filter between each dish to prevent scratching.

Prevent silver from tarnishing. You love using your grandmother's good silver when company comes but hate having to polish it after every use. Try putting a piece of chalk in the drawer with the silver. The chalk will absorb moisture and slow down the tarnish. Put some in your jewelry box, and your jewelry won't tarnish as quickly, either.

Save a minute one room at a time. To save time when you clean, carry all your tools, sprays, and detergents with you when you move from room to room. Then you won't have to backtrack to get what you need to clean.

For serious supplies. Minimize clutter and keep dangerous cleaning solutions from spilling by standing cleaning supplies upright in a plastic crate under your sink. If there are some supplies you need to use throughout the house, store them in a plastic tool carrier so you can easily use them on cleaning day.

Handy storage for your broom. Attach a magnet to your broom with a screw, about halfway down the handle. Then you can store it attached to the side of your refrigerator, between the refrigerator and the wall.

Double your cabinet space. Screw hooks into the bottoms of your cabinet shelves, and hang coffee mugs from them. Your kitchen cabinets will hold twice as much.

Rejuvenate your closet. Motivate yourself to clean out your closet. Buy a can of your favorite color paint, empty the closet, and repaint the whole thing. As you refill the closet, you'll have the chance to throw out unnecessary items and reorganize the things you keep.

Round up your electrical cords. Here's another handy use for those cardboard tubes inside toilet tissue rolls. Use them to tidy up all those electrical cords on your bathroom counter. Stuff the cord for your hair dryer, curler, or electric razor inside the roll, leaving out just enough cord to reach the outlet.

Keep extension cords under wraps. Put a paper towel or toilet paper tube around your looped-up extension cords, and they won't unravel in the drawer. This is also a great way to store cords to appliances you're not using. Just label the tube with a marker so you'll know which cord goes to which appliance.

Pack your bags for more storage space. Just because you're not going anywhere doesn't mean your suitcase gets to take a vacation. Suitcases are made to hold things, so use them to store holiday decorations, last season's clothes, spare towels and sheets, or anything else you can think of.

Make a two-point basket. Add a window seat and some extra storage space with a pillow and a large wicker basket. Just put the pillow on top of the basket's lid. It can work with a trunk, too.

Take inventory with index cards. A few index cards could be all you need to keep track of everything you have in storage. Start by labeling each box with a number. On an index card, write this number and then list everything you packed in that box. Keep all your index cards together, and make copies just to be safe. It's a convenient system — and it comes in handy for insurance purposes.

De-stink your trunk. Can't get that musty odor out of a storage trunk? Fill a coffee can with cat litter deodorizer, and leave overnight.

Give your garage a facelift. Treat your garage like your bedroom closet and go through it regularly. Donate things you don't use anymore, and rearrange everything that's left so it's organized and easy to find. If you come across something valuable, take it inside. Your garage won't protect it from cold, heat, and dampness.

File away extra furniture. Put a file cabinet in your bedroom, and cover it with a decorative tablecloth. Not only can it store your important papers, it can also moonlight as a nightstand.

Divide up your desk drawer. Keep track of all your pens, pencils, erasers, and other items in your desk drawer. Put them in a cutlery tray or drawer organizer with several compartments.

File away your home office. Don't despair if your house doesn't have a den or office. You can turn any room into a temporary office with ease. Just keep a rolling file cabinet in a closet. That way, you can roll it out when you need it, and it stays out of your way the rest of the time.

Organize essentials using cans. Looking for a neat and inexpensive way to organize your office supplies? Save and clean a few tin cans of varying sizes — such as a tuna can, soup can, and large juice can. Either wrap them in felt or spray paint them. Then glue the cans together with a hot glue gun to make a nifty office supplies holder for your desk. Use it to hold pens, pencils, rulers, paper clips, staples, push pins, and the like.

Go back to school for great deals. "Back-to-School" sales aren't just for kids. You can take advantage of these seasonal low prices to load up on office supplies for the whole year. Notebooks, loose-leaf paper, pens, pencils, sticky notes, and even computers can be found for a fraction of their usual cost. After snapping up all those bargains, you'll feel like the smartest kid in class.

Wipe away desk clutter. Your hands are clean — now it's time to make your desk the same way. An empty, hand-wipe container can help. Those upright, cylindrical containers are perfect for holding pens, pencils, or markers.

Fight identity theft with a shredder. One of the most common crimes of recent times is identity theft. Thieves can use your personal information to steal from your bank account, run up your credit card bill, ruin your credit, and generally make your life miserable. Protect yourself by guarding your garbage, where thieves rummage for personal information. Invest in a small, cheap paper shredder from an office supply store. Use it to shred bills, advertisements, and credit card offers that include your personal information. You can even use the shredded mail for packing boxes or mulching your lawn.

Hide your PIN within a phone number. It's tough to remember all your PIN numbers for bank cards, phone cards, and whatnot. Of course, it's not a good idea to write the PIN on the card itself. And it's not practical to carry small slips of paper with the PINs written on it everywhere you go. But you can use a simple trick to keep track of all your PIN numbers. Enter fake names in your address book and list what appear to be phone numbers — but are actually PIN numbers — beside it.

Organize your recipe clippings. Put an end to scraps of recipes sticking out of books by making your own cookbook. Simply place your favorite recipes in a photo album. The albums in which you lift the plastic sheet and insert your clipping work great. Arrange them into categories, such as entrees, side dishes, salads, and desserts. When you clip a new recipe, you'll know exactly what to do with it and where to find it later.

Bind your warranties. Save your appliances' warranties and manuals by punching holes in them and filing them all in one three-ring binder.

Rustproof your iron skillet. A cast-iron skillet is great, old-fashioned cookware for even the most modern kitchen. Keep yours rust-free by storing it with a paper coffee filter inside.

Shield walls from grease spatters. Use sheets of clear contact paper over the wallpaper behind your stove. It will protect the pattern from grease and food stains. If the wall is painted, coat it with furniture polish for a no-hassle cleanup.

Easy-clean the top of the fridge. You finally found time to clean the top of your refrigerator. Now take one more step to make this the last time. Cover the top with overlapping sheets of plastic wrap. Next time, you simply remove them, throw them in the trash, and roll out new layers.

Keep garbage bags secure. To keep your garbage bags from slipping down inside the can, cut the elastic waistband from a pair of pantyhose. It makes a giant rubber band that you can put over the rim of the garbage can to hold the bag in place.

Discover a 'vintage' spot for towels. Just because you don't drink wine doesn't mean you can't use a wine rack. Keep one around to store spare towels.

Speed up selection in your linen closet. Instead of pawing through stacks of mismatched sheets when it's time to change your bed linens, try this handy tip. Fold matching fitted and flat sheets, and slip them inside the matching pillowcase. Fold over the end and stack in the closet. Next time your bed needs a change, just grab and go.

Turn with the seasons. Use the seasons as reminders to turn your mattress. For example, in spring, switch the ends, putting the head where the foot was. In summer, turn it over, keeping the head at the top. In the fall, swap ends without turning it over. And when winter comes, just turn it over again. Your mattress will last longer and be more comfortable.

Lick your envelope problem. Your bill is ready to be mailed. You've made sure the company's address is peeking through the window, you've slapped a stamp in the upper right corner, and you've sealed the envelope — but you forgot to include the check. No problem. Just put the sealed envelope in the freezer for a few hours, then slide a knife under the flap. You can put your check in and reseal the envelope.

Perfect placement. Experts in household management live by the axiom "a place for everything and everything in its place." Follow their lead by creating specific places for the everyday necessities. For instance, hang car keys on a hook next to the back door, put mail that hasn't been read in the wicker basket on the desk, stack the newspaper on the television. Make sure you also create permanent "homes" for frequently used items, like light bulbs, batteries, or cleaning supplies.

Pack with precision. When packing your stuff for a move, keep all related items together. Cable cords should stay with the television, lids with their pans, and remote controls with the stereo. Prevent small items, like screws, from getting lost by putting them in a sandwich bag and taping the bag to a larger item, like a bookshelf. Or you could keep all little things, like cords, cables, controls, nails, and screws, in a separate, labeled box.

Write an autobiography in every album. While you're putting together a photo album, make sure to write a little story on the back of each picture. Who are the people in the picture? What are they doing? Where are they doing it? It will take a little longer, but it will make your album a true keepsake.

Get positive results from negative storage. Here's a tip to keep all your negatives together. Punch holes in the side of the plastic sleeve that they usually come in. Of course, make sure not to punch holes in the negatives themselves. Label each sleeve with the date and occasion. Then store the plastic sleeves and negatives in a three-ring binder.

Wipe out your weekly grocery list. Here's a tip if you sometimes forget to buy what you need at the supermarket. Hang a small chalkboard or wipe-off board in your kitchen. When you run out of something during the week, write it down on the board. Then, on shopping day, copy the list onto a piece of paper. Add anything else that you're running low on or that you'll need for meals.

Pop plastic bags in tissue boxes. Plastic grocery bags come in handy, but they also tend to accumulate in large piles. Take control of your plastic bags by filling old tissue boxes with them. Insert one bag at a time, making sure to leave the handles of the last one sticking out of the box. When you insert each bag, thread it through the previous bag's handles and then push it into the box. That way, when you remove one bag, the next bag's handles will pop out for easy access.

Milk that jug for all it's worth. Make a handy dispenser for your plastic grocery bags from a clean, plastic milk jug. Cut a hole about 4 inches in diameter in the side. When you finish putting away groceries, just push the empty bags through the hole one at a time. When you are ready to use one, it will pull out neatly while the others stay put.

Coupons straight from the horse's mouth. Contact manufacturers for coupons. By calling the toll-free number on their products, you may receive several dollars worth of coupons and product samples.

Hold it right there. Use the plastic cases from rolls of 35-millimeter film to store small objects, like paper clips, buttons, or thumbtacks. Recycle metal coffee cans to hold nails and screws.

Store small items in drawers. Separate paper clips, safety pins, thumbtacks, and marbles. Egg cartons make great organizers for a catchall drawer.

Provide a place for everything. Get the stuff in your drawers organized cheaply. Wash and dry plastic yogurt or pudding cups. You can use them for storing pantyhose, jewelry, hair accessories, baby socks, office items — the possibilities are endless.

Stash your valuables securely. Hide your spare cash, jewelry, and other valuables somewhere less predictable than under your mattress. Be creative. Try stuffing them inside an empty frozen vegetable box in your freezer. Or put them in an empty cereal box on your pantry shelf. Cut out a portion of some of the pages in a book you don't read, or stuff your valuables inside a full tissue box. The inside of your vacuum cleaner bag, a stuffed animal, and a tennis ball make great options, too.

Take stock of household possessions. Keep tabs of everything in your home in case of a fire or robbery. If you can, videotape every room, as well as the outside of your home. Take pictures of your most valuable possessions and keep a copy of the receipts. Make a list of all your property, including its worth. Store these important documents in a safe-deposit box.

Protect prized papers. To save valuable papers from dust and creases, roll them up and stash them in cardboard tubes.

Best bets for banishing pests

Send 'em scurrying with cinnamon. Ants hate the smell of cinnamon. But you will love it — and the way it keeps ants out of your kitchen. Just sprinkle some cinnamon where you see ants, and they will turn the other way.

Plant plants that stop ants. Use your green thumb to squash ants. Plant mint or onion around the foundation of your house to keep ants away. Other plants that thwart ants include spearmint, southernwood, and tansy.

Stymie ants with vinegar. Make life a little more sour for ants. Splash vinegar around door and window frames, under appliances, and anywhere else you've noticed ants marching. It should deter them.

Gum up the works to control bugs. Keep bothersome insects out of your cabinets with a chewy, mint-flavored repellent. Just leave a few sticks of mint chewing gum where the bugs seem to be entering. It doesn't matter if you unwrap the gum or leave it wrapped. Either way, the bugs will avoid the area.

Give ants the slip with baby oil. Next time ants invade your home, don't let it slide. Let them slide instead. Apply baby oil to areas where the ants tend to march. The little pests will have trouble making their way across the slippery surface. Eventually, after you repeat the baby oil trick a few times, the ants will give up and retreat.

Lemon-fresh solution. Who says lemons are only good for cooking? They're also great for ant-proofing your kitchen. No insecticides needed. Just squeeze lemon juice in the holes or cracks where ants are getting in. Scatter small slices of lemon peel around the entrance, too. The ants will catch on that they're not wanted. Lemons also help with roaches and fleas. Squeeze four lemons into a half-gallon of water and toss in the rinds. Then rub the mixture on your floors. The pests can't stand the smell, and they will abandon your house.

Hide pet's food dish. Why tempt ants? Pick up the dishes of dog food or cat food between meals. If left on the floor, your pets' food dishes make inviting targets for hungry ants.

Halt ants with salt. It's easy to stop ants. All it takes is some reasoning — and some seasoning. Figure out where ants are entering your house. Then dump a layer of salt in their path. The invading ants will stop and turn back in defeat.

Use dryer sheets outdoors. If you let them, ants will get into anything — including the sugary syrup you put in your hummingbird feeder. Put a stop to those antics with a dryer sheet. Wrap the dryer sheet around the feeder's hanger and fasten the ends with either tape or rubber bands. Ants will stay out of the forbidden territory.

Kill fire ants with Southern hospitality. Make those pesky fire ants feel at home. Feed them a nice helping of instant grits. Just sprinkle some on the fire ant hills in your yard. The ants will nibble on the grits, then seek out water. When that happens, the grits expand inside the ants and kill them. Seconds anyone?

Attack them in their home. Ants invade your home all the time. Why not attack theirs? Pour some ammonia down the ant hole in your yard. You'll kill the ants before they have a chance to mount an assault on your house.

Surprise them with spices. Set a spicy trap for those black ants roaming through your home. Shake some ground red pepper or curry powder at their point of entry. Chances are, they won't come back any time soon.

Try a peppermint patty. Raise a stink to get ants out of your house. To an ant, nothing stinks more than peppermint. Squirt some peppermint flavoring or place some peppermint tea bags inside your home where ants seem to enter. Do the same outside your house. The ants will smell that they're not wanted there.

Rattle ants with baby powder. Guard your house the gentle way. Simply sprinkle baby powder wherever ants might enter. The baby powder smells good and won't harm children or pets — but it stops ants, who will not crawl through the powder.

Corner ants with cloves. Ant-proof your kitchen for a whole year. Just put bay leaves or whole cloves in the corners of your cupboard shelves and windowsills. These long-lasting spices will foil any ant invasions.

Keep problems at bay with bay leaves. Bay leaves are great for cooking. But who ever figured they'd ant-proof your pantry, too? Ants can't stand the smell of bay leaves so they'll avoid them at all costs. Crumble some bay leaves on your windowsills to keep ants out of your kitchen. For extra protection, you can also toss a bay leaf or two into your flour or sugar canisters.

Draw a line of flour. Guard your house from an ant invasion. Just make a line of flour anywhere you think ants might enter. It will keep ants outside looking in because they will not cross the line.

Show ants you mean business. Ants usually will not cross a line of bone meal, powdered charcoal, cream of tartar, red chili pepper, paprika, or dried peppermint either. So find out where they are entering and create your own barrier.

Wipe out wasps with ammonia. Give your wasps a housewarming present they won't forget. Attach a hose-end spray bottle filled with ammonia onto your garden hose and turn on the water. Then soak the wasps and their nest. The ammonia shower will kill the wasps at once and eventually topple the nest.

Force fleas to flee. If you've ever had a flea infestation in your house, you know how hard they are to get rid of. They can even multiply in your vacuum cleaner bag. To keep that from happening, place a flea collar in the bottom of the bag.

Say good-bye with salt. If you're worried about fleas or ticks in your home, give the pests a salty welcome. Pour several boxes of salt in a blender and blend until you get a fine powder. Shake the powder onto your carpet and under your appliances. With a broom, work the powder deep into the carpet, where flea eggs hatch. Let the salt do its job for a few days before you vacuum. The salt should dehydrate the pests and kill them.

Flea-proof your home with basil. To repel fleas, grow a pot of basil in your kitchen window. Water it regularly from the bottom for a stronger smell. Or it works just as well to put crushed dried basil leaves in small bowls or hang some in muslin bags.

Give pests a clean sweep. Add salt to your vacuum cleaner bag to kill insect eggs and larvae that may be trapped inside.

Halt fruit flies with household herb. Stop those annoying fruit flies from swarming all over your fruit bowl. Just add some fresh basil to the fruit bowl, and fruit flies will stay away. You can also grow basil in pots outside your door to keep fruit flies from entering your house.

Blow away backyard bugs. Don't let flies, gnats, or mosquitoes wreck your backyard barbecue. Drive them off, naturally, without smelly bug sprays. Just use a portable electric fan. Aim it at the center of the party to keep your guests cool and the bugs away. For even better results, aim a second fan toward the same area from another direction.

Scare off critters with cat litter. Trick mice into smelling danger. Gather some used cat litter from your cat's litter box and put it in several containers around your garage. Mice will smell a cat and run for their lives.

Stop mice with this pleasant aroma. Keep your garage in "mint" condition. Just put peppermint extract on items you want to protect from mice. Mice can't stand the smell of peppermint and won't go near those areas.

Banish mice with baking soda. You've probably heard of several amazing uses for baking soda. Here's one more — it deters mice. Simply sprinkle baking soda around the edge of your basement walls, in dresser drawers, or any other area where you spot evidence of a mouse. An added bonus is the easy cleanup. Just vacuum.

Mouseproof your house with mothballs. To stop mice from scurrying around your garage or attic, put mothballs along the walls to discourage them. In addition to deterring mice, the mothballs will also keep spiders away.

To catch a mouse. Forget the stereotype of the cheese-loving mouse. What mice really love is the same thing most kids really love — peanut butter. Use some to bait your traps and the mice will come running.

Banish mosquitoes with plants. Discourage mosquitoes from buzzing near your home. Plant some tansy or basil around your patio and house. The mosquitoes will steer clear of the area.

Repel mosquitoes. Rub a fabric softener sheet on your skin to keep mosquitoes at bay.

Use 'common scents' on moths. Don't let moths feast on your wool coats, hats, and sweaters when they're tucked away during warm weather. Place whole cloves in coat pockets and in bags containing sweaters. Moths don't like the scent, and they'll avoid your wool. You can also put cloves in your dressers to keep moths from nibbling on your everyday clothes.

Curb moths with herbs. Safeguard your clothes from moths with a fragrant herbal remedy. Mix half a pound of rosemary, half a pound of mint, one-quarter pound of thyme, one-quarter pound of ginseng, and two tablespoons of cloves. Scoop the mixture into cheesecloth bags and put them in closets or drawers. Moths will stay away.

Repel insects naturally. If you don't like spraying chemicals on your skin to keep the bugs at bay, try one of these. Mix 1 ounce of oil of spearmint, peppermint, citronella, or pennyroyal with a few drops of baby oil, vegetable oil, or a bit of petroleum jelly. (Never use the herbal oils full-strength.) Rub this onto your skin before you go outside.

Chase roaches with a cucumber. It's easy to repel roaches without dangerous pesticides. Just combine cucumber skins with chopped bay leaves. You'll end up with a natural roach repellent. Sprinkle the mixture around the cockroaches' usual hangouts. They won't stick around for long.

Make a lethal snack for roaches. To control cockroaches in your home, combine equal parts oatmeal, flour, and Plaster of Paris. Put the mixture in dishes where cockroaches are likely to hide. Just make sure children and pets don't eat the mixture. Or mix two tablespoons of flour, four tablespoons of borax, and a tablespoon of cocoa. Leave this deadly treat on dishes around your house. Make sure you keep borax out of the reach of children and pets because it will poison them.

Silence cockroaches with mums. Chrysanthemums look pretty — unless you're a cockroach. That's because these flowers double as natural insecticides. To put mums to work for you, let them dry out before slightly shredding them. Then sprinkle some wherever cockroaches hang out — in your garage, under appliances, or in storage areas.

Rid your dig of roaches. Control roaches by scattering a mixture of equal parts baking soda and powdered sugar in the infested area. (The sugar attracts them; the soda kills them.) Or repel these creepy critters by cutting hedge apples (Osage orange) in half and placing them in the cabinets, in the basement, or under the house.

Go fishing for silverfish. Silverfish rarely show themselves in the day. If you want to stop them, you have to attack their hiding spots. Pour boiling water down the drain in your bathtub and sink. Use the nozzle on your vacuum cleaner to get at holes and cracks. Aim a hair dryer or fan heater into known silverfish hangouts. Keeping your house cool and dry also helps discourage these pests.

Attack attic pests with mothballs. Your attic, with all its boxes and papers, makes an ideal playground for silverfish. One way to help control these pests is to put some mothballs in the boxes in your attic.

Polish off silverfish with cinnamon. No one wants to use dangerous pesticides in their home, especially in the kitchen. So how do you get rid of those annoying silverfish? Just put a little cinnamon inside your drawers and cabinets. Although silverfish eat everything from glue to clothing, they hate cinnamon and will stay away.

Silverfish take the big chill. Get rid of silverfish and other insects that have infested your books or valuable papers. First seal the items in a plastic bag. Then put them in the freezer for 72 hours.

Boot out squirrels in bird feeder. Tired of squirrels getting all the food you put in your bird feeder? Try this. Cut a pole-size hole in the bottom of an empty, plastic, gallon milk jug. Then put the bird feeder pole through the jug, moving it up near the food, and placing the pole back in the ground. Squirrels won't be able to climb over the jug without slipping off, and the birds will finally enjoy their feast.

Take the termite test. Relax. That critter you just spotted might not be a termite after all. Winged ants are often mistaken for winged termites. Here's how to tell them apart. Ants have bent antennae, thin waists, and longer front wings than back wings. Termites, on the other hand, have straight antennae, thick waists, and front and back wings that are equal in size.

Top-notch tips for healthy pets

Help for a messy birdcage. To keep your bird from tossing seeds all over your floor, wrap a length of nylon net around the cage. Don't cover the cage entirely — just a few inches near the food dish.

Put pet pictures in your purse. A photo of your pet can be a great conversation starter on an airplane, but if the pet is traveling with you, it can be much more than that. On the off chance that your pet becomes lost or misplaced, you'll be able to show airline employees a photo for quick identification.

Greasy kid stuff. Hairballs can annoy your cat and make your life harder when you have to clean up the aftermath. Help lessen your cat's chances of having hairballs by adding a teaspoon of bacon grease or vegetable oil to his food once a day.

Healthy pet food supplement. If you add a little Crisco oil to your pet's food every day, it will help his coat become shiny and lustrous.

Play a neat trick on your kitty. If you've tried to give your cat liquid medicine and failed, let her need for cleanliness help you along. Just squirt the medicine onto her coat with an eyedropper, and watch her lick it clean.

Keep countertops cat free. Does Fluffy insist on walking all over your clean countertops? Put down double-sided sticky tape. She won't like the way it feels on her paws. Or, for a noisier solution, assemble a collection of tin cans or aluminum cookware near the edge. Next time she pounces, all that crashing metal will give her a start. She'll think twice about getting up there again.

Take a swipe at shedding pets. Does your dog shed hair all over you and your furniture, even though you brush him outside regularly? Try this. Swipe a dryer sheet over his fur each day. The dryer sheet will pick up stray hairs and keep them from landing on your clothes and couch.

Chase bad smells from your dog. Until dogs stop rolling in stinky things, pet owners will need tips like this. After washing a bad-smelling dog, add lemon juice, vinegar, or baking soda to the rinse water. And for a dog with long, thick fur, add a creme rinse with a conditioner to keep his hair tangle free.

Wash your dog without water. Whew! Fido needs a bath, but it's below zero outside, and he really hates to get wet. Don't suffer through the winter with a smelly dog. Use this trick. Take him outside or into the garage and pour plenty of baking soda on his coat. Work it into his fur, then brush his coat thoroughly. Much of the dirt will leave with the baking soda, and he'll smell a whole lot better, too.

Clean your dog's ears at home. There's no need to take your dog to the vet to get his ears clean. Make this simple rinse at home. In a small squirt bottle, mix equal parts water and vinegar, then label the bottle. Squirt the solution over the outer portion of your dog's ears, then stand back. It's best to do this outside, since most dogs will shake their heads to get the liquid out.

Recycle those plastic bags. Neat and simple poop scoop for dog owners — plastic grocery bags! Take them along when you walk the dog; just put the bag over your hand and pick up the waste. Then turn the bag inside out, knot it, and throw it out at home.

A dog's doormat. Keep an old, clean rag by the back door for when you take your dog for a walk. When you come in from rainy or snowy weather, you can wipe your dog's feet before he gets into the house and tracks the day's weather all over your carpet.

Give pet hair the brushoff. Pet hair on the furniture can be a mess and an embarrassment. An easy way to get rid of it is to put on a rubber glove and rub your hand over the upholstery. You'll find the pet hair rolled up into an easily removable ball.

Protect your dog's feet. Exposure or dry skin can cause your dog's soft footpads to crack or peel. A little petroleum jelly will help soothe the discomfort and encourage healing.

Hair care for Fido. Give your dog glossy, thick hair by adding just a bit of apple cider vinegar to his drinking water. It will also help get rid of doggy odor.

Ditch the itch. If your pet has dry, itchy skin, add a tablespoon of olive oil to his food every day. You should see an improvement within a couple of weeks.

First aid for clothing. You've been romping with Rover, and now your clothes are covered with dog hair. If they are clean otherwise, just take them off and toss them in the dryer with a damp cloth. The pet hair should end up in the lint catcher, and your clothes are ready to wear again.

Vinegar to the rescue. Vinegar also removes pet urine from carpet. Follow this three step process: (1) Absorb as much liquid as possible by putting layers of paper towels over the spot and stepping on them until each stack of papers is soaked. (Blot gently; never scrub.) Repeat until the papers come up virtually dry. (2) Spray or sprinkle on generous amounts of vinegar, either straight or diluted and absorb the same way as before. (3) If further cleaning is needed, use a solution of liquid dishwashing detergent and water or a commercial carpet cleaner. This treatment should remove the urine's odor so well that the animal will not return to the spot again based on the familiar smell.

Relief for itchy pets. Soothe your pet's dry, itchy skin with gentle, all-vegetable Murphy's Oil Soap.

Salt your dog to repel fleas. If you hate fleas and those chemical-laden flea collars for dogs, wash your pet in salt water instead. Fleas will quickly look for another victim. For added protection, rub some baker's yeast into his coat once it's dry.

Natural flea remedies. Make a lemon tonic to get rid of your pet's fleas. Slice a whole lemon and place it in a pint of almost boiling water. Let it sit overnight. Next morning, apply it to the pet's skin with a soft cloth. Repeat daily as needed for bad infestations. (Don't use this remedy on irritated or broken skin from too much scratching.)

Oil just 'mite' be a cure. Is your pet scratching or pawing at its ears a lot? It may have ear mites. Here's a great natural remedy for ear mites in cats and dogs: mineral oil. Just apply with a dropper or well-soaked cotton ball. Fold outer ear over ear opening and massage gently to get oil down into ear canal. Repeat every four or five days for a few weeks in order to kill newly hatched mites.

Ward off fleas and ticks. Help keep your dogs or cats pest-free with a little garlic. If they'll tolerate it, place a few cloves in their bedding. And try mixing a touch of garlic juice in with their drinking water.

Remove ticks from your dog. If a tick has a hold on your dog, dab a little alcohol on its back, then pull it out with tweezers. Make sure you pull it out straight and clean. Anything you leave behind can become infected.

Control fleas and ticks. Add a little vinegar to your four-legged friend's water bowl. Fleas and ticks should stay clear after he drinks this unusual potion.

Give your pet's coat a lustrous sheen

When buying dog food, look for quality ingredients. Vegetable oils are important because they contain fatty acids that dogs need. Corn oil, wheat germ oil, and linseed oil are good choices. There should also be some animal fat in your dog's diet, such as chicken or turkey fat. The combination of fats will keep your dog's skin soft and his coat shiny.

Pop pet food in popcorn tins. Don't throw out those giant tins of popcorn you get every Christmas. Recycle them. After you wash and dry them, they work great as containers for dog food or birdseed. Not only are they sturdier than a bag, but with the lid on, they don't attract bugs and rodents like an open bag of food does.

Make a disposable pet bowl. Want a disposable bowl for your pet while traveling? Cut the top off a gallon milk jug, leaving a few inches at the bottom. When you return home, simply throw the already recycled bowl into the recyclable trash.

Surviving the water bowl battle. Does your dog constantly knock over his outside watering dish, then give you reproachful looks when you come home because he's out of water? Try using an angel food cake pan for your angelic pet. Put a stake in the ground through the hole in the middle of the pan, and his efforts to turn it upside down will be thwarted.

Travel doggie dish. An old margarine tub makes a great temporary food dish for Fido when you take him on the road.

Pass up the plastic. Many animal experts agree that using plastic bowls for feeding and watering your pets at home is a no-no. Plastic may harbor harmful bacteria. Metal or ceramic is a more sanitary choice.

Tame pet odor. If you notice a powerful animal odor when you open your front door, maybe it's time to do something about it. Try mixing brewers yeast into your pet's food. Use a teaspoon of yeast for a cat and a tablespoon for a dog. Your pet's scent will become much less noticeable.

Easy way to clean your pet's bed. Simply sprinkle baking soda on the bed, leave it for at least an hour, and then shake it off. Your pet's bed will be as fresh as new.

Have a pretty yard and healthy pets. Keep Fido and Fluffy away from newly fertilized lawns and gardens. That goes for pesticides, too. If possible, keep them in a fenced backyard and forego the chemicals there. Too many pets become sick and even die after eating plant food or fertilizer. And before adding ornamental plants to your yard, find out if they're toxic to animals.

Catch a cat quickly in an emergency. Buy a pet carrier for your cat and keep it handy. In an emergency, transporting pets quickly and safely can be a life or death situation. In a pinch, you can tuck a cat into a pillowcase, but it won't want to stay there very long.

Picture your pet safe. Keep a snapshot of your pet with your valuable papers. During an emergency, your pet might run away in fear. But if you have a picture of the animal, you'll be able to make fliers to help find it.

Plan for disaster with pets in mind

When disaster strikes, pets frequently get lost in the mad dash for safety. But with a little planning, you can save yourself and your pet. Keep your pet's immunization and health records in the same place you keep your valuable papers. If you have to leave home suddenly, you can grab one box and go. Most emergency shelters won't take pets so you'll have to make arrangements at a kennel, which will require your pet's medical records. As an alternative, locate in advance a motel that allows pets.

Protect electrical cords. Rub down your electrical and extension cords with liquid laundry detergent to keep curious pets from munching on the cords and shocking themselves.

Medicate with care. When pets aren't feeling well, don't be tempted to give them your pain relievers to save money. Acetaminophen, such as Tylenol, is generally harmless to humans, but it's extremely toxic to cats. They don't have enough of an enzyme required to break down the drug. And while vets often prescribe aspirin or ibuprofen for some animals, the doses are much lower than for humans. Always check with your vet before giving your pet any pain reliever.

Be careful about flea control. Cats and dogs react very differently to some insecticides. A product made for dogs — even in very small amounts — could be deadly for your cat. Always read the product label carefully and follow instructions. If in doubt, ask your vet.

Lock up the antifreeze. One of the most common reasons for an emergency trip to the vet's office is antifreeze poisoning. Antifreeze contains ethylene glycol, which is toxic to both humans and animals. Unfortunately, it also tastes sweet, so innocent pets will happily lap up any you spill on your garage floor. It only takes half a teaspoon per pound to poison a dog and even less for a cat. Remember to keep containers tightly closed and clean up spills immediately.

Protect your pet from sunburn. With all the warnings about skin cancer, you wouldn't think of going outside in the summer without sunscreen. But what about your pale pet? Animals with light-colored coats and skin can get sunburns and skin cancer, too. If your pet is light-colored, put a bit of sunscreen on his nose and on the tips of his ears when taking him out in strong sun.

Spare your furry friend's feet. Your pet relies on you for relief from summer's heat. Don't let him down by walking him on a sizzling sidewalk. He could burn the pads on his feet and become overheated in the process. Keep him in the shade and on grass whenever possible, and move quickly if you must take him on the sidewalk or road.

Give your dog a cool haircut. You can help your dog beat the heat of summer by shaving her long, thick fur to about one inch in length. You'll also be able to easily see any fleas or ticks. Just don't shave off all her hair since it's her natural protection from sunburn.

Help pets with heatstroke. People aren't the only ones who get heatstroke. Your pet can be overcome by hot weather, as well. If your pet pants rapidly, twitches, barks for no reason, or stares with a crazed look, he may be experiencing heatstroke. Pour cool water on him every few minutes, but don't try to place him in a tub of water or put ice on him. That could send him into shock. Offer him water to drink, and let him rest near a fan while you call your veterinarian.

Prolong pet's life with good oral hygiene. Did you know that keeping plaque off your pet's teeth can add two or three years to his life? And that's in people years! Experts say bacteria in plaque can get into an animal's bloodstream, damaging internal organs and cutting short his life. But brushing and checking your pet's teeth and gums regularly can keep bacteria at bay. Ask your veterinarian about keeping your pet's teeth in tiptop shape.

Stop your pup from chewing. Save your furniture and your sanity by rubbing a little oil of clove onto wooden furniture — not fabric — your puppy is chewing. He won't like the smell or the taste.

Protect paws from chemicals. If you take your pet outside in the winter, beware of chemicals used on driveways and roads to melt snow and ice. Your pet's bare paws could be injured. Wipe his paws before he comes in the house, too. He might try to lick his pads clean and irritate his mouth, as well.

Money savers around the house

Outwit air conditioner mold. If your window air conditioner is putting out a moldy odor, its drain hole could be clogged. Unplug it, take off the front panel, and look for the hole underneath the evaporator area. Then poke it clear with a wire hanger or a long bottlebrush.

Filter out dust. Remove the front panel of your air conditioning unit and take out the filter. Hold it up to the light. If you can't see through it, vacuum it with a brush attachment or replace it with another filter.

Made in the shade. If your air conditioning unit is exposed to direct sunlight, you can boost its performance by building a privacy or lattice work fence beside it to provide shade and ventilation, as well as protection from rain and snow. However, don't let leaves, shrubs, and grass grow too close to the unit. They will cut down on the air circulation around it and make the unit work harder.

Peak protection for window units. Window air conditioners need attention, too, or they won't run at peak efficiency. At the start of the cooling season, get out your owner's manual and learn how to clean the fan blades and the evaporation coil. Check the caulking and weather stripping around the unit. Oil the motor and fan. Then clean the air filter each month throughout the summer.

Cool down your upstairs

Hot air in your attic will heat up the ceilings of the rooms below and jack up the temperature. To keep your cool, open all the vents in your attic. The hot air trapped under the heated roof tiles will cool, relieving your overworked air conditioning unit. Or install a reversible fan to suck hot air out during the day and blow cool air in at night.

Boot out cold air. Don't tiptoe around drafty doors. Sock it to them. Fill an old tube sock or stocking with sand, rice, or beans, and tie up the loose end. Lay it against a leaky door or window to stop drafts dead in their tracks.

Dodge drafts with wall quilts. Cover drafty windows with a favorite quilt or blanket. Simply tack the blanket to the wall around a window, and stuff a rolled up towel in the window cracks behind it. The quilt will keep you warm and add a soft touch to otherwise stark walls.

Unclog drains with thrifty threesome. Don't waste money on expensive drain cleaners when this pantry trio clears clogs just as well. Mix a cup of baking soda, a cup of salt, and three-quarters of a cup of white vinegar, and pour the mixture into your congested drain. Let it soak in for about 20 minutes, and rinse with a gallon of boiling water.

Break up hair clogs with bleach. Dissolve hairy gunk in your drains with a monthly dose of bleach. Carefully pour a cup of bleach down the drain. Five minutes later, rinse with cold water. This treatment will stop clogs before they start. Better yet, pry the cover off your drain and remove most of the hair by hand. Then let the bleach finish the job for you.

Clean without toxic chemicals. Clogged drain becoming a pain? Here's the safest solution around. Simply boil a gallon of water, and pour half of it down the drain. Wait five minutes, and pour in the rest. Pour directly into the drain so you don't crack the porcelain basin. Do this once a week. It's the simplest method to keep drains running clean — and it requires no harsh chemicals or hard work.

Sweeten 'drain breath.' Ever notice a slight stench wafting up from your tub or sink drain? You can prevent this by giving your drains a monthly dose of baking soda. Rinse it through with hot water and wash away that odor.

Arrange furniture for a lower heating bill. If you're trying to cut costs on your heating bill, check to see if any of your furniture is blocking a heating vent. If a couch or chair is pushed up against a vent, the furnace will keep running as it tries to regulate the room temperature. Arrange furniture away from vents to keep the air circulating and your heating bills low.

A clean sweep for your system. Your regular heating and air conditioning inspection should include vacuuming the heater vents and return air grills. They gather dust over time, slowing down the flow of air and keeping dust loose in the system. Remove the vents and grills and vacuum the area every few months to promote efficient heating and cooling.

Bring springtime indoors all winter long. To get rid of musty winter odors throughout your house, place a fabric softener sheet in your heating vents. It will also help control the static electricity inside, too.

Blow away grime from your fan. Your window fan needs a thorough cleaning every year. Start by removing the grills and vacuuming them with a shop vac. Next, wipe the dust off the blades. If they're really dirty, use an ammonia or an ammonia-based cleaner — not a petroleum-based one. Then attach the pointy nozzle on your shop vac and use it to get into the slots in the back of the fan engine, where a lot of dirt, dust, and hair can build up. When you can see clearly through the slots, they're clean. Finish the job by checking to see if there are oil holes on the top of the engine case, or in a dimple in the front or back. If there are holes, squeeze in 10 to 20 drops of three-in-one oil. If there aren't any oil holes, the motor is self-lubricating, and you're finished.

Let in a breath of fresh air. Choose a balmy day to replace the stale air in your house. Open all the windows and doors, turn on the fans, and enjoy the fresh breeze for five to 10 minutes. Remember, it's more energy efficient to change all the air at once than to do it bit by bit.

Down in summer, up in winter. In summer, set your ceiling fans to blow down so that you'll feel cooler. In winter, reverse them to pull air up, which will keep blankets of cold air from forming near the floor. Both settings keep the air moving, which will keep you more comfortable. You'll find the switch that reverses the fan blade direction on the side of the fan motor housing.

Even out the wobble. If your ceiling fan insists on wobbling, try taping a coin to one of the blades. Experiment with each blade until you eliminate the annoying problem.

Silence squeaky faucets. Does your faucet screech in protest every time you turn the handle? Unscrew the handle from its base and smear petroleum jelly on both threaded sides. The extra lubrication should soothe your grumpy faucet and your aching ears.

Keep your faucet flowing freely. If you have an aerator on your kitchen faucet, be sure to clean it periodically. Simply unscrew it, and rinse out any particles that could be clogging your water flow.

A trick of the tap. Want to make it seem like you have lots more water pressure while you use half the water? Install a low-flow faucet aerator. One of these devices will reduce water flow by 50 percent but your water pressure will seem stronger because air is mixed with water as it leaves the tap. A family of four typically saves 3,300 gallons of water a year. You can find low-flow faucet aerators at your local hardware store. Only one caution: Don't install a low-flow aerator on your kitchen faucet if you have a portable dishwasher that hooks up to it. The reduced flow would affect the dishwasher's performance.

Don't let a leak sneak up on you. To keep your hot water heater in top shape, drain two to three gallons of water from the valve at the bottom to remove any sediment that may have collected. If you do this about every six months, you may save yourself the trouble of repairing a leaky faucet valve. Removing sediment will also help the heater work more effi-ciently, saving you money each month on your power bill.

Dodge flying dander. If you keep a pet indoors, you should change your heating and air conditioning filter often, perhaps every month. Otherwise, your pet's hair and dander will keep circulating throughout your house, lessening air quality and possibly worsening allergies in the human inhabitants.

Pull the plug on heat loss. Finish sealing your house by insulating your outlets. Turn off all the electricity, remove the face plate, and fill the hole around the socket with fireproof insulation. You may discover, with a shock, that you've just saved a bundle on your heating bills.

Put a damper on heat loss. Santa Claus may come in through your chimney, but heat can exit the same way. Keep your damper closed when it's not in use to keep hot air from heading up the chimney. If possible, cover your grate with glass doors to further insulate your house.

Turn valve to prevent disaster. The last thing you need when your bathroom is flooding is a rusty shut-off valve that won't budge. To keep the valve in working order, turn your water off and on again once every six months.

Test your toilet. You suspect a leak somewhere in your toilet, but you can't find it. To check if the leak is coming from the inside valves, dribble a few drops of food coloring into the tank. Now don't flush, just wait it out. If the coloring comes into the bowl without your flushing, you've found your leak.

Thaw frozen pipes. When your pipes freeze, your hair dryer may be the best tool to thaw them out. A hair dryer set on high will thaw frozen pipes slowly. If you use a propane torch, you could heat the water too quickly, causing steam to form and bursting your pipes.

Plant trees to chop down utility bills

Take advantage of the natural cycles of trees to lower your utility bills. Plant trees around the south and west sides of your house. In the summer, the shady boughs will keep your house cool. In the winter, the sun will peek through the bare branches and warm up your house.

Heat up for summer savings. Want to save up to 25 percent on your next cooling bill? Set your thermostat at 78 degrees instead of 72 degrees in the summer.

Draw the curtain on blinds. Layering is the key to conserving energy. Whether you are braving the snow, trekking through the desert, or sitting in your own living room, more is better. Take your windows, for instance. Hanging blinds behind your drapes will increase your protection from heat in the summer and cold in the winter.

Cool your house with a new coat. If you love the winter because your utility bills drop, it's time to improve your cooling system. Paint your house a light color, which will deflect hot sun rays, instead of a dark shade, which will absorb heat. You might also want to put lighter shingles on your roof. Lighten up, and those summer heat waves will roll right over you.

Steam away winter's chill. Turn up the heat without touching the thermostat. Just set a pot of water on the stove to simmer. Throw in some cinnamon sticks for a cozy, homey feeling.

Flip the switch for cool savings. Any light source produces heat. That's why leaving an extra light on puts an extra strain on your air conditioner — and your electric bill. To keep your electric bill under control, turn off any lights you don't need.

Cleaner air is cheaper air. Clean or replace your heating and air conditioning system filter every one to three months. A dirty filter makes the system work harder and use more energy than a clean one. Home improvement stores and discount stores carry inexpensive standard filters as well as special filters that are designed to last as long as several months. You can also buy permanent metal filters that can last years because they're washable. Whatever kind of filter you have, keep it clean.

Don't do windows this summer. Do your window cleaning in late fall or winter. A clear window will let in more light and heat, which will lower your winter heating bill. In summer, a little film of dirt won't hurt, deflecting some sunlight and letting in less heat.

Fan-handle your whole house. If you want to get tough on cooling costs, consider getting a whole-house fan that exhausts through your attic. The idea is to operate it in the evenings when outside temperatures cool off but your house is still warm inside. By opening a few windows, you can pull in the cool, night air and force the accumulated warm air out through the attic. In some areas, it can be used instead of air conditioning for a good cost savings. In really hot climates, it can be used in addition to air conditioning.

Turn up your radiator's heat. If you have a radiator in your home, you can increase the amount of heat put out into a room very simply. Here's how. Cut a piece of rigid insulation or poster board the same size as the radiator. Cover it with aluminum foil and slip it between the radiator and the wall. You've just made your own insulated reflector.

Soak your shower head. If you have mineral deposits built up on your shower head, they can block the flow of water. To get rid of them without taking apart your fixture, fill a plastic sandwich bag with vinegar. Pull the bag up so that the shower head is completely immersed in the vinegar. Use a rubber band to attach the bag. Leave it to soak for several hours or overnight. Remove the bag and, if necessary, use an old toothbrush and toothpicks to clean all the holes.

Show your thermostat you mean business. If your thermostat seems to have a mind of its own, its connections may be clogged with dust or dirt. To clean it, remove the cover and run a business card through the connectors. With no dirty little excuse, your thermostat should quit its crazy behavior.

Get with the program. You can reduce heating and cooling expenses by 20 to 30 percent just by changing your thermostat setting while no one is home and while you sleep at night. In winter, set it back 15 degrees (maybe from 70 to 55 degrees). In summer, raise it from 70 to 75 or 80 degrees. To make this cost savings easier, consider investing in a programmable automatic thermostat. It will take care of the desired temperature changes in the house before you get up in the morning and before you get home in the evening. With the money you'll save on utility bills, the thermostat should pay for itself in about six months.

Watch out for space heater dangers

Space heaters top the list of home fire hazards, but you'll be safer if you follow these tips.

- Keep the heater at least 3 feet away from anything flammable, including furniture, rugs, clothing, and curtains. Dangerous liquids, like gasoline or kerosene, should be used and stored far away from the space heater.

- Avoid plugging it into an extension cord, but if you must, make sure it's the correct wire gauge size and type.

- Lastly, turn the heater off and unplug it any time you're not using it and when you go to bed.

Thermostat alert. To make sure your heating and cooling system's thermostat is helping your system operate at peak efficiency, check inside the wall behind where it's mounted and make sure the wall is properly insulated. If it's not, hot air or cold air could creep in from outdoors and alter the thermostat reading, causing the system to work harder than necessary.

Help out your septic system. If you have a septic tank, help keep it fresh by flushing a cup of baking soda down the toilet every so often.

Save on your water bill. If the toilets in your house are the older models that use over three gallons of water for every flush, you may want to try this water-saving tip. Fill a plastic soda bottle with water and set it in your toilet tank. This will cut the amount of water used.

Crisis reminders for flooded bathrooms

When your toilet overflows, don't just reach for the plunger. Turn the shut-off valve on the water pipe clockwise to stop the flow of water into the tank. Next, reach into the holding tank and make sure the rubber seal on the flush valve is closed properly. When the water stops running, use your plunger to unclog the drain.

Maintain a healthy septic system. A good rule of thumb for the health of your septic system is to never use any product labeled "antiseptic." Bleach and other chlorine-containing products can also keep your system from working properly. These substances kill the bacteria that work to break down waste products in your septic system.

Make time for fun

Outsmart jet lag with simple tactics. You can avoid jet lag by fooling your body. For example, if you're going to land in the morning, sleep as much as possible during your flight. If you're going to land at night, try to stay awake with your overhead light on while you're in the air. That way, your body will be adjusted to the new time zone.

When 'bumping' pays off. Know your rights if you are bumped from a flight. You are entitled to one-half the cost of your round-trip ticket (up to $200) if you arrive at your destination between one and two hours later than your original flight or the entire cost of your round-trip ticket (up to $400) if you arrive more than two hours late (four hours for international flights).

Land a prime seat on next flight

Make sure you always get the safest and most comfortable seat on any airplane. It's easy — just ask for it. When you book your flight, ask to sit in the first row (the bulkhead) or an exit row. You'll have plenty of leg room. Keep in mind that, in case of emergency, certain responsibilities come with an exit row seat. If you don't think you can handle those responsibilities, choose an aisle seat in the row behind or in front of an exit row. That way, you'll have some leg room, and you're still close to an exit — but you won't have to open the exit door or direct people during an emergency.

Reserve your weekend. The best time to call for airline reservations is evenings or weekends. Reservation agents aren't as busy then and can give you more time and better service.

Fly the friendly skies. Flying is one of the safest forms of transportation you can choose. To make it even safer, follow these tips. (1) After boarding, locate the nearest emergency exit door and count the rows of seats to it. In an emergency, the lights may go out, and you may have to feel your way to the exit. (2) Pay attention to the preflight instructions, no matter how often you've heard them before. (3) Make sure you know how to operate the emergency exit. (4) Keep your seat belt fastened whenever you are seated. (5) If an emergency does arise and you have to evacuate the plane, don't attempt to take your luggage with you. Your luggage can be replaced. You, however, are irreplaceable.

Bag your toys for the beach. A mesh bag is one of the neatest ways to take toys to the beach. When you're done for the day, dip the bag and its toys in the ocean or spray them with a hose. The sand and water will just drip away.

Make a splash with Velcro. Stick with this simple plan while you're on vacation. Get a fabric fastener, like Velcro, and sew or iron it onto the pockets of your swim trunks. That way, you can keep your keys and spare change safe while you take a dip in the pool or ocean. You can also use a fabric fastener on your regular pants to thwart pickpockets.

Brush away sand. No need to get sand in your car when you go to the beach. Keep a paintbrush handy to brush off your feet before you get in.

Great for vacation souvenirs. Fill an old, clean pantyhose leg with your collection of seashells from the beach or rocks from a wilderness trail. Knot the end and you've got a great way to transport your treasures home.

Leave sand at the beach. Take a mesh bag along when you go to the seashore. When it's time to gather your belongings, put small washable items — like suntan lotion, sunglasses, and any shells you've collected — into the bag. Dunk them in the water or under a faucet to remove any sand sticking to them.

Make sure you're paying the lowest price

Just because you've already booked your flight doesn't mean you should stop checking prices. Call and see if the price has come down. Even if you have to pay a $100 fee to change your ticket, you might end up saving money if the new fare is dramatically lower.

Get more mileage from bike tires. Don't store your bicycle near a refrigerator, freezer, or electric heater. They give off ozone, which can cause the rubber tires to crack.

Get frequent perks as a frequent flier

Even if you're not really a frequent flier, sign up with airlines' frequent-flier programs. Besides free trips, you can earn discounts on hotels and car rentals. You might also be able to earn frequent-flier miles by using your credit card or switching your long-distance phone company.

Feed your feathered friends a feast. Give hungry birds a treat during the winter by coating pine cones with peanut butter and leaving them outside. For a tasty dessert, smear hardened bacon grease on pine cones and roll them in birdseed.

Save your valuables from sinking. When you're boating, place your valuables in a resealable, plastic bag. Before you close it, blow into it and fill it with air. That way, if the bag ends up in the water, it will float.

Keep your keys afloat. Whenever you go boating or swimming, attach your keys to a cork. Then if they fall overboard, they'll float and you can retrieve them easily.

Save your books, come humidity or high water. If a valuable or treasured book becomes damp, move it to an airy place where it can dry gradually. Stand the book on end and fan out the pages so air can get to them. If the book is very damp, you can sprinkle baby powder between the pages. Let it sit for several hours and then brush it off the pages with a clean, soft cloth.

Low light is right. Sunlight is one of the worst things for paper — it quickly damages inks and dyes and makes paper brittle. But it's not always practical to store valuable paper treasures in the dark. To help guard against the UV rays in sunlight and fluorescent light, keep your books and papers out of direct light and use heavy draperies in the rooms where they are stored. Keep individual papers in acid-free file folders away from direct light.

Camp with great balls of fire. Before you go camping, smear petroleum jelly on a bunch of cotton balls and seal them in a plastic bag. They're fail-safe fire starters if you get stuck in the rain or can't start a fire for some other reason.

Sleep in a clean, dry tent. A painting dropcloth is a must for your next camping trip. Bring one the same size as the floor of your tent and set your tent on top of it. It will protect you and your tent from wetness and dirt.

Evict musty smells from sleeping bag. Stick a fabric softener sheet in your sleeping bag before you roll it up and put it away. That will keep it smelling springtime fresh the next time you use it.

Feel clean without water. On long camping adventures, sometimes bathing isn't an option. To feel clean and refreshed, wash yourself with flat cotton pads soaked in witch hazel.

Waterproof your matches. Anyone who has camped in the rain knows that waterproof matches come in handy. Make your own by dipping match heads in candle wax.

Bowl over your camping buddies. Cut off and clean out the bottoms of empty, plastic soda or milk containers and pack them in your backpack. They'll make great cereal bowls on your next camping trip.

Add pantyhose to camping gear. Old pantyhose makes great rope. It's easy to find space for it in your camping gear and strong enough to bundle together your sleeping bag or cooking utensils. You can even use it to hang your food in a tree to keep it safe from animals.

Get tough on tent mildew. Mildew is one of your tent's worst enemies. As soon as you see it growing, hand wash the tent with a gentle, detergent-free soap in as little water as possible. Then sponge the mildew spot with a half-cup of disinfectant cleaner in a gallon of warm water. Dry the tent in direct sunlight. If the mildew has caused your tent to start peeling, treat it with a stronger solution — one cup of salt plus one cup of lemon juice in a gallon of hot water. After the tent dries in the sun, peel off the damaged, flaking sections of the tent's coating and cover these spots with a new layer of water sealant.

Zap a stuck zipper. Don't get trapped in your tent because of a stuck zipper. Make it an easy slider by rubbing it with candle wax. In a fix, lip balm will work, too.

Spice up camp cuisine. Dinner at the campsite doesn't have to be bland and boring. Before you leave home, remember to fill several plastic film canisters with your favorite spices. The airtight canister will keep the spices fresh and make them easy to pack.

Clean your lint trap and feed a fire. Take along a ball of laundry lint with you on your next camping trip. On days when you can't find dry tinder, the lint makes a great substitute.

Freshen your sleeping bag. If you put a bar of soap in your sleeping bag and leave it there for the entire camping season, your sleeping bag won't smell musty.

Eliminate foul odors from your canteen. Dump three teaspoons of baking soda and a little bit of water into your canteen and shake it around. After an hour, dump this mixture out and rinse your canteen thoroughly. It will smell as fresh as a mountain stream.

The care and cleaning of sleeping bags. Keep your sleeping bag clean and help it last longer by placing a folded sheet inside the bag to sleep in and by putting a ground cloth under it when using it outdoors. During camping trips, it's a good idea to hang up the bag and let it air out every day. Always be sure your sleeping bag is completely dry before you roll it up for storage.

Keep toilet paper dry. When you're camping out there "in the rough," one luxury you don't want to be without is dry toilet paper. An empty coffee can makes a perfect waterproof travel container for this precious commodity.

Pack a handy camping tool. Toss in a few coat hangers, the kind with cardboard tubes on the bottom, the next time you go camping. When you get settled, unhook the tube from the wire, slip a roll of paper towels over the tube, and hook the wire back in. Hang it up on a convenient tree branch, and you've got towels at your fingertips. This idea works for toilet paper, too.

Stay organized when camping. A hanging shoe bag should be the first thing you pack on your next camping trip. This versatile item can save you from lost socks, misplaced toothbrushes, or cluttered piles of clothing. Hang one inside your tent or camper, and fill the bags with each person's necessities for the next morning. Use another one for bathroom items. Even if the family has to take turns in the shower, at least the shampoo, soap, etc. will all be in the right place.

Expose film to the cold. Keep rolls of unused film in the refrigerator until you need them. They will stay fresh longer that way.

Good batteries gone bad. Camera batteries can leave invisible chemical deposits inside your camera. Clean the batteries and the contacts regularly and replace batteries once a year.

Cover up fishing lure scents. Lure scents and dyes can ruin the rest of your tackle if you're not careful. Keep these secret weapons to themselves in a resealable bag.

Grab a mint and save the tin. After you're done freshening your breath, use that empty mint tin to store your small hooks and weights in one easy-to-find place. Then maybe you won't get stuck fishing for them at the bottom of your tackle box.

Turn softball into a splash-fest. Score big points with your grand kids this summer. On a hot day, supply them with water balloons to replace balls in traditional games, such as softball or volleyball. Even a simple game of catch becomes exciting when the ball threatens to explode with icy water.

Win in the game of croquet. Colorful drinking straws can make croquet more fun and easier to play. Slide a straw onto each wicket leg before you place them in the ground. When it's your turn to shoot, you'll be able to find the wickets a lot easier.

Powder your playing cards. A light dusting of baby powder keeps cards from sticking together. Shuffling will go more smoothly, too.

Whiten your golf balls. Get your golf balls as clean as they were on their first putt. Dip them in a mixture of one cup water and one-quarter cup ammonia. Let them sit until they are clean, then rinse and dry.

Chip dirt off your golf clubs. Give your metal golf clubs a bath in a bucket of water and laundry detergent. Soak your clubs for no longer than a minute and then towel them off. The laundry detergent contains the same active ingredient as fancy, store-bought club cleaners.

Personalize golf balls inexpensively. Never get your golf balls mixed up with somebody else's. Make a dot on them with a touch of nail polish. This is a great idea for tennis or racquet balls, too.

Store golf balls. Empty egg cartons make perfect storage containers for your golf balls.

Photocopy credit cards for extra protection. Always keep photocopies of your credit cards with the rest of your financial information. If your cards are ever lost or stolen, you'll have your account numbers and expiration dates handy. That means no problems reporting the incident. When you travel, make two copies — one to bring with you and one to leave at home.

Copy documents before you go. Besides making plans and reservations for your trip, you should also make some photocopies. Guard against theft or loss by making copies of your driver's license, passport, travel tickets, traveler's checks, and other important documents. Keep one set of copies at home and put another in your luggage.

Diabetics — stash syringes in plastic jar. If you have diabetes and take insulin, you have special travel concerns. In addition to the usual traveler's worries, you have to deal with syringes and medication. You can bring along an empty peanut butter jar to dispose of your used syringes. Any plastic jar with a screw-on lid should do the trick. While you're at it, get a note from your doctor saying you need to carry syringes because of a medical condition. That way, you won't get hassled by airport security. Also, buy a small, thermal-insulated lunch bag to keep your medication cool.

Stop hotel intruders with doorstop. Feel secure in your hotel room. Bring along a small rubber doorstop and wedge it under your door from the inside. For added protection, use two doorstops. That should stop anyone from getting in.

Foil pickpockets with a rubber band. Keep tabs on your wallet during your travels. All it takes is a thick rubber band. Just wrap it around your wallet. If someone tries to slip it out of your pocket, you'll feel the rubber band rub against your pants.

Give your valuables maxi-mum protection.

Camouflage your valuables from snooping thieves. Keep them in a tampon or maxi-pad box in your hotel room. No one will want to rummage through it. Leave half the tampons in the box and fill the rest of it with jewelry and other valuable items.

Protect cash with pantyhose.

Get a leg up on airport pickpockets. Cut a leg off an old pair of pantyhose and slide your credit cards and cash inside. Then tie the leg around your waist under your clothing. Since you don't need to access your credit cards or cash right away — and no thief will be able to get at them — you'll have a worry-free trip through a crowded airport.

Try a towel to prevent bathtub slips.

Worried about slipping in a hotel bathtub? You don't have to take up precious suitcase space with sandals or flip-flops for the shower. Just lay a hand towel in the bottom of the tub.

Track down belongings with matchbooks.

You don't have to smoke to take advantage of hotel matchbooks. Take one from each hotel you stay in during your trip. That way, if you leave something behind, you'll have the name and address of every place you've been.

'Watch' out for tricky time zone changes.

Just because you change time zones doesn't mean you have to change your medication schedule. Instead of struggling with any confusing adjustments, bring an extra watch set to the time zone where you live. That way, you can take your medicine at familiar times without any problems.

Foil pickpockets' plans.

Women should carry a handbag that will fit under their arm. Put your arm through the strap, and carry the bag close to your body.

Foreign exchange.

When traveling to a foreign country, exchange some of your money before you leave. Criminals often watch for people exchanging large amounts of money at airport banks and currency exchange windows.

Avoid malaria and other maladies. Planning a vacation to exotic locales? Call the Centers for Disease Control (CDC) at least six weeks before you depart for current health information on the areas you plan to visit. (404) 332-4559.

Save your sight. If you wouldn't drink the water when traveling abroad, you most certainly shouldn't store your contacts in it. Contaminants in water may cause eye infections or even blindness. Make sure you take your sterile contact solution with you when you travel.

Luggage leave-outs. Don't pack your medications or extra glasses in your luggage. In an emergency, you may need them. You're better off keeping them in your carry-on bag or purse.

Keep your camera dry. Place your camera, keys, wallet or other valuables into a coffee can (with lid) while you're at the beach or on a boat. An empty coffee can will also keep your silverware and napkins dry and bug free on a picnic.

Hold the ice, please. When traveling outside the country, protect yourself from "Montezuma's revenge" — traveler's diarrhea. Drink only bottled beverages, well-cooked foods, and fruits you peel yourself. If you have access to a stove, boiling water for three to five minutes will ensure its safety. One source of contaminated water that many people overlook is ice cubes. Putting ice cubes made with local tap water into your bottled water can defeat your efforts to defend your stomach.

Guard your maps from bad weather. If you plan to go for a hike — or just a leisurely stroll — while on vacation, pack your maps in a large zip-lock bag. That way, if it rains, your map won't get soggy and hard to read.

Escape altitude sickness. Traveling to the mountains can cause altitude sickness in people who live at sea level. Symptoms include headache, shortness of breath, and nausea. To avoid altitude sickness, spend a day at a lower elevation before traveling higher, and drink plenty of fluids, especially water.

Plug in some protection. Groping through the darkness to find the bathroom in a strange motel room can be dangerous. To be safe, bring a night light with you on your travels. Plug it in before bed to shed some light on any nighttime bathroom trips.

Feel welcome with hotel deals. Next time you're taking a trip by car, stop at a state welcome center. It's usually one of the first rest stops off the interstate once you enter a new state. Often, welcome centers offer discount booklets for hotels. You might be able to find a real deal.

Don't brake for breakfast. Breakfast might be the most important meal of the day — but it doesn't have to be the most expensive or most time consuming. Save both time and money on breakfast while you're on vacation. Pick up some juice and a muffin at night, and store the juice in your hotel room's ice bucket. The next morning, enjoy a quick, cheap breakfast before starting your day.

It pays to ask. You know to shop around for good deals on airfares and car rentals, but did you know you should also shop around for hotel rates? Besides comparing hotel prices, ask about discounts. Every hotel offers them, but they won't tell you about them or give you a better rate unless you ask.

Drop a few coins for clean clothes. It's hard to return home to your regular chores after a fun, relaxing family vacation. And knowing you have all those dirty clothes to wash can really add to the dread. Why not take your dirty duds to a self-service laundry and use those big machines to make fast work of this unpleasant task.

Wash your clothes in your trunk. Don't waste time on a road trip doing laundry. Before you hit the road, get your hands on a sealable, plastic bucket. Fill it with hot, soapy water and add your clothes. Secure it in a corner of your RV or your trunk. A day's worth of sloshing around in the bucket should be all it takes to clean your clothes.

Say 'bon voyage' to spills. The last thing you want to think about on vacation is laundry. But don't forget to bring a trial-size bottle of liquid laundry detergent with you. It comes in handy if you spill food on your shirt or if you run out of clothes and need to wash something by hand.

Turn your pillowcase into a hamper. Storing your dirty laundry in an airtight plastic bag while you're traveling might keep the rest of your clothes in the suitcase smelling better. But it could leave your dirty clothes moldy. Try tossing them in a pillowcase instead.

Stash trash bags in your luggage. Next time you pack for a trip, bring a few large garbage bags. They won't go to waste. You can use them to store dirty laundry during your return trip. A garbage bag also serves as a waterproof layer inside your luggage to protect your stuff. You can even make an emergency raincoat out of a garbage bag by cutting slits for your head and arms.

Wash your clothes in your hotel room. You don't want to waste time at a Laundromat while you're on vacation. But you might need to freshen up your clothes a little, especially on a long trip. Pack an empty spray bottle and a few ounces of laundry detergent in a plastic travel bottle. Fill the spray bottle with water, mix in some detergent, and spray your clothes with the mixture. Rinse them in the shower and let them drip dry overnight. The next day, they should be ready to wear.

Iron on the go. When traveling, it's easy to pack a travel iron but not an ironing board. Make one no matter where you are by sliding a stack of magazines or newspapers inside a pillowcase. Lay it on the floor or a bed and press those wrinkles away.

Include ID inside your bags. Don't assume that the name tag on the outside of your luggage will stay on. In case it falls off, have a back-up plan. Write your name, address, and phone number on an index card, slip it into a zip-lock bag, and put it in your suitcase. Do the same for all luggage you're taking with you. The airlines check inside lost bags for ID.

Make your suitcase stand out. Give your luggage a colorful makeover. Wrap some brightly colored electrical tape around the handle of your suitcase before you check it at the airport. That way, even if another passenger has the exact same suitcase and grabs yours by mistake, he'll realize he has the wrong one. You could also braid some brightly colored yarn and tie it around the handle.

Decorate your suitcase. Does your suitcase look like everybody else's? Transform your bland bag into a work of art. Paint flowers, stars, or any other design you can think of on your luggage. You can use stencils to make the designs or just express yourself freehand. You definitely won't grab the wrong bag at baggage claim anymore. No passenger will take your bag by mistake, either. And no thief would think of making off with such a unique piece of luggage.

Freshen your bags with fabric softener. It's time for one of your rare vacations. But you're dreading the prospect of packing because of your musty, smelly suitcase. Luckily, there's an easy way to protect your nose. When you store away your luggage, toss in a fabric softener sheet. Next time you travel, your luggage will smell fresh and ready to go.

Tag your bags. You can make attractive, low-cost I.D. tags for your luggage from recycled greeting cards. Select brightly colored ones so they'll be easy to spot. Write your name and address clearly on the back of each, and cover them completely with strips of transparent tape. Punch holes, and tie or tape them to the handles of your suitcase.

Put a sparkle on your piano's smile. The keys on your piano were once an elephant's tusks, so what do you do if they turn yellow? That's right. Brush them with toothpaste. Rub very gently with a soft cloth and use as little as possible, being careful not to get any paste stuck down between the keys. When you're done, buff the new pearly whites back to their original glory.

Keep track of credit card expenses. Remember, when traveling in foreign countries and using your credit card, you need to keep careful records of your expenditures. People have actually been arrested for unknowingly going over their credit limit! Keep a list of your credit card numbers and cancellation instructions in case of theft and store it in a safe place during your trip.

Topple tangles with toilet paper roll. Do you spend most of your unpacking time trying to untangle your costume jewelry chains? Instead of tossing them in a jewelry case when you travel, wrap them around a cardboard toilet paper roll and secure them with tape. When you reach your destination, accessorizing is a breeze.

Bag wrinkles with packing secret. Clothes made of thin fabric can be a wrinkled mess when you take them out of your suitcase. Keep them wrinkle-free with this simple secret. Save leftover plastic dry cleaner bags and put them between folds of clothing as you pack.

Roll your way to wrinkle-free clothes. Roll, don't fold, clothing when you travel, and you'll arrive wrinkle free. For items on hangers, put them in a plastic dry cleaner bag and roll it up. You can also fold in the sleeves and collars of shirts and roll them with a layer of tissue paper.

Pack your toothbrush in a pill bottle. You need to pack your toothbrush, but you don't have a toothbrush holder. Make a handy holder out of an old plastic pill bottle. Just cut a slit in the cap and slide the toothbrush handle through. Then snap the cap back on the bottle with the toothbrush bristles inside.

Bring newspaper bags on your route. Chances are you recycle your daily newspaper. But you probably don't save those long, narrow plastic bags that come with it. Maybe you should start. You can use those narrow bags to pack your shoes or hairbrushes or to stash last-minute purchases on your vacation.

Travel with disposable cloths in Europe. A European vacation has many charms. Unfortunately, an abundance of soft, cushy washcloths isn't one of them. Because European hotels and bed-and-breakfasts rarely provide washcloths, you could bring your own. But it gets tiresome lugging a wet, soggy washcloth in a plastic bag from place to place. Instead, buy a package of disposable cloths, like Handy Wipes. Cut each of them in half, and you'll have a fresh washcloth each night of your trip. You can even use it to wipe your shoes before tossing it out the next morning.

Save space with samples. Why bring bulky bottles of moisturizer, cleanser, and other beauty aids on your trip? Just grab a few samples that they give out at cosmetics counters in department stores. These smaller portions should last through your vacation without any problem.

Keep bugs away with cotton balls. Save precious suitcase space while saving yourself from mosquitos and other pests. Instead of bringing a whole bottle of insect repellent, just moisten some cotton balls with the stuff and pack them in a small zip-lock bag.

Make the most of luggage space. Stuff your underwear and socks into your shoes when you pack. It not only saves precious suitcase space, it also preserves the shape of your shoes.

A little squeeze'll do it. You probably already know that you can save space on bulky essentials, such as shampoo, conditioner, and body lotion, by transferring the contents to smaller, plastic containers. Here's a neat trick you may not know: Once the contents are inside, squeeze a little air out of each mini bottle and reseal. This creates a vacuum that cuts down on messy spills and leaks.

Travel light with a portable clothes dryer. No need to pack a lot of undergarments. Just wash those unmentionables in the bathroom sink and quick dry them with your hair dryer.

Arrive at your destination in style. Snap snaps, button buttons, and zip zippers on all clothes before putting them in the suitcase. That will help them maintain their shape better.

Prepare piping hot food for picnics. If you're bringing a hot dish to a picnic, keep it warm by tightly wrapping the container in several sheets of newspaper. Tape it closed and then carry it in a paper bag.

Protect your tender tomatoes. Don't want to bruise your tender produce on the way to the picnic? Drop your cherry tomatoes, plums, apricots, and various other small items in an empty egg carton for a safe voyage.

Build a picnic moat. Are ants crawling up the legs of your picnic table trying to join the feast? Stop them cold with mini moats. Pour an inch of water into four empty margarine tubs, cottage cheese containers, coffee cans or tuna cans, and stand each leg of the table in one of the pools.

Seal in salt and pepper. You're unpacking your picnic lunch when you find the salt and pepper have fallen over and emptied into your picnic basket. Next time cover the holes with tape. The salt and pepper will stay put until you are ready to sprinkle them on your potato salad. This also works to hold salt in when refilling shakers.

Make a portable grill. If you don't have a charcoal grill, you can still cook out if you have a metal wheelbarrow. Just put the charcoal in the wheelbarrow, and put an oven rack on top of it, and have "grilling to go."

Reuse lemon-shaped squeeze bottles. When you have used all the lemon or lime juice, refill that handy little squirter with salad dressing to take on a picnic. And refill another with children's shampoo, and toss it in the beach bag for a quick wash-down at an outdoor shower. The possibilities are endless.

Find your map in a snap. Do you need a map to find your road maps? Keep them filed alphabetically by state in a folder or three-ring binder. Then, when you begin a trip, you can easily find the map you need. Folding it up again, however, might not be so easy.

Make your own money bags. Handling foreign currency during your travels can be difficult, especially if you pass through several countries on your trip. To help keep your money organized, slip some plastic sandwich bags in your purse or travel bag. You can use them to hold the various currencies and keep them separate from each other. If you pass through a country again on your way back, just reach for the appropriate bag.

Organize more than shoes in shoe holder. A hanging shoe holder comes in handy if you're staying in one place for your whole vacation. You just fasten the holder's Velcro strap around your room's closet bar and let it hang there. But you don't have to use it just for shoes. The rectangular slots can also be used to store belts, underwear, socks, and pantyhose.

Stop scrambling for important info. A hole-puncher and a soft binder could make the difference between a smooth, well-organized trip and total chaos. Just punch holes in important documents — such as your itinerary, addresses of places you plan to stay, and phone numbers you'll need — and put them in a binder. Choose a brightly colored binder so you can spot it easily in your carry-on bag. Arrange the documents in the order you'll need them. You'll have all the information for your trip in one easy-to-find place.

Protect posters with cardboard tube. The wrapping paper is all gone, but the cardboard roll it came on still has some value. When you go on a trip, cut the roll so it fits in your suitcase. If you buy a poster of the place you're visiting, you can roll it up and store it in the wrapping paper tube. As an added bonus, you can roll your clothes around the tube when you're packing to keep them wrinkle-free.

Drive robbers crazy with this trick. Keep robbers guessing by having your neighbor park her car in your driveway while you're away. The trick will work even better if she moves the car regularly.

A deal of a lifetime. Don't be taken in by travel scams! Watch out for these danger signals when someone offers you a free or low-cost vacation deal: A price that's too good to be true. It is. Pressure to make a decision right away. A request for your credit card number. Vague or unnamed hotels, airlines, or other travel services.

Credit card delay — a warning signal. Another travel scam to avoid: If someone offers you by phone or mail a vacation deal of a lifetime, take note if they say you can't take the trip for at least two months. If the trip is going on your credit card, they may be scamming you. Why? Because there's a 60-day deadline for disputing credit card charges, and they probably know it. If something goes wrong, you won't be able to deny them payment.

Know your insurance requirements. Before you leave on vacation, especially if it's going to be an extended one, be sure you know what's required by your insurer to protect your unoccupied house. Some companies require a certain level of attention if you're away for an extended period. For example, turning off the water or having a neighbor check your house daily. Others will refuse to pay any claims for damage from vandalism if you've been away for more than 30 days.

Rejuvenate a sluggish slide. If your kids' slide has lost its zip, try this. Give your children a sheet of wax paper and have them sit on it on their way down the slide. They'll get a fun ride and a faster slide all in one.

Fill 'er up. Check into refueling options at the end of your rental. Watch out for refueling service by the rental company; it may charge a per-gallon service fee. You'll probably save if you do it yourself.

Steer toward safety and savings

Improve your driving skills and save money on your auto insurance premiums with a simple strategy. Just enroll in the AARP 55 ALIVE Driver Safety Program. The eight-hour course, which includes two four-hour sessions in two days, is designed especially for drivers over 50. You don't have to be a member of AARP to take the course, and there are no tests. It costs $10, but you might qualify for a discount on auto insurance when you complete the course. Check your state for details.

Picnic in the park. A picnic kit is a handy item to carry along on car trips. In a small bag or picnic basket, include paper plates, plastic knives forks and spoons; can opener; bottle opener; salt and pepper; premoistened towelettes, paper towels, or napkins; and a few extra plastic bags for trash. With your prepacked picnic kit, you can stop anytime and enjoy a feast when you run across any specialty food shops or fresh fruit stands you just can't resist trying.

Packing pointers. When traveling by car, leave your clothes on hangers and slip a large plastic trash bag over them. Lay them flat in your trunk. This makes unpacking easier and uses less trunk space.

Layer for smarter traveling. When packing a pillow for the car, slip on several pillowcases. Your pillow will be more comfortable, and you can peel off the top pillowcase when it gets dirty and use it as a laundry bag. This will keep stains and odors from getting onto your clean clothes in your suitcase.

Free fun. You can enjoy your free time without spending a fortune. Begin by making a list of free activities in your area: libraries, parks, your city's recreation department, museums, or municipally supported concerts.

Be your own mechanic

Freshen car with laundry detergent. You carry a spare tire in your trunk — but you might want to carry a spare box of laundry detergent, too. Next time you shop for powdered laundry detergent, buy two boxes and keep one in your trunk. It makes a great air freshener for your car.

Extinguish car odors. Even if you don't smoke, you can still make use of your car's ashtrays. Fill them with baking soda to absorb any stale odors.

Expel cigarette smell with ammonia. Nothing lingers like the smell of cigarette smoke. To rid your car of the odor, fill a shallow pan with ammonia and leave it in your car overnight. The next day, take out the pan, roll down the windows, and let your car air out. It'll be smoke free and ready to drive.

Filter in freshness. Give your car a fresh, pleasant smell. Just slip a dryer sheet in your air filter.

Help your antenna slide. The music you listen to when you drive may be smooth — but the way your car's antenna pops up is anything but. To help your antenna slide out easier, rub it with wax paper.

Get a jump on corrosion with petroleum jelly. Your car won't start, and you need a jump. But your battery posts are so corroded the jumper cables can't get a good connection. Don't be left stranded with corroded battery posts. Prevent corrosion by rubbing petroleum jelly on them.

Use common cents for car maintenance. Protect your car's battery for only a penny. Just tape a copper penny to the top of your battery. Corrosion will be drawn to the penny and leave your electrodes clean.

Jump right in. You hope you'll never be in the situation where you have to jump-start your car. But if the worst happens, a little knowledge about the proper procedure can save you towing or service charges and possibly some expensive car damage. Here are the steps: (1) Ask someone with a car engine larger than yours if possible to help you out. (2) Line up the cars so the jumper cables can reach both batteries. Make sure the cars are not touching. (3) Do not smoke or allow any open flame near the area. (4) Start the car with the good battery and let it idle. (5) Connect the red (positive) cable to the positive terminal (the post with the "+" mark) on the idling car's battery. Then attach the black cable to the negative terminal. Make sure the jumper cable is not in the way of any moving parts. (6) Holding the remaining metal clamps away from each other, hook the red one to the positive battery terminal in your car and the black to the negative terminal. Be careful. If you make a mistake and hook a positive to a negative (called "reversed polarity"), you could cause some serious and costly damage. Also, if you touch the metal clamps together, you'll cause severe sparking and could injure yourself. (7) Try to start your car's engine.

(8) Once it's running, let your motor idle for a few minutes to recharge the battery, then disconnect the jumper cables. (9) If your car won't start after a few tries, it's time to call for service.

Take action after an accident

Nobody wants to be in an automobile accident. But everybody should know what to do in case you are. Here's a quick rundown of steps to take.

- First, do not leave the scene.

- Call for medical help if there are injuries.

- When a police officer arrives at the scene, get his name and precinct address and ask how to get a copy of the accident report.

- Keep a notebook in your car to jot down the details of the accident — the date, time, street, city, weather, road conditions, and a description of what happened. Include the speed you were going and the direction you were traveling.

- Also, make sure to get the names, license plate numbers, and insurance information of the other drivers involved.

Put the brakes on costly repairs. Make sure you change your brake fluid every two or three years or every 30,000 miles. Otherwise, the combination of age and moisture will turn your brake fluid into a dangerous substance that can damage your car's expensive brake components. It's up to you. You can spend a little money on preventive maintenance — or a lot of money on replacement parts.

Make decals disappear like magic. Those decals that stubbornly stick to your windshield seem as if they've been attached by magic. Fortunately, you have something even more magical in your kitchen. Just soak a paper towel with white vinegar and lay it on top of the decal. You'll be able to peel it off before you can say "Abracadabra."

Slide bugs off bumper with cooking oil. Bugs getting caught on your bumper and grill? Get rid of them easily with a little spray of cooking oil. Just spray some onto your car's clean bumper and grill. Your next cleanup job will be a snap.

A dirty car's best friend. There's nothing quite like picking flattened bugs off the grill and headlights with your fingernails. Avoid this unpleasant task with the magic of baking soda. Apply this mild abrasive with a nylon net and watch the splatter marks disappear. Baking soda also works wonders on chrome and enamel.

Unfreeze a lock. When you're dealing with a frozen lock, why not try a burning key? Heat your trunk or car door key with a match, then quickly put it in the lock and turn.

Clean up a messy car. Movie rentals, magazines, clothes, cleaning supplies, mail, and other random items can really clutter up your car. Put a plastic crate or laundry basket in your trunk or backseat to hold all your stuff.

No more scrounging for coins. Fumbling for change at a toll-booth is embarrassing and annoys people waiting behind you. Keep quarters handy for tollbooths, parking meters, and phone calls by storing them in an empty film canister in your car. No more digging through your pockets or purse for loose change.

Organize your car. Wrap a couple of rubber bands around the sun visors, and you'll have a handy place to slip maps, pencils, directions, tickets, etc.

Check fuses first. Next time you have a problem with your car's electrical system, don't blow a fuse. Check to see if your car did. Fixing the problem might be as simple as replacing a broken

Fix your car for free

Thanks to secret warranties nobody's telling you about, you might be entitled to free auto repairs. Here's how it works. Secret warranties are a response to a common problem in particular vehicles. For example, maybe the brakes are shoddy or the paint peels in certain models. The manufacturer agrees to fix the problem for free — but doesn't tell the public. The automakers profit from this strategy, because most times, the consumer gets stuck with the bill.

At any time, there are at least 500 secret warranties out there. The tricky part is finding them. Because only four states have laws requiring automakers to tell you about secret warranties, you usually have to uncover them on your own.

Your best bet is to look for technical service bulletins (TSBs) that deal with the model and year of your vehicle. These documents from the manufacturer let dealers know about common problems with certain cars — and, sometimes, how to fix them. TSBs are available to the public. Just ask your dealer for copies. Other good sources of help include the Center for Auto Safety, the National Highway Traffic Safety Administration, and the Federal Trade Commission. Also, keep your eyes open for stories in the media or trade magazines about automobile defects.

Remember, these warranties are secret. So they're not going to be called "secret warranties." They might be called "goodwill adjustments" or something similar. But you can find enough evidence to show your dealer that you know a secret warranty exists. The key is to be well-informed and persistent. Often, only those who loudly demand their rights get treated fairly.

or blackened fuse. You might save a great deal of money by not towing your car to your dealer or a garage for repairs.

Head for the open road. Too much stop-and-go city driving isn't good for your car's electrical system. Treat your car to a weekly 20- or 30-minute jaunt on the highway. That should be enough to give the charging system a boost.

Walk away to drive a bargain

Buying a new or used car off the lot? Salespeople admit this simple but powerful secret gets you the lowest price practically every time — just walk away. Your willingness to walk out the door might be your best bargaining chip. Once salespeople realize you're prepared to leave rather than settle for an unreasonable price, they often sweeten the deal.

Take the ordeal out of getting stranded. When cold weather hits, always store the following items in your car trunk or back seat in case of emergency — an extra blanket, gloves, a heavy coat, boots, motor oil, antifreeze, a cell phone, water, and food. And make sure you have enough for everyone who rides with you.

Keep bulging trunk closed with pantyhose. Every once in a while, you need to transport something just a little too big for your trunk. Keep an old pair of pantyhose in your trunk for just such an occasion. You can use them to tie down your trunk during your journey.

Drive like a Boy Scout: Be prepared. Other than gas, what's the most important thing to keep in your car at all times? An emergency kit. You can design your kit to contain whatever you think you'll need most often, but a few essentials should never be overlooked. Be sure to include: spare tire, flashlight, tool kit, jumper cables, fire extinguisher, road flares, gallon of water, first aid kit, blanket, towel, stand-up emergency reflectors, umbrella and waterproof parka.

Make an emergency heater. Keep an empty coffee can, a candle, and some matches in the trunk of your car. If you're ever stranded during bad weather conditions, you've got a great little source of light and heat.

Dealing with dealers

The factory invoice price is an important number to find out. This figure reflects what the dealer actually paid for the car, and it is the same for all dealers. It is not their actual cost, however, so even if you paid this price, the dealer would still make money. There are dealer hold-backs and incentives in place that allow the dealer to haggle with smart shoppers. Because it can be pretty tough to keep all these figures straight in your head, the best way to go about buying a new car is to get prices from several different dealers. If a dealer thinks he's in competition with other car dealerships, he's much more likely to give you a competitive price.

Oil your hands after an oil change. You've probably heard of the health benefits of olive oil. Well, here's another bonus — it helps clean your hands. Keep some olive oil in your garage. After you're done working on your car, pour some olive oil on your hands and rub them together. This should dislodge the grease. Wipe the gunk off with a paper towel, then wash your hands with soap and water.

Battle greasy hands easily. Your car is fixed, but now your hands are a greasy mess. Before you work on your car again, prepare this economical grease remover. Combine one-half cup of vegetable shortening, one-third cup of cornmeal, and one-quarter cup of powdered soap. Keep the mixture in a covered container, and use it whenever you need to get grease off your hands.

Turn on the AC in winter. It's the middle of December. The last thing on your mind is your car's air conditioner. However, you might want to turn it on for 10 minutes or so, just to keep it in shape. If you leave your air conditioner off for too long a stretch, you risk damaging it. That's because the lubricant won't move through the system. Play it safe — run your AC every few weeks all year long.

Keep an eye on the antifreeze. Antifreeze helps keep your car running well, but did you know it also helps prevent rust and corrosion? To make sure your antifreeze works its best, have it changed every two years or 24,000 miles, whichever comes first. If you change it yourself, use a 50-50 antifreeze-water mix, using distilled water, not tap water.

Energize an overheated engine. If your car begins to overheat in traffic, don't panic. Put it in neutral, then rev the engine a few times. This should get the coolant moving again. If this doesn't work, try running your heater at full blast. This will push more of the heat away from your engine. You might want to roll your windows down first, though.

Pop goes the oil stain. Your car has certainly left its mark on your driveway. Get rid of those unsightly oil stains with soda pop. Just pour some soda on the stains, then hose them off with water.

Put a lid on it. Your car needed some oil, but you didn't need to use the whole can. Save the rest by covering the can of motor oil with a one-pound coffee can lid.

A slick drip trick. What's filthier than a garage floor? Nothing, if you've got an oil leak. Even a tiny drip can cause a major stain in a pretty short time — a stain that's very easy to track into the house. Head this problem off at the pass by making a drip pan. Place a few sheets of corrugated cardboard in a cookie sheet and arrange this pan under your car's drip. You can also use cat litter, oatmeal, or sawdust in the pan. If you already have a major oil slick in your garage or driveway, spread one of these thirsty substances all over the spot, wait for a while, then sweep up and discard it.

Jump at junkyard deals. Your car might need a part — but that doesn't mean you have to pay top dollar for a brand new one. Check around at junkyards or salvage yards. You might find a perfectly usable part for a fraction of the cost. Buy it and bring it to your mechanic to install. It takes a little extra effort, but it might be worth it in savings. Not all garages install junkyard parts, so ask before you buy anything.

Coddle cargo with shower power. It's curtains for clanging cargo — literally. Use a spring-loaded shower curtain rod to keep items in the back of your pickup truck from banging all over the place. You can use one rod to secure large items against the back of the passenger compartment or use several rods as dividers throughout the bed of the pickup.

KO tar with mayo. During your travels, your car might pick up an unwanted passenger — road tar. Luckily, a common household condiment can take care of that. Just slather some mayonnaise over the tar. Let it sit a few minutes, then wipe it with a clean rag.

Low tar, no tar. Ugh! Road tar on your beautiful paint job. Makes you almost wish they wouldn't fill those potholes in front of your house. But calm down, you've got a secret weapon. Laundry pre-wash sprays successfully remove tar from car surfaces.

Guard against trouble with monthly checks

You know the basics of car maintenance — change your oil every 3,000 miles and get regular tune-ups, usually every 30,000 miles. But you can do a little bit more to keep your car running smoothly. Stay on top of things by making a few monthly checks. Fill your car's fluids, such as the oil, coolant, brake fluid, windshield washer fluid, transmission fluid, and power-steering fluid. Check the pressure in your tires, including the spare, and look for any leaks on the engine or under the car. With this monthly plan, it will be a lot harder for car trouble to sneak up on you.

Don't forget the dipstick. Quite simply, your engine needs oil. Check your oil every two weeks or whenever you fill up your car with gas. If you change your own oil, catch it in a clean, plastic milk jug and take it to a local service station or recycling center.

An idling engine is the devil's playground. What's one of the worst things you can do for your car's engine? Idling. Or at least frequent or long-term idling. If you have to stop your car for more than a few minutes, turn it off. And on cold winter mornings, keep "warming up" to just a minute or so; today's cars are designed to warm up quickly. This will save on gas as well as protect your engine.

The road best travelled. If you want to know just how long your car can last, pay a visit to Bill Desch. As a refurbisher of old cars, Bill is delighted to show people that, in most cases, it's not the car that quits on the owner but the other way around. So how do you keep that from happening? "Change your oil" Bill says. "Every 3,000 miles no matter what your manual says. I don't care if it's just off the showroom floor or a classic in your garage. That's the number one thing you can do to lengthen your car's life." And don't forget to replace the oil filter when you change the oil, he adds. That's where the gunk collects that will cause your engine problems. So take it from an expert. Just like you watch what you eat, take care of what goes into your car. It's the best way to keep it healthy for the long haul.

Tune up for the long haul

Did you know? Keeping your car properly maintained translates into a more efficient safer car that will last up to 50 percent longer. That means thousands of free miles! Something as small as a misfiring spark plug can reduce your gas mileage up to 30 percent. But you can prevent such a problem with regular tune-ups. Check your owner's manual to see how often you should have a tune-up. Then mark the dates on your calendar and keep the appointments.

Remember to keep your coolant. The most frequent cause of summertime breakdowns is overheating. Have your cooling system checked, flushed, and refilled every 24 months. Periodically, check the level of coolant just to make sure you don't have a leak.

Buy the book. One of the most important things you can do for your car is read the owner's manual. It's the most reliable source of information about caring for your car. If you don't have an owner's manual, call a dealership that sells your kind of vehicle, and order a manual from the parts department.

Bust rust with a screwdriver. If you want to stop your car from rusting, you should go down under. Not to Australia

— just underneath your car. Look for drain holes that allow water to drip out and moisture to evaporate. When these holes get plugged up, rust sets in. Poke them with a small screwdriver or wire hanger to open them up again.

No rust for the weary. Remember, the hood and bumpers aren't the only parts of your hard-working car that need attention. Rust can creep up where you least expect it or where you're least likely to look for it. Salt, dirt, and road oils can build up on the exposed underside of your car and do some serious damage. Keep rust away by flushing out the undercarriage of your car every so often. Toss the sprinkler underneath and turn it on, moving it around every now and then so that each part gets good and clean.

Your car's castle. Your garage is as important to your car as your house is to you. Storing your vehicle in a spot where it is protected from the elements can improve the performance, preserve the appearance, and extend the life of your car. Rain, snow, wind, hail, extreme heat, and extreme cold cause damage that can be prevented by keeping your car in a sheltered place. If your garage is full of things other than your car, clean it out and use it for storing this very important possession.

Prevent slams with a tennis ball. Loading up the car for a family trip can be hectic, especially with little children around. Protect little fingers by wedging a tennis ball between the car door and the car. The door will stay open, even if the wind blows or somebody bumps it.

Ace parking with simple trick. You're slowly inching your car into the garage. You pull in a little further... a little further... a little further... and BANG. Your car hits the back wall of the garage. Again. You can stop this from happening. First, park your car exactly where you want it. Then hang a tennis ball from the garage ceiling so it gently rests on your windshield. From now on, when you pull into the garage, you'll know to stop when the tennis ball touches your windshield.

Address your forgetfulness with labels. You've often been told you'd lose your head if it wasn't screwed on. Imagine what might happen to your car's gas cap. Consider taping an address label to your gas cap in case you accidentally leave it at the gas station. That way, someone can return it to you.

Reflect on defective headlight. A burned-out headlight can mean more than a ticket from the police. It can also spell danger. Make sure you're visible to other drivers by covering your headlight with reflector tape until you make it to a service station or auto parts store.

Keeping your car in line. To help guide your car into perfect parked position, paint a stripe down the middle of the back wall of your garage. This bearing will help you center your car when you pull into the garage and should keep you from ramming your door into something because you parked too far left or right.

Map out your plans. It's always a good idea to plan ahead before you travel. Maps are pretty inexpensive and can save you time, trouble, and terrible headaches down the road. Always buy a map if you are traveling to a new area by car. But what about your hometown? If you live in a large urban area, it's likely you don't know your way around every neighborhood, so a few local maps are good to have along just in case. You can photocopy local maps at the library or out of the front of the local telephone book and keep them in your glove compartment.

Hang your maps out to dry. If you want a real challenge, try getting a parking stub out of your pocket with your seat belt on. If you want to do it the easy way, snap a big clothespin on the visor over your steering wheel. It makes a convenient holder for parking stubs, toll tickets, maps, or that list of forgotten items you've gone back to the grocery store to get.

Take it easy. If you want your car to last longer, take it easy when you first start driving. Since most engine wear occurs while the cold engine is warming up, accelerate gently until your engine reaches its normal operating temperature.

Drive with ears wide open. When driving in fog, roll down a window. You'll hear cars coming before you'll be able to see them.

Camouflage car scratches with crayons. The paint scratches on your car need to be fixed, but you're short on cash. No problem. Here's an amazing way to get rid of scratches on your car — without spending a cent. Just reach for a box of crayons. Find a crayon that matches the color of your car and rub it on your car to cover the scratches.

A manicure for your car. Ouch! A shopping cart took a nip out of your car's beautiful finish. Doesn't look too bad, but how do you keep it from getting worse? Nail polish. That's right. A quick coat of clear fingernail polish will help prevent rust from forming and keep that small scratch from getting worse.

Use oven cleaner on whitewalls. Put the white back in your whitewall tires. Simply spray them with oven cleaner, hose them off, and admire.

Can you handle the pressure? Here are some tips for keeping your tire pressure in check. Use a reliable pressure gauge when checking your tires. Don't use the one at the gas station; you don't know who's been mistreating it or how well it works. Here's something that's often overlooked. When you check the pressure on your four tires, check your fifth one, too. What good is a spare if it's not properly inflated and ready to roll when you need it? Always check tire pressure when tires are "cool." If your tires are warmed up from a long period of use, the heat can cause a false reading. Be sure to check tire pressure at least once a month. Make it a natural part of your service routine, every three or four times you fill up, to give your tires the once-over.

Increase your gas mileage for free

Get 5 to 10 more miles per gallon when you drive. Just check your car's tire pressure frequently. Underinflated tires increase resistance, which causes your tires to wear out quicker and your car to consume more gas. Try to keep your tires filled to the recommended level. It's a cheap and easy way to improve your mileage. While you're at it, make sure you get regular tune-ups for your engine, too. A misfiring spark plug can lower your gas mileage by 30 percent.

Save gas, your tires, and the environment. You can accomplish all three of these goals just by keeping your tires at the correct air pressure. Underinflated tires wear out more quickly, and they cut fuel economy by as much as 2 percent per pound of pressure below the recommended level.

Repair tears for less. Don't let a small tear in your car's upholstery make a big rip in your pocketbook. Instead of taking it to the dealer for an expensive repair job, try mending your seat with iron-on patches. You can find them in discount stores or fabric stores. Just look for patches that match your car's interior.

Oil leather to keep it together. Sometimes you have to baby your car. If your car has leather seats, cover them with a thin coat of baby oil every once in a while. It will help prevent rips and tears.

Curb car odors with baking soda. Next time you clean the inside of your car, clean more than meets the eye. Sprinkle some baking soda on the seats and carpet before you vacuum. You'll suck out the smell of cigarette smoke and other odors that have seeped into the upholstery.

Wash your car with a helping hand. You care enough about your car to wash it by hand. But why not make your job a little easier? Make your own special car-washing mitt. Just take two washcloths, put one on top of the other, and sew them together. Leave enough space on one side to slip your hand in between the washcloths, but make your mitt tight enough so it won't slip off when you dunk it in the suds bucket.

Leave the detergent under the sink. Detergents meant for washing dishes or clothing have a pH content designed to cut grease. This could also cut through your car's wax coating and harm its clear-coat finish. Use specially formulated car wash products instead. It's also important to rinse your car before washing it because dirt and grit caught under your sponge or towel can scratch the paint.

Hey... you clean up nice. For a shine that looks like it just came off the showroom floor, rub down the vinyl and hard plastic parts of your car's interior with aerosol furniture polish. Not only does it look great, the coating helps keep dust from gathering, too.

Brush up on wheel polishing. This will make you smile. The same stuff you use to brighten your teeth does wonders for your car's chrome or aluminum wheels. Instead of buying expensive wheel polish, just use some plain, white toothpaste. Your wheels will sparkle — and they won't get cavities.

Foil dullness with aluminum foil. Make your chrome hubcaps shine again. Crumple up some aluminum foil and rub it on your hubcaps to polish them. If your hubcaps are rusty, you can get rid of the rust by dipping the aluminum foil in cola first.

Help hubcaps find their way home. If one of your hubcaps flies off, chances are you'll never see it again. But if you take one simple precaution, your odds skyrocket. Inside your hubcaps, write your name, address, and phone number in permanent marker. You also might want to include the word "reward." Someone might find your hubcap and return it to you.

Erase steamy windows. Go back to school to solve a common car problem. If your windows get steamed up, clear them with a chalkboard eraser. You'll be able to see all the way to the head of the class.

Repel rain from your windshield. Rain, rain, go away. Dump some baking soda on a damp rag and wipe your windshield. It will keep rain from collecting on it.

Patch holes with nail polish. Pebbles and other flying debris can make things rough on your car. You won't believe what you can use to fix a crack in your windshield or window — and you can find it right in your cosmetic bag. To fill small holes in your windshield, simply apply some clear nail polish. It also works for holes in your car's paint job.

Fight windshield grime with homemade fluid. Keep your windshield clean with a simple, homemade washer fluid. Just add two tablespoons of liquid detergent, three cups of rubbing alcohol, and enough water to fill a clean gallon milk jug.

Pull the plug on windshield bugs. Splat! Your windshield is starting to look like a graveyard for bugs. Get rid of them with some common kitchen items. Squirt a little bit of dish detergent and water on your windshield and scrub it with a mesh onion bag. The mesh won't harm your windshield, but it will scrape off the bugs. When you're done, wipe the windshield with a clean rag.

Shield your wipers from ice. When your windshield wiper blades get grungy, clean them with rubbing alcohol. You'll get more than just clean wipers — you'll also prevent ice from forming on the blades.

Ward off ice with vinegar. Keep ice off your car during those cold winter months. Before you go to bed, spray a mixture of three parts white vinegar and one part water on your car's windshield and windows. The next morning, your car should be in the clear.

Wipe out streaks with ammonia. Smears and streaks on your windshield can hamper your ability to see while you drive. Avoid them by keeping your windshield wipers clean. Get rid of the dirt, sap, and grime by rubbing both sides of each wiper with a rag soaked in ammonia.

Steer clear of streaks. Are your windshield wipers doing more harm than good? If your wipers cause streaks, wash them with a solution of baking soda and water. You'll clearly see the difference.

'Club' grease from your windshield. The trunk of your car probably contains several handy items. Here's one more — a bottle of club soda. You can use it to get grease off your windshield.

Banish snow and frost. If scraping snow and ice off your windshield in the morning isn't your favorite way to start the day, try covering your windshield at night with a plastic garbage bag or sheet of plastic. Hold it in place by closing the doors on the edges. In the morning, lift off the garbage bag, and you'll have a perfectly clear windshield.

Banish windshield haze. Want to get a like-new sparkle on that hazy windshield? Simply give it a good wash with white vinegar, rinse with water, and dry it off.

Use a straw to thaw frozen lock. Your car door lock is frozen again. Try shouting, "That's the last straw." Then reach for a plastic drinking straw. Blow warm air through the straw directly onto the lock to heat it. Your door will be ready to open in no time. Keep your "last straw" handy during the winter months.

Find a helper on your car's floor. Your floor mats have it easy. They just lie on the floor of your car all day. Next time you get stuck on a patch of ice, put them to work. To get the traction you need, lay a floor mat under your tire. You'll be able to drive off the slippery area, and your floor mat will be able to return to the car floor for a well-earned rest.

Help yourself out of snow. Make use of those old carpet scraps sitting in your basement. Cut them into strips measuring 1 by 4 feet and keep them in your car's trunk. If you get stuck in the snow, just put a strip under each tire.

Slash scraping time with an onion. Avoid the dreaded winter task of scraping by rubbing half an onion all over your windshield. It will help stop ice from forming.

Battle winter elements with sand. Fill plastic milk jugs with dry sand and keep them in your trunk for weight. They're much easier to move than sandbags, and they won't break open and spill. Plus, if you need help getting past a slippery area, you can just sprinkle some of the sand under your tires.

Foil frozen locks with all-purpose oil. You've heard of a lube job for your car — but what about for your car doors? Squirt an all-purpose lubricant, like WD-40, into your car's locks to prevent them from freezing. If the lock is already frozen, spray it with lubricant at room temperature to thaw it. Keep bottles of spray lubricant in your home and office, as well as in your trunk. That way, if your trunk lock is frozen, you still have access to some.

Let it snow, let it snow, let it snow. After a good night's snowfall, the best way to clear away the flakes is with a broom. A tiny window scraper doesn't pack much muscle, and a snow shovel could easily scratch your windshield or paint job. Keep a sawed-off broom in the trunk of your car for those heavy snow days but keep an extra one in the house. After a really cold night, there's bound to be more than just snow on your car, and that sawed-off broom won't do you much good if the trunk is frozen shut and you can't get to it.

Ease the freeze. To keep your car's trunk from freezing shut in winter, wipe down the rubber gasket with vegetable oil.

Keep a clear view in winter. When you wash your windows during cold weather, add a half-cup of rubbing alcohol to every quart of wash water. After washing them down, polish the windows with newspaper. This will keep them free of frost all winter. If you don't have alcohol handy, try the same recipe with antifreeze.

Wiper fluid works wonders. Keep windshield wiper fluid in a spray bottle in your car in winter. It comes in handy for de-icing windows and thawing frozen door locks.

Ingredient Substitutions

Ingredient	Amount	Substitution
allspice	1 tsp	1/2 tsp cinnamon, 1/2 tsp ground cloves
apple pie spice	1 tsp	1/2 tsp cinnamon, 1/4 tsp nutmeg, 1/8 tsp cardamom
arrowroot	1 1/2 tsp	1 Tbsp flour or 1 1/2 tsp cornstarch
baking powder	1 Tbsp	1 tsp baking soda and 1 tsp cream of tartar
baking powder	1 tsp	1/4 tsp baking soda, 1/2 tsp cream of tartar or 1/4 tsp baking soda, 1/2 cup sour milk or buttermilk (decrease liquid in recipe by 1/2 cup)
brown sugar	1 cup	1 cup white sugar, 1 1/2 Tbsp molasses
buttermilk	1 cup	1 cup plain yogurt; 1 cup sweet milk, 1 3/4 tsp cream of tartar; or 1 cup minus 1 Tbsp warm milk, 1 Tbsp vinegar or lemon juice; let stand for 5 minutes
cake flour	1 cup	1 cup stirred all-purpose flour minus 2 Tbsp
catsup	1 cup	1 cup tomato sauce
catsup (for cooking)	1 cup	1/2 cup sugar, 2 Tbsp vinegar

continued...

Ingredient	Amount	Substitution
catsup	1/2 cup	1/2 cup tomato sauce, 2 Tbsp sugar, 1 Tbsp vinegar, 1/8 tsp ground cloves
chili sauce	1 cup	1 cup tomato sauce, 1/4 cup brown sugar, 2 Tbsp vinegar, 1/4 tsp cinnamon, dash ground cloves, dash allspice
chocolate chips	1 oz	1 oz sweet cooking chocolate
chocolate, semisweet	1 2/3 oz	1 oz unsweetened chocolate, 4 tsp sugar
chocolate, semi-sweet baking	1 square	3 Tbsp unsweetened cocoa powder, 1 Tbsp shortening or oil, 3 tsp sugar
chocolate, semi-sweet chips, melted	6 oz package	2 squares unsweetened chocolate, 2 Tbsp shortening, 1/2 cup sugar
chocolate, unsweetened	1 oz square	3 Tbsp cocoa, 1 Tbsp fat
cocoa	1/4 cup	1 oz square chocolate
coconut cream	1 cup	1 cup whipping cream
coconut milk	1 cup	1 cup whole or 2% milk
corn syrup	1 cup	1 cup honey or 1 cup sugar, 1/4 cup liquid
cornstarch	1 Tbsp	2 Tbsp all-purpose flour; 2 tsp arrowroot; or 2 Tbsp granular tapioca
cracker crumbs	3/4 cup	1 cup dry bread crumbs

continued...

Ingredient	Amount	Substitution
cream, half-and-half	1 cup	1 cup evaporated milk, undiluted, or 7/8 cup milk, 1/2 Tbsp butter or margarine
cream, heavy	1 cup	3/4 cup whole milk, 1/3 cup melted butter
cream, light	1 cup	1 cup evaporated milk, undiluted or 3/4 cup milk, 3 Tbsp butter or margarine
cream, whipped		evaporated milk (13 oz) chilled, 1 tsp lemon juice, whipped
egg	1 whole	2 Tbsp oil, 1 tsp water or 2 yolks, 1 Tbsp water
flour, all-purpose	1 cup sifted	1 cup plus 2 Tbsp cake flour; 1 cup rolled oats; or 1 1/2 cups bread crumbs
flour, cake	1 cup sifted	1 cup minus 2 Tbsp sifted all-purpose flour
flour, self-rising	1 cup	1 cup minus 2 tsp all-purpose flour, 1 1/2 tsp baking powder, 1/2 tsp salt
gelatin, flavored	3 oz package	1 Tbsp plain gelatin, 2 cups flavored fruit juice
herbs, fresh	1 Tbsp	1 tsp dried herbs
honey	1 cup	1 cup sugar, 1 cup water or 1 1/4 cups sugar, 1/4 cup liquid

continued...

Ingredient	Amount	Substitution
lemon juice	1 tsp	1 tsp vinegar
mayonnaise for salads	1 cup	1 cup cottage cheese, pureed; 1 cup sour cream; or 1/2 cup yogurt, 1/2 cup mayonnaise
milk, whole	1 cup	1 cup fruit juice; 1 cup potato water; or 1/2 cup evaporated milk, 1/2 cup water
molasses	1 cup	1 cup honey
mustard, dry	1 tsp	1 Tbsp prepared mustard
pimento	2 Tbsp	3 Tbsp fresh red bell pepper, chopped
pumpkin pie spice	1 tsp	1/2 tsp cinnamon, 1/4 tsp ginger, 1/8 tsp allspice, 1/8 tsp nutmeg
sour cream	1 cup	1 cup plain yogurt or 3/4 cup milk, 3/4 teaspoon lemon juice, 1/3 cup butter or margarine
sugar, white	1 cup	1 cup brown sugar, packed; 1 cup corn syrup (decrease liquid in recipe by 1/3 cup); 1 cup honey (decrease liquid in recipe by 1/4 cup); or 1 3/4 cups powdered sugar
tomato juice	1 cup	1/2 cup tomato sauce, 1/2 cup water
yogurt, plain	1 cup	1 cup buttermilk; 1 cup sour cream; or 1 cup cottage cheese, pureed

Index

Index

Index

E

Egg beaters 160, 238
Egg cartons 123, 194, 220, 288, 325, 333
Egg stains 27, 51, 269
Egg whites 77, 246
Eggplants 200
Eggs
  for Easter 239
  for pest control 186
  for plants 203
  for stains 28, 265
  peeling 86, 87-88
  preparing 86, 87, 88
  storing 86, 87, 88
Eggshells 41, 164, 168, 178, 183, 187, 195
Electric mixers 6
Electric razors 232
Embroidery floss 118
Emergency kits 241
Emery boards 220, 229
Energy savings 250, 252, 253-254, 257, 278, 309, 312, 313
Epsom salt 187, 201, 202-203
Erasers 14, 22, 43, 55, 56, 66, 154, 273, 354
Eucalyptus oil 209
Evaporated milk 85
Eyeglasses 210, 327

F

Fabric softener sheets 9
  for car care 339
  for clothing care 76, 255
  for crafts 131, 133

Fabric softener sheets *(continued)*
  for household care 9, 20, 24, 46, 54, 255
  for odors 43, 44, 45, 69, 72, 258, 259, 310, 321, 330
  for pest control 291, 295
  for pet care 299
  homemade 255
Fabric softener, liquid 31, 47, 54, 69, 142, 150, 255, 257
Fabrics 120, 125, 131, 132, 139, 142, 242, 250, 263, 273, 277
Fans 243, 294, 308, 310, 314
Faucets 34, 310
Felt 158
Ferns 164, 178, 193, 195, 198, 204-205
Fertilizers 168, 169, 190, 203, 205, 303
Fiberglass 22
Figs 107
File cabinets 284
Film 323
Film canisters 123, 288, 322, 341
Fingernails 34, 173
Fireplaces 40, 198, 312
Fires 101-102
First-aid kits 279
Fish 89, 94, 113
Fish tanks 203
Fishing supplies 323
Fleas 17, 291, 293, 301, 302, 305
Flies 189, 243, 294
Floors 30, 33, 39, 53, 54, 155, 156, 220-221
Flour 26, 78, 80, 121, 169, 184, 293, 296
Flowerpots 190, 205
Flowers
  African violets 175, 189
  azaleas 167

Index

Index

Index

Index

Index

Tongs 193

Toolboxes 227

Toothbrushes 16, 19, 34, 54, 66, 67, 74, 155, 161, 217, 231, 266, 274, 314, 332

Toothpaste

   cleaning and polishing with 48, 65, 67, 73, 158, 230, 331, 353

   for odors 100, 113

   for pimples 209

   for stains 267, 273

Toothpicks 118, 148, 155, 205, 314

Topiary 202

Towels 155, 205, 251, 274, 276, 280, 286, 308, 326

Toys 5, 34, 248, 250, 279

Trash compactors 8

Travel documents 325, 334

Trees 136, 137, 169, 191, 197, 198, 199, 203, 312

Trellises 193, 199

Trivets 157

Turkey basters 196

Turpentine 272

TVs 14

Tweezers 302

Twist ties 199, 210, 225

U

Umbrellas 199

Upholstery

   car, repair of 352

   care of 160, 300

V

Vacuum cleaner bags 16, 17, 289, 293, 294

Vacuum cleaners 16, 17, 19, 35, 39, 44, 126, 230, 309, 310

Vanilla 13, 142

Varnish 149, 157

Vases 41, 136, 137, 239-240

VCRs 14, 15

Vegetable oil 11, 30, 83, 106, 158, 295, 298, 357

Vegetables 97, 99, 111, 199, 206

Velcro 15, 62, 230, 319

Velvet 67-68

Videotapes 15

Vinegar

   for appliance cleaning 3, 5, 10, 11, 17, 18, 50

   for bathroom cleaning 19, 21, 22, 24, 34, 52

   for car care 341, 355

   for clogs 8, 309, 314

   for clothing care 74

   for cut flowers 170

   for dishes 38, 51

   for floors 30, 54

   for food preparation 78, 85, 87, 88, 96, 109, 113

   for glassware cleaning 41, 46

   for household cleaning 32, 34, 37, 43, 50, 54, 55, 162

   for laundry 76, 211, 251, 255, 256, 258, 266, 277

   for odors 45, 107, 113, 259

   for paintbrushes 147

   for personal care 213

   for pest control 184, 188, 199, 290

   for pet care 299, 300, 301, 302

   for polishing furniture 156

   for pots and pans 26, 34, 45

   for rust removal 223, 227

   for scorch mark removal 64

   for sinks and drains 49

   for soot 40